1001 Chess Exercises for Club Players

Frank Erwich

1001 Chess Exercises for Club Players

The Tactics Workbook that Also Explains All the Key Concepts

New In Chess 2019

© 2019 New In Chess

Published by New In Chess, Alkmaar, The Netherlands
www.newinchess.com

Cover design: Volken Beck
Supervision: Peter Boel
Editing and typesetting: Peter Boel
Proofreading: Sandra Keetman
Production: Anton Schermer

Have you found any errors in this book?
Please send your remarks to editors@newinchess.com. We will collect all relevant corrections on the Errata page of our website www.newinchess.com and implement them in a possible next edition.

ISBN: 978-90-5691-819-4

Contents

Explanation of symbols

The chessboard
with its coordinates:

	White stands slightly better
±	White stands slightly better
∓	Black stands slightly better
±	White stands better
∓	Black stands better
+−	White has a decisive advantage
−+	Black has a decisive advantage
=	balanced position
!	good move
!!	excellent move
?	bad move
??	blunder
!?	interesting move
?!	dubious move
≥	stronger is
≤	weaker is
△	with the idea

- ☐ White to move
- ■ Black to move
- ♔ King
- ♕ Queen
- ♖ Rook
- ♗ Bishop
- ♘ Knight

Introduction

For the things we have to learn before we can do them, we learn by doing them – Aristotle.

If you agree with the famous Greek philosopher, then this is the right book for you! By working through these 1001 (!) exercises you will train your tactical skills extensively, and I am sure this will make you a much stronger chess tactician.

I have always had a great love for the royal game, and I have been a professional chess teacher in the Netherlands since 2012. During these seven years, I have collected thousands of tactical fragments from tournament chess practice for my pupils to study. A broad selection of these fragments have made it into this book. It is primarily aimed at club players. Of course, this is a broad concept, as the levels of club players diverge enormously. It is not easy to offer appropriate teaching material for such a broad range of readers. Nevertheless, with the huge amount and variety of these exercises, their difference in difficulty, and the hints given below the diagrams, I am convinced that this book will be of great value to any player with an Elo rating ranging from 1500-2000.

Every game fragment highlights a certain area of the tactical spectrum. Each chapter has a different theme, and within this theme the exercises are divided into subthemes. The names of these subthemes can be found in the hints; in the second part of the hints (behind the '+') the aim or point of the move is given. These subthemes are arranged in order of increasing difficulty. Of course, the notion of 'level of difficulty' is partly subjective. But you can be pretty certain that any last exercise from any set in this book will be more challenging than the first.

   In Chapters 1-9 you will learn and practice how to win with the most fundamental tactics: Eliminating the defence, Double attack, and so on. In Chapter 10, you are invited to take the opposite side, and required to *defend* against such tactics. Here, you will be facing your own newly-acquired weapons! Chapter 11 is what we might call the Grand Finale. Here, every exercise involves a combination of several different themes, and you won't find any hints below the diagrams. It's almost like playing a real game! So, in this chapter you can test your ability to use the skills you have gained in the previous chapters. The solutions to all the exercises are given in Chapter 12.

   For the execution of the right tactic in the right way, one or more preparatory moves are needed in many cases. This means that for most exercises the solution is at least 2½ moves deep (i.e., 5 ply or more). The reason why I have provided hints below the diagrams is that I want you to look in a specific direction. The more you are focused on a particular kind of tactic, the better it will be incorporated into your system, and the better you will be able to apply it in your own games. If you prefer a bigger challenge, you can cover the hints with a piece of paper or a carbon card.

To group the tactical themes in this book I have largely used the categorization introduced by Cor van Wijgerden and the late Rob Brunia in their Step-by-Step Method. As a young player, I grew up with these great chess teachers by my side, and I still implement their method in my lessons regularly.

Naturally, I have given my own twist to this material by introducing several new categories. Moreover, not only do the types of positions vary widely, but also the players range from elite grandmasters to post-beginners. In some cases I have distilled an exercise from the analysis of a game. In other cases I had to adjust one or two pieces in the original to make an exercise more sound, or more thematic.

I would like to thank Allard Hoogland and Remmelt Otten from New in Chess for their confidence, and for giving me the opportunity to write this book. Of course I also have to mention the editorial team and their efforts to mold the manuscript into a publishable form. They have done a wonderful job! In particular, I would like to express my gratitude to Peter Boel for his useful advice and for fine-tuning my work. Last but not least, I want to thank my parents for their support. Whether it is about chess or something else: they are always there for me.

I sincerely hope you will enjoy working through this book, and that you will reap the benefits of the acquired knowledge and skills in your own games. Have fun, and good luck!

Frank Erwich
Leiden, February 2019

CHAPTER 1

Elimination of the Defence

Defenders can be eliminated in several ways and with different intentions. Important goals are to win material or to deliver mate (as indicated in the hints in the Exercises section). In the following example these goals are nicely combined.

Anna Muzychuk   2566
Viktorija Cmilyte   2514
Beijing blitz W 2013 (24)

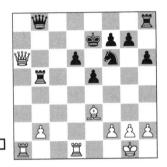

The black queen is **overloaded**. She has to defend the rook on b5 and the d6-pawn. By **chasing away** the defender White ensures that Black cannot protect both:

22.♗a7!

A) 22...♛c7 23.♛xb5, winning the rook; or

B) 22...♛b7 23.♛xd6+ ♚e8 24.♛d8#. 22.♖xd6 was played in the game. With this move, White **lures away** the defender of the rook. After 22...♛xd6 (not capturing the rook is too dangerous with the king in the middle; Black is happy to remove an attacking piece from the board) 23.♛xb5 ♖b8 24.♛c4 White has the better chances, and eventually she won the game, but 22.♗a7 would have been winning at once!

In the following example we will see a mix of ways to eliminate defenders. Here again, either White wins material or Black will get mated:

Dmitry Andreikin   2683
Sergey Karjakin   2760
Moscow Wch blitz 2010 (2)

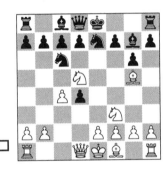

7.♘xd4
Surprise! White's idea is to lure the bishop to d4, or to **lure away** the c6-knight. As White is threatening to take the knight on c6, **capturing the defender** of the knight on e7 and thus winning material, Black opted for the most logical reply:

7...♗xd4
7...♘xd4 fails to 8.♗xe7 and the queen is trapped.
Best is 7...f6, but after 8.♗xf6 ♗xf6 9.♘xf6+ ♚f7 10.♘e4 Black is a pawn down and his kingside is weakened.

8.♛xd4!

The point! White captures the defender of the dark squares in order to checkmate Black: 8...♘xd4 9.♘f6+ ♚f8 10.♗h6#.

8...0-0

Still allowing a forced mate:

9.♘f6+ ♚h8 10.♘g4+!

Clearing the f6-square for the bishop. Black resigned due to 10...♘xd4 (10...f6 11.♗xf6+ ♖xf6 12.♕xf6+ ♚g8 13.♘h6#) 11.♗f6+ ♚g8 12.♘h6 – *Suffocation mate.*

In the following example, Black first needs to make a preparatory move before he can eliminate the defence:

Alexander Grischuk   2782
Fabiano Caruana   2799

St Louis 2017 (2) (analysis)

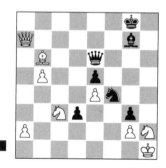

42...♕h6!

Black lures the white bishop to g1, where it *blocks* the escape of its own king.

43.♗g1 ♕h3!

Threatening mate on g2. Of course, this move would have made no sense on the previous move.

As now 44.gxh3 (the g2-pawn being lured away) leads to 44...g2# (44.♕b8+ ♚h7 does not change much), the only way to defend against mate is

44.♕f2

But now again Black can use the method of **luring away** an important defender:

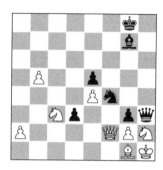

44...♕xh2+!

White's bishop is overloaded! This device, drawing the guard away from a square where it is protecting a piece, is also called **deflection**.

Not good is 44...gxf2 as after 45.gxh3 fxg1♕+ (45...f1♕? 46.♘xf1) 46.♚xg1 Black has won back the piece, but the remaining position is lost.

45.♗xh2 gxf2−+

And White cannot prevent the black f-pawn's promotion. This is another reason why capturing the knight on h2, the defender of the f1-square, was such a strong move.

Besides capturing, chasing away and luring away, **interference** and **blocking** are two other ways to eliminate the defence:

Viswanathan Anand   2781
Kaido Külaots   2597

Tallinn rapid 2004 (2)

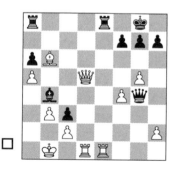

27.♗d8!
White interrupts the connection between the rooks. This is called **interference**.
27.♖g1 was played in the game.
27...♖axd8
27...♖xe1 28.♖xe1 does not solve Black's problem. The a8♖ is still under attack, while 29.♖e8# is the other threat.
28.♕xd8 ♖xd8 29.♖xd8+ ♗f8 30.♖ee8 h5
Creating luft for the king.
After 30...♕g1+ 31.♔a2 ♕c5, White liquidates to a winning pawn endgame: 32.♖xf8+ ♕xf8 33.♖xf8+ ♔xf8 34.b4 ♔e7 35.b5 (breakthrough! More about this in Chapter 7) 35...♔d6 36.b6 ♔c6 37.♔b3+−.

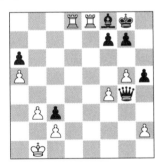

31.g6!
First of all White is threatening mate by 32.♖xf8, as the text takes away the h7-square from the black king.
Secondly, if Black takes the pawn with either 31...fxg6 or 31...♕xg6, a black piece will be in the way of the king's escape: 32.♖xf8+ ♔h7 33.♖h8#.
Blocking is the only way of eliminating the defence where you do not have to actually eliminate a piece which is protecting a square or another piece. All in all, this means Black has to play the ...♕g1+-c5 manoeuvre to prevent mate, but as we saw on move 31, the pawn ending is lost for Black. In this

case, Black is even too late to stop White promoting by b3-b4-b5, as he has to lose time to remove the g6-pawn first.

We conclude this chapter with a spectacular move:

Li Chao	2746
Nigel Short	2666

Baku ol 2016 (7) (analysis)

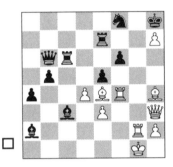

36.♕e6!
This is called a **Novotny interference!** The queen is sacrificed on a square where it can be captured in four ways, but whichever black piece makes the capture, it interferes with the range of the other pieces:
36...♖/♘xe6 interrupts the a2-g8 diagonal and allows 37.♖g8#, while 36...♗xe6 closes off the sixth rank and runs into 37.♗xf6+ ♖g7 38.♗xg7#. 36...♖g7 prevents immediate mate, but after 37.♗xf6 Black will also have to lay down his king before long.

More 'special' interferences can be found in the exercises of this chapter, but there is also one included in Chapter 9 – the fragment from the game Van Osch-Werle (Exercise 592). The reason for including that fragment in the 'Mate' chapter is that in this case the interference leads straight to mate.

Exercises

It is important to keep in mind that when we eliminate a piece that is involved in defending against mate, this does not necessarily lead to mate. When this tactical operation ensures material gain, another main goal is achieved. Thus, when making the exercises, don't be fixated on 'mate' hints concerning 'mate'. Sometimes there will be a forced mate, but not every time.

To distinguish between the exercises in this chapter and those in Chapter 9 (the chapter on Mate), I have decided to classify in Chapter 9 all exercises where the elimination of the defence involves nothing but checks (see, for instance, Exercise 570: Andriasyan-B.Burg).

Furthermore, please note that in most exercises you will first have to prepare a winning 'elimination of the defence' tactic, as for example in the above-mentioned exercise. There are also cases where preparatory moves are not needed – this is either because the exercise in question marks the beginning of a new sequence of exercises (new topic), or because there is still some work to be done after the elimination of the defence.

The hint 'away' indicates either 'luring away' or 'chasing away'. Hints like 'mate' and 'material' (i.e. material gain) indicate the goal or point of the tactic.

Good luck!

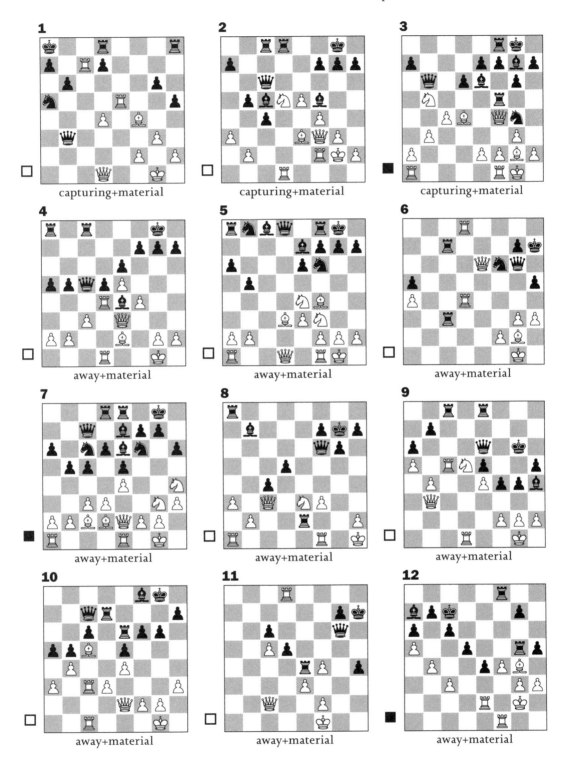

1

capturing+material

2

capturing+material

3

capturing+material

4

away+material

5

away+material

6

away+material

7

away+material

8

away+material

9

away+material

10

away+material

11

away+material

12

away+material

13

14

15

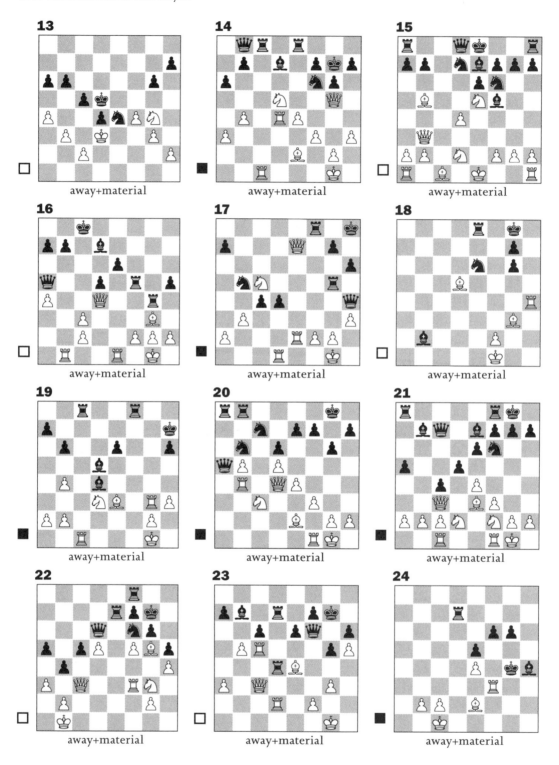

away+material

away+material

away+material

16

17

18

away+material

away+material

away+material

19

20

21

away+material

away+material

away+material

22

23

24

away+material

away+material

away+material

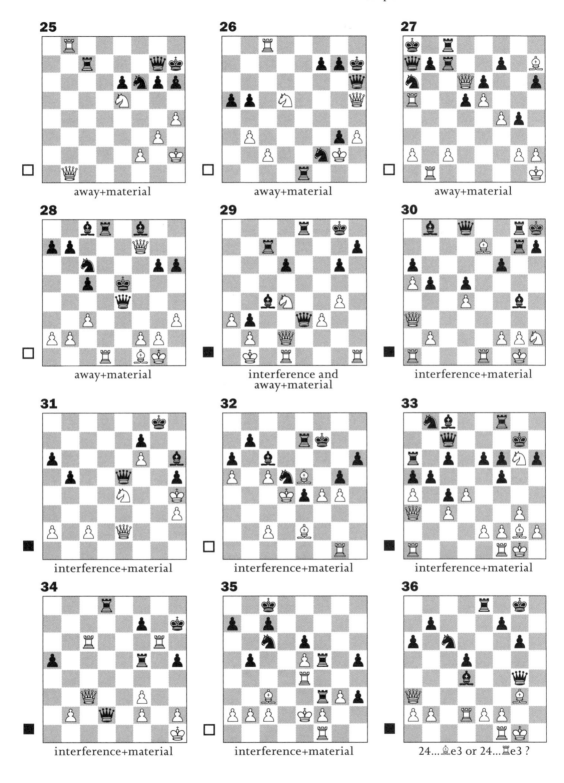

25

away+material

26

away+material

27

away+material

28

away+material

29

interference and
away+material

30

interference+material

31

interference+material

32

interference+material

33

interference+material

34

interference+material

35

interference+material

36

24...♗e3 or 24...♖e3 ?

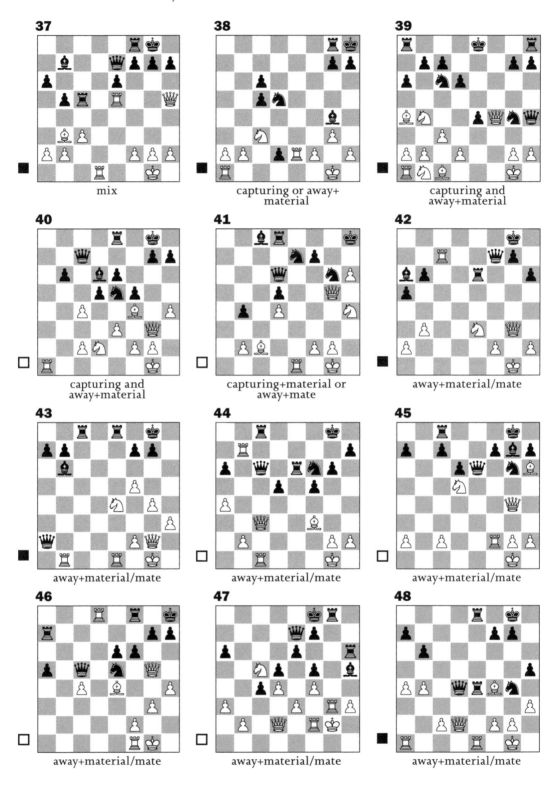

37

mix

38

capturing or away+
material

39

capturing and
away+material

40

capturing and
away+material

41

capturing+material or
away+mate

42

away+material/mate

43

away+material/mate

44

away+material/mate

45

away+material/mate

46

away+material/mate

47

away+material/mate

48

away+material/mate

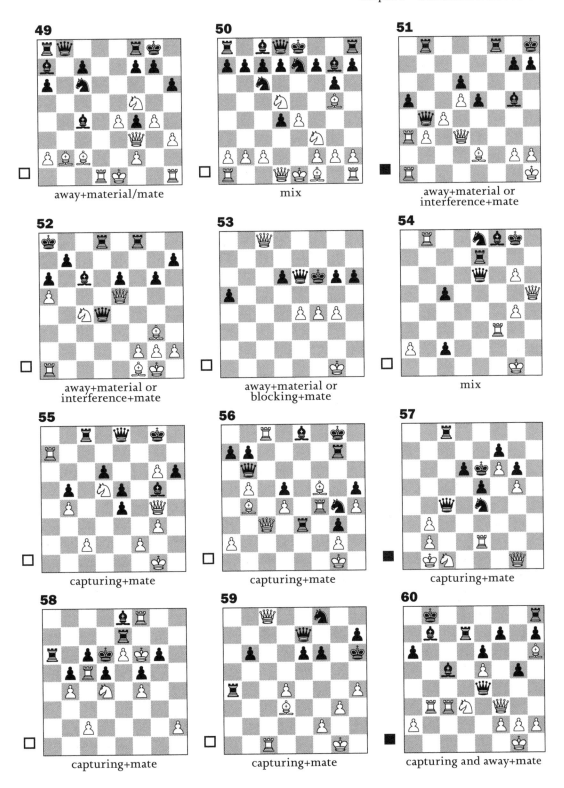

49

away+material/mate

50

mix

51

away+material or
interference+mate

52

away+material or
interference+mate

53

away+material or
blocking+mate

54

mix

55

capturing+mate

56

capturing+mate

57

capturing+mate

58

capturing+mate

59

capturing+mate

60

capturing and away+mate

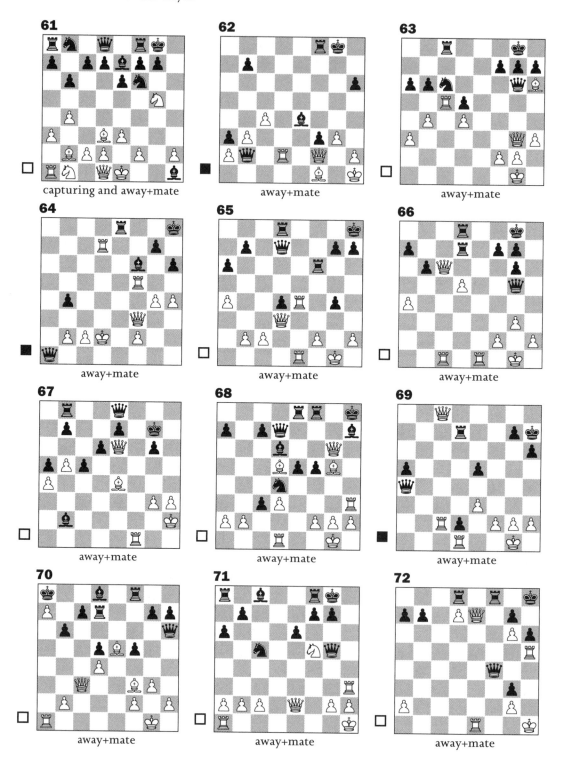

61

capturing and away+mate

62

away+mate

63

away+mate

64

away+mate

65

away+mate

66

away+mate

67

away+mate

68

away+mate

69

away+mate

70

away+mate

71

away+mate

72

away+mate

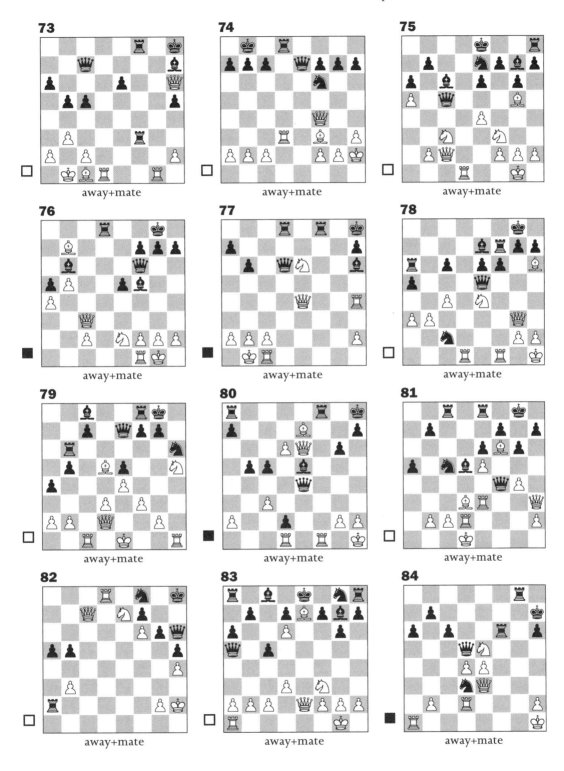

73

away+mate

74

away+mate

75

away+mate

76

away+mate

77

away+mate

78

away+mate

79

away+mate

80

away+mate

81

away+mate

82

away+mate

83

away+mate

84

away+mate

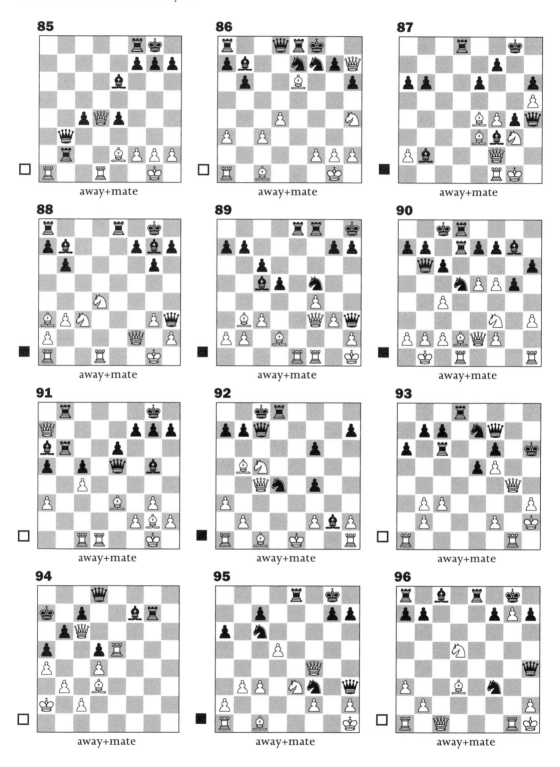

85

away+mate

86

away+mate

87

away+mate

88

away+mate

89

away+mate

90

away+mate

91

away+mate

92

away+mate

93

away+mate

94

away+mate

95

away+mate

96

away+mate

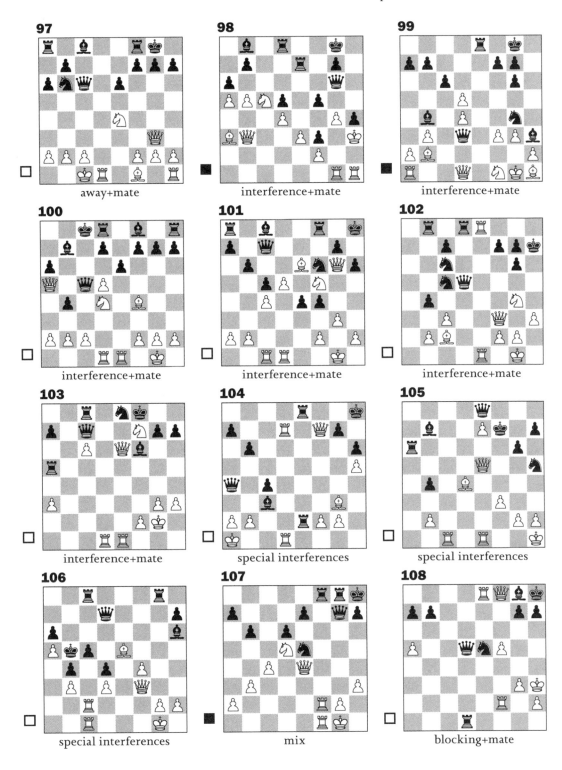

97

away+mate

98

interference+mate

99

interference+mate

100

interference+mate

101

interference+mate

102

interference+mate

103

interference+mate

104

special interferences

105

special interferences

106

special interferences

107

mix

108

blocking+mate

109

110

111

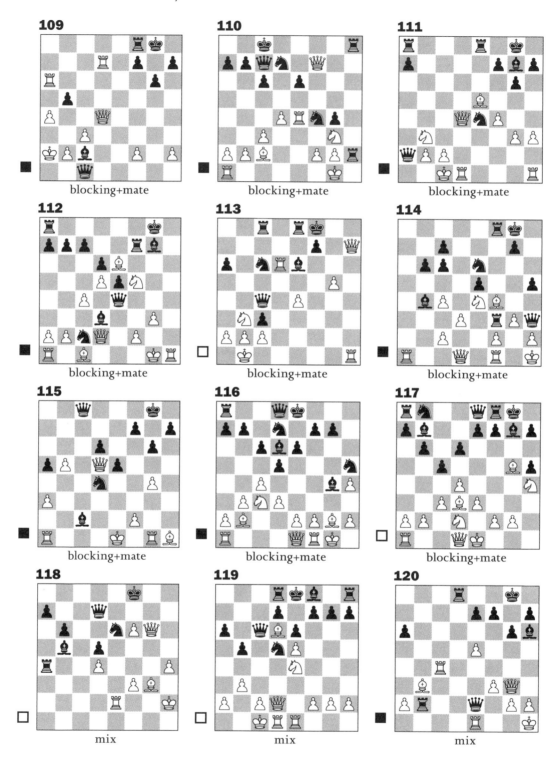

blocking+mate

blocking+mate

blocking+mate

112

113

114

blocking+mate

blocking+mate

blocking+mate

115

116

117

blocking+mate

blocking+mate

blocking+mate

118

119

120

mix

mix

mix

CHAPTER 2

Double Attack

A double attack is an attack in which one piece attacks two targets at the same time, or one move creates two different threats at the same time (see the next chapter about the discovered attack).

Possible targets can be the enemy king, a piece, or an important square. In case of the latter, most of the time a mating square or a promotion square is targeted, but it is also possible to attack a square with a threat. See also the second example in this introduction. In Exercise 894 (Mchedlishvili-Aliyev in the Mix chapter), a square is targeted from which Black can give perpetual check.

To set up a double attack, preparatory moves may be needed. In this chapter, the – in my opinion – most important ones will be discussed, and we will see them return in the next chapters. Sometimes you may need several preparatory moves to succeed, or a preparatory move can serve more than one purpose.

Let's start with **luring** and **chasing**!

Jonathan Gottfried	1653
Quinten Ducarmon	2482

Jerusalem Ech 2015 (1)

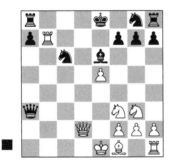

15...♛a1+!

There are two ideas behind this move. The first one is **chasing** the king to e2. After 16.♔e2 the white king and queen become easy targets for the queen: 16...♛a6+–+.
The second idea is to **lure** a white piece to d1, after which another double attack becomes possible:

16.♕d1 ♛xd1+ 17.♔xd1 0-0-0+! 0-1
It's always nice to finish a game by castling!

In the following example we get acquainted with **clearing** and **targeting**.

Justus Van Klaveren
Karl Baak

The Hague 2016

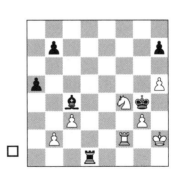

After 49.♔g2 the players agreed to a draw, but winning would have been:
49.♘g2!

with a double threat. White **clears** the f4-square for his rook, while also threatening 50.♘e3(+). Black cannot cope with both threats:

A) 49...♔xh5 50.♘e3+−. An attack on two pieces with a knight (or a pawn) is called a **fork**;

B) 49...♖d3 50.♖f4+ ♔xh5 51.♖xc4. Setting up a winning tactic, in this case a double attack, to enable the attacking piece to move to its purpose square with gain of tempo, is called **targeting**.

In the previous chapter we were presented with **elimination of the defence** as an independent tactic. But it can also serve as a preparation for a double attack:

Matej Sebenik   2528
Sergei Tiviakov   2608
Reykjavik Ech tt 2015 (5)

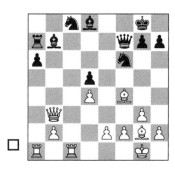

25.♖xc8 was played in the game, but
25.♗b8!
wins material. First White *chases* the rook *away* from the square on which it defends the bishop.
25...♖a8
Now he makes use of *interference*:
26.♗c7! ♗xc7 27.♕xb7
White has eliminated two defenders in order to set up a double attack.

27...♖b8 28.♕xc7+− (or even 28.♕xb8 ♗xb8 29.♖xc8+ ♘e8 30.♖xb8+−); 27...♖a7 28.♕xc8++−.

Other independent tactics can also be used to prepare a double attack – or another tactic. In the coming chapters we will discuss the most important of these tactics. As a teaser for the next chapter, here is an example of a discovered attack as a preparatory move:

Thomas Kubo   2038
Christoph Krings   2165
Germany tt 2016/17 (6)

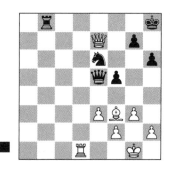

44...♘d4!
Attacking both the queen and the bishop. But isn't the black queen unprotected? Yes, it is, but after
45.♕xe5 ♘xf3+,
forking the king and queen, Black wins back the queen with interest:
46.♔g2 ♘xe5
and Black won.

Luring an enemy piece onto a poisoned square by means of a sacrifice on that square, is called **decoying**. In the above example, the queen is the target for a double attack, but in the next chapters we will see that a decoy sacrifice can also be a preparation for another tactic (i.e. a pin, the trapping of a piece, and so on).

By the way, it is important to note that after 44...♘g5, with the same idea as in the game, White can avert material loss with an in-between check: 45.♖d8+! ♖xd8 (45...♔h7 46.♕xe5 ♘xf3+ 47.♔g2 ♘xe5 and compared to the game, now Black's rook is en prise: 48.♖xb8+–) 46.♕xd8+ ♔h7 and as now the white queen is not hanging, White has all the time in the world to save his bishop. The move 44...♘d4! prevents this trick as it shuts off the d-file.

Exercises

As preparatory moves, **luring**, **chasing**, **targeting** and **clearance** moves play an important role in setting up a double attack.

I have also added **elimination of the defence** to the list. This motif appears frequently, not only as an independent tactic, but also as a preparation for a different tactic. I am aware that there are other independent tactics that may also serve higher goals, but in my opinion they occur not as frequently as elimination of the defence.

These five types of preparatory moves will return in almost every chapter from here on. I have also indicated them in the hints to the exercises. To summarize, here is a description of each of these types of preparatory moves.

Luring forces a target to move to a bad square or line, most of the time by means of an exchange or a sacrifice, after which the position of the target can be exploited by a tactic. In case of a sacrifice, we also speak of a **decoy**.

Chasing forces the king or a piece to a bad square or line by attacking it. On that bad square or line, the piece or king will be a target for a tactic.

Targeting is setting up a winning tactic through gaining a tempo. For instance, if a white knight can fork two rooks on the e4-square and a black king is on g8, then ♘f6 check enables the knight to go to e4 without wasting time.

Clearance involves freeing lines (a file, rank or diagonal; = line clearance) or a square (= square clearance) by moving away one of the player's own pieces that is obstructing that line or square. The removal and/or sacrifice of this piece is followed by a tactical blow.

Elimination of the defence can take on different forms. From Chapter 1 we know the methods of **capturing**, **chasing away**, **luring away**, **interference** and **blocking**. Using one or several of these methods enables the attacker to follow this up with another tactic.

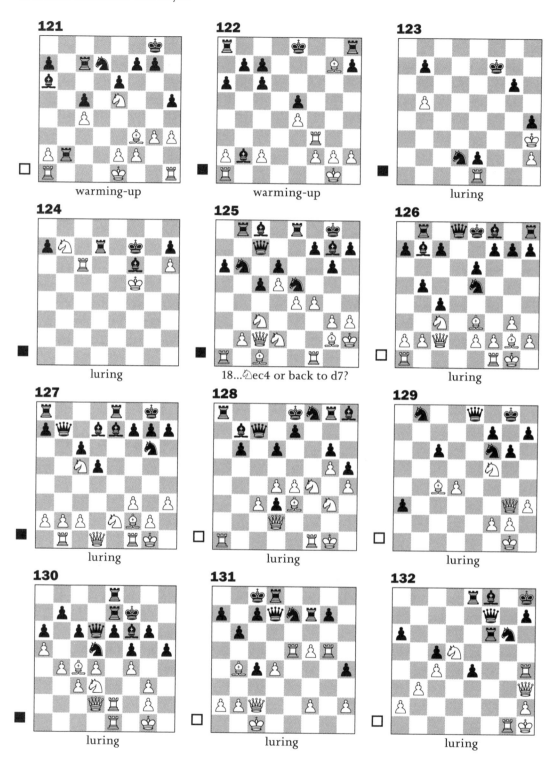

121

warming-up

122

warming-up

123

luring

124

luring

125

18...♘ec4 or back to d7?

126

luring

127

luring

128

luring

129

luring

130

luring

131

luring

132

luring

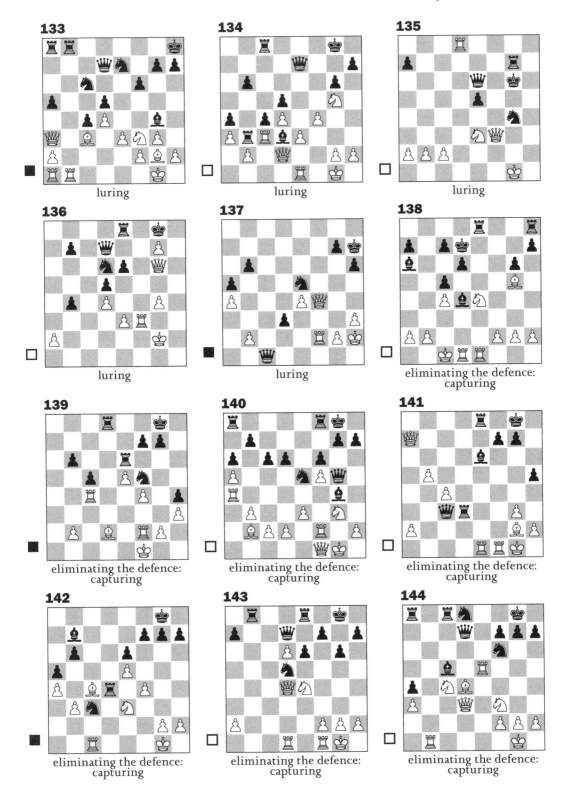

133

luring

134

luring

135

luring

136

luring

137

luring

138

eliminating the defence:
capturing

139

eliminating the defence:
capturing

140

eliminating the defence:
capturing

141

eliminating the defence:
capturing

142

eliminating the defence:
capturing

143

eliminating the defence:
capturing

144

eliminating the defence:
capturing

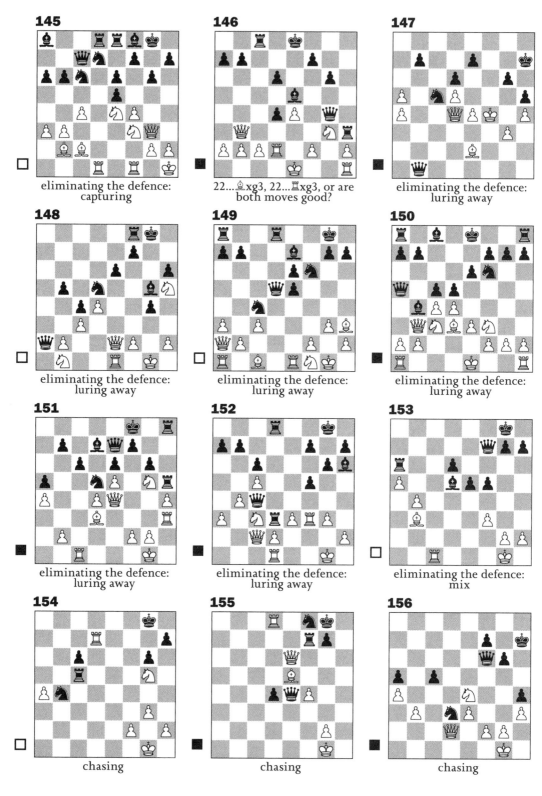

145

eliminating the defence:
capturing

146

22...♗xg3, 22...♖xg3, or are
both moves good?

147

eliminating the defence:
luring away

148

eliminating the defence:
luring away

149

eliminating the defence:
luring away

150

eliminating the defence:
luring away

151

eliminating the defence:
luring away

152

eliminating the defence:
luring away

153

eliminating the defence:
mix

154

chasing

155

chasing

156

chasing

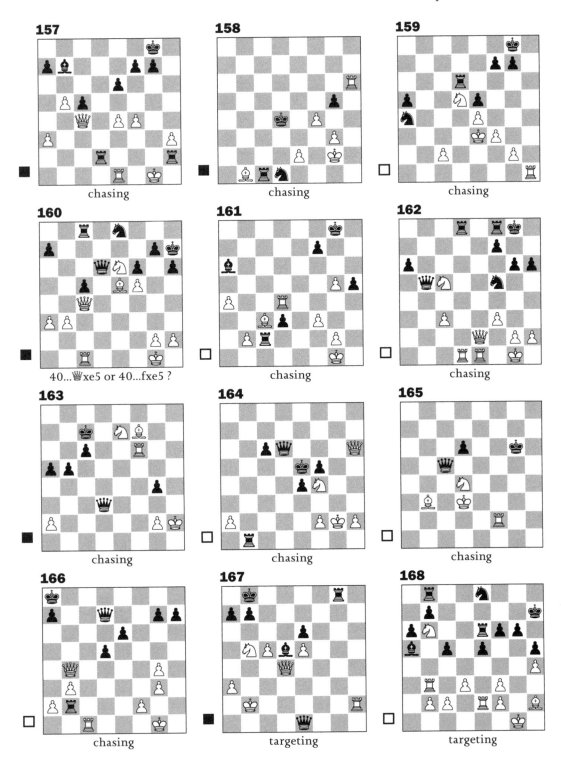

157

chasing

158

chasing

159

chasing

160

40...♕xe5 or 40...fxe5 ?

161

chasing

162

chasing

163

chasing

164

chasing

165

chasing

166

chasing

167

targeting

168

targeting

29

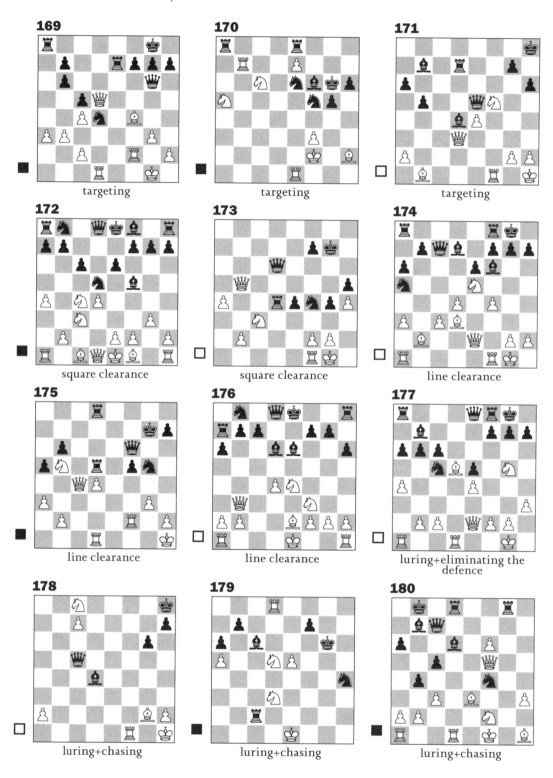

169

targeting

170

targeting

171

targeting

172

square clearance

173

square clearance

174

line clearance

175

line clearance

176

line clearance

177

luring+eliminating the defence

178

luring+chasing

179

luring+chasing

180

luring+chasing

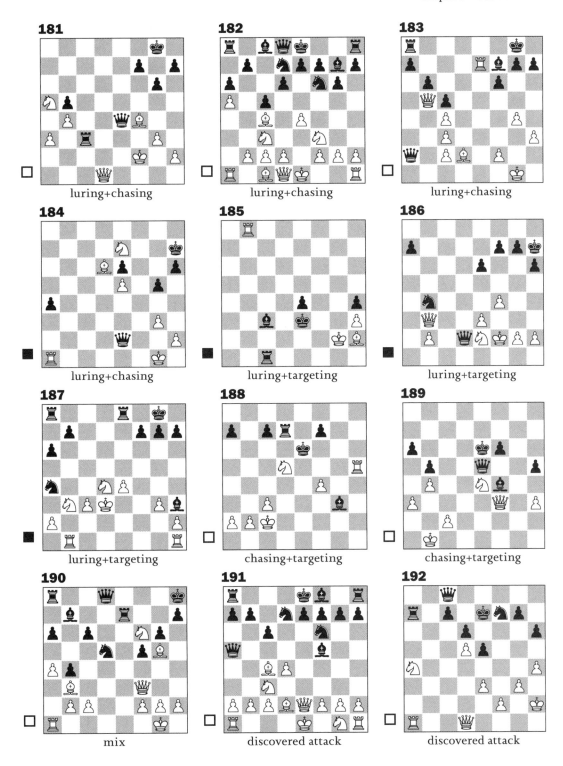

181

luring+chasing

182

luring+chasing

183

luring+chasing

184

luring+chasing

185

luring+targeting

186

luring+targeting

187

luring+targeting

188

chasing+targeting

189

chasing+targeting

190

mix

191

discovered attack

192

discovered attack

193

194

195

discovered attack

discovered attack

discovered attack

CHAPTER 3

Discovered Attack

A discovered attack is a double attack for which the attacker uses two pieces. By moving one piece, an attack by another piece is 'discovered'. A picture tells more than a thousand words, so let's move on immediately to the first example.

Marc Erwich	2364
Marinus Kuijf	2357

Germany tt 2013/14 (6)

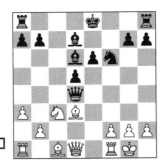

After the previous moves 11...♘xd4 12.♘xd4 ♛xd4, it seems Black has just captured a poisoned pawn. Black's queen is a target, as it is loose, and lined up vis-à-vis White's queen. The only piece standing between the queens is the white bishop. The white bishop and white queen form a **battery**, the bishop being the *front* piece and the queen the *back* piece. As soon as the bishop moves, the back piece attacks the queen. With the black king in the middle it is not difficult to spot a target for the front piece: 13.♗g6+, a **discovered attack** (when the *back* piece is the one that gives check, we speak of a **discovered check**). His king being in check, Black has no time to move away his queen. Normally this will do, but here Black had a devilish trick up his sleeve: 13... hxg6 14.♛xd4 ♗xh2+ 15.♔h1

analysis diagram

and suddenly Black is the one with a battery. After 15...♗e5+ Black's bishop attacks the white queen and also 'discovers' the rook's check on the white king. Black wins back the queen with interest!

Thus, in the game White played

13.♘b5

Now 13...♗xb5 would be a real howler, as after 14.♗xb5+ White wins the queen by means of a discovered attack. This time Black is not able to surprise White! If 13...♛b6, then 14.♗e3 and Black is in trouble. After 14...♛a6 White again has a discovered attack with 15.♘c7+; 14...♛c6 15.♖c1 does not help Black either. This means 14...♗c5 is forced, but now White wins an exchange with 15.♗xc5 ♛xc5 16.♖c1 ♛b6 17.♘c7+.

Therefore,

13...♛e5

is the only move and after

14.f4 ♗c5+ 15.♔h1 ♛b8 16.b4

an exciting struggle arose.

In some of the previous exercises (see No. 7, Jongste-Hilwerda, and No. 75, Smirin-Kunche, in Chapter 1, as well as the final example from the introduction of Chapter 2, Kubo-Krings), a discovered attack was used as the first step of a combination. In this chapter we mainly focus on the discovered attack as the final step of a combination. The preparatory moves we know from the previous chapter come in handy.

In the next example, White could have won material with a **decoy**:

Pieter Nieuwenhuis   2216
Ewoud de Groote   2330

Netherlands tt 2014/15 (4)

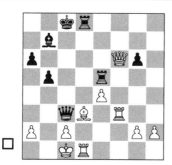

27.♕xd8+! ♚xd8 28.♗e2+

(or 28.♗f1++−) Combining a discovered attack with a discovered check! White wins back the queen on the next move. 27.♖g3 was played in the game.

There are circumstances in which, after one of the players has gained material by a discovered attack, there is still some work to do:

Helge Andreass Nordahl   2340
Aloyzas Kveinys   2526

Norway tt 2012/13 (9)

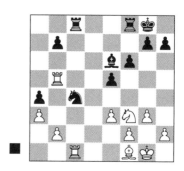

21...♘d2! 22.♘xd2

White could have tried 22.♖xc8 ♘xf3+. Black captures the knight with check while the c8♖ is still hanging, but that's not the end of it! With 23.♔g2 White attacks the knight, and so 23...♖xc8 24.♔xf3 is just equal. Luckily for Black he has an intermediate check: 23...♘e1+!, saving the knight, and after 24.♔g1 ♖xc8 Black is winning.

22...♖xc1 0-1

So, no preparatory move(s) in this case, but a direct discovered attack with a follow-up for which some extra calculation is needed. Exercises 223-229 are similar exceptions; here, the discovered attack is not preceded by preparatory moves, and a follow-up is needed to finish the operation.

In some positions, a battery can be set up with some care:

Wesley So 2540

Abhijeet Gupta 2521

Dubai 2008 (7)

12.♖d1!

White puts the 'back piece' in position, threatening 13.♗a6+.

Moving away the queen, e.g. with 12...♕e5, does not help Black, as White still plays 13.♗a6+ and Black has to abandon the defence of his rook: 13...♔b8 14.♖xd8+ ♗c8 15.♖xc8#. However,

12...♔b8

does not save Black either. The rook on d8 is loose and White exploits this with

13.♗c2!

Protecting his own rook, while skewering the black queen and rook! This is actually another type of double attack, which will be discussed in the next chapter.

13...♕xd1+ 14.♗xd1

and White won.

Besides the discovered attack and the discovered check, there is also the **double check**. In this case, both the front piece and the back piece are giving check at the same time. As a consequence, the enemy king cannot get out of the check by interposing a piece or by capturing an attacking piece. The double check is often used in the mating process, and therefore I decided to give more attention to this weapon in Chapter 9 (Mate), although of course a double check can also be instrumental for winning material, see Exercise 217 (Skripa-Buksa) in this chapter, and Exercise 256 (Navara-Bacrot) in the next chapter, or even for making a draw (Exercise 505, Sreeves-Gupta, in Chapter 8).

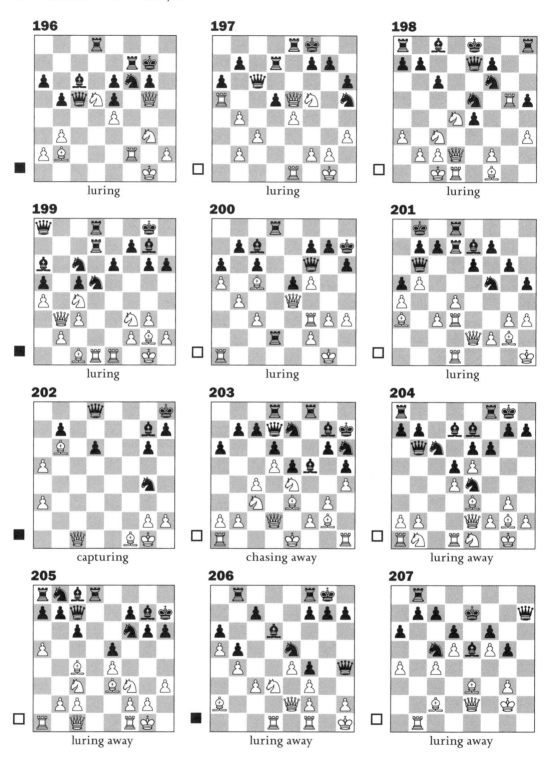

196

luring

197

luring

198

luring

199

luring

200

luring

201

luring

202

capturing

203

chasing away

204

luring away

205

luring away

206

luring away

207

luring away

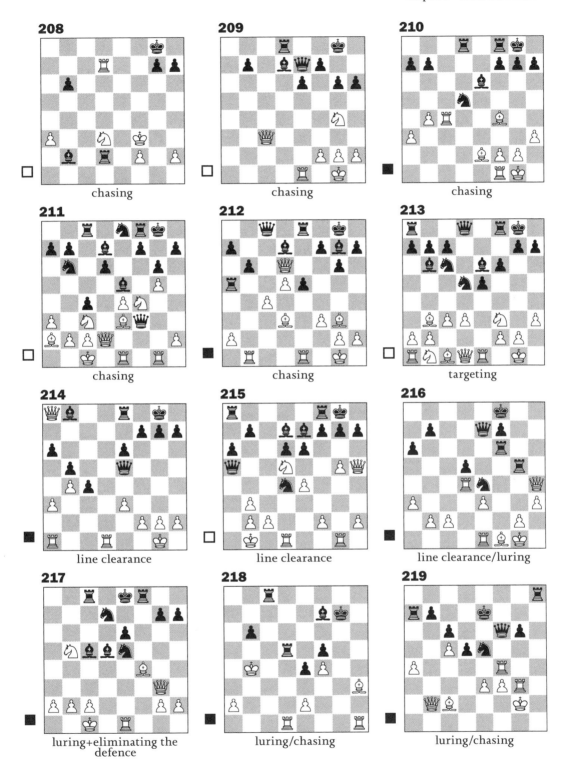

208

chasing

209

chasing

210

chasing

211

chasing

212

chasing

213

targeting

214

line clearance

215

line clearance

216

line clearance/luring

217

luring+eliminating the defence

218

luring/chasing

219

luring/chasing

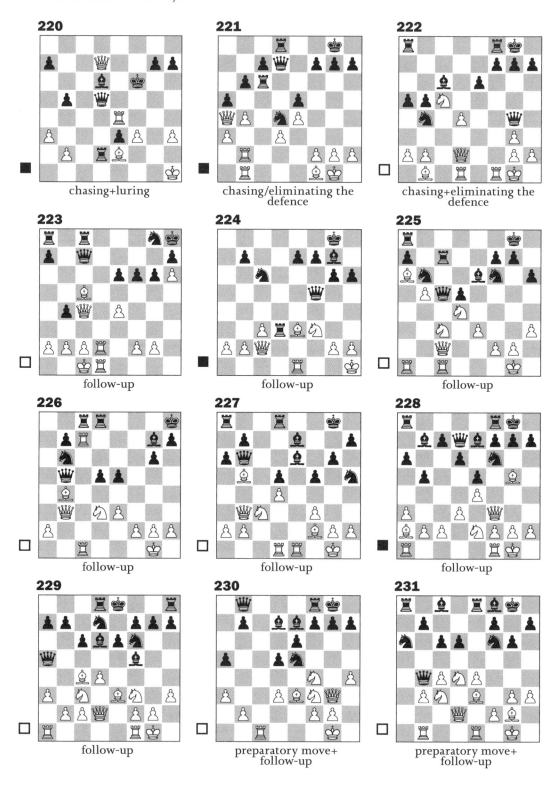

220

chasing+luring

221

chasing/eliminating the
defence

222

chasing+eliminating the
defence

223

follow-up

224

follow-up

225

follow-up

226

follow-up

227

follow-up

228

follow-up

229

follow-up

230

preparatory move+
follow-up

231

preparatory move+
follow-up

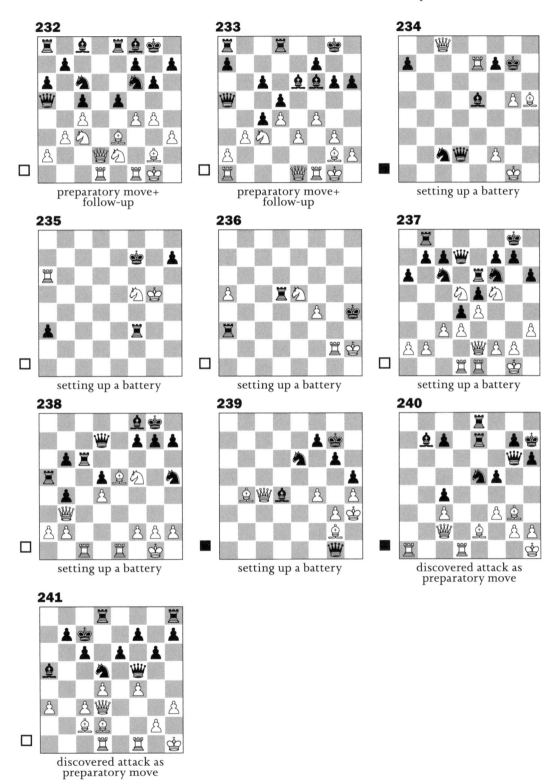

232

preparatory move+
follow-up

233

preparatory move+
follow-up

234

setting up a battery

235

setting up a battery

236

setting up a battery

237

setting up a battery

238

setting up a battery

239

setting up a battery

240

discovered attack as
preparatory move

241

discovered attack as
preparatory move

CHAPTER 4

Skewer

The skewer is another form of double attack. This tactic is also known as an 'x-ray attack': a piece attacks an enemy square or piece 'through' another enemy piece along a line (file, rank or diagonal). With a skewer, either the more valuable enemy piece is the one standing in front, or the front and back pieces are of the same value. When the enemy king (in front) is in check, we are dealing with an 'absolute skewer', otherwise it is called a 'relative skewer'.

In Exercise 46 (Matlakov-Shomoev) in the chapter on Elimination of the Defence, we saw a skewer serving as a preparation for another tactic. In this chapter the roles will be reversed!

Thomas Willemze
Frank Erwich
Training game blitz 2012

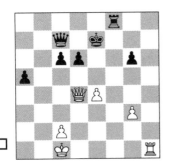

The black king and queen are on the same rank, and White can attack them both by putting the queen or rook on the seventh.

After 34.♖h7+ ♖f7 Black holds, e.g. 35.♖xf7+ ♔xf7 and the black king covers the g7-square, so 36.♕g7+ does not make sense. 35.♕g7 is an inventive try, but after 35...♖xg7 36.♖xg7+ Black can protect the queen with 36...♔d8 and the remaining pawn ending is lost for White.

However, reversing the move order is a good idea. White should start with
34.♕g7+!,
luring the rook,
34...♖f7
and now
35.♕xf7+,
removing the defender of the seventh rank. Moreover, now the distance between the king and rook has been increased, so after
35...♔xf7 36.♖h7+
the black king can no longer protect its queen. White will be a rook up.

In this blitz game I was lucky because my opponent missed this opportunity. Play continued 34.e5.

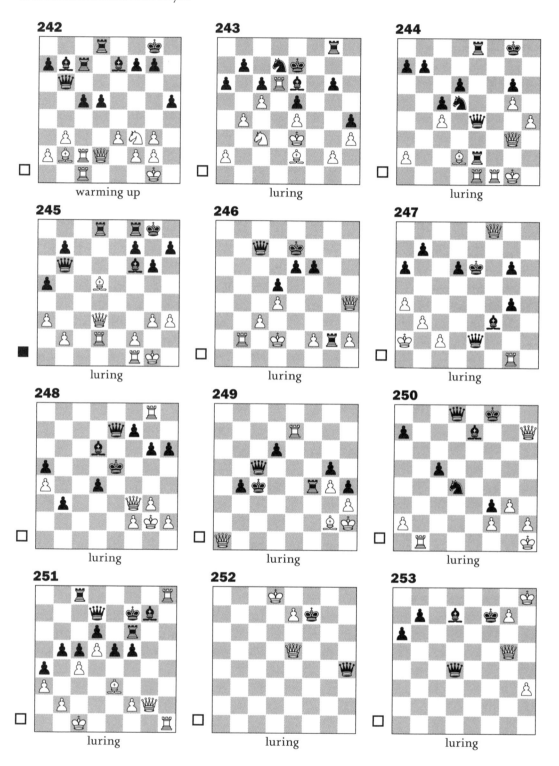

242

warming up

243

luring

244

luring

245

luring

246

luring

247

luring

248

luring

249

luring

250

luring

251

luring

252

luring

253

luring

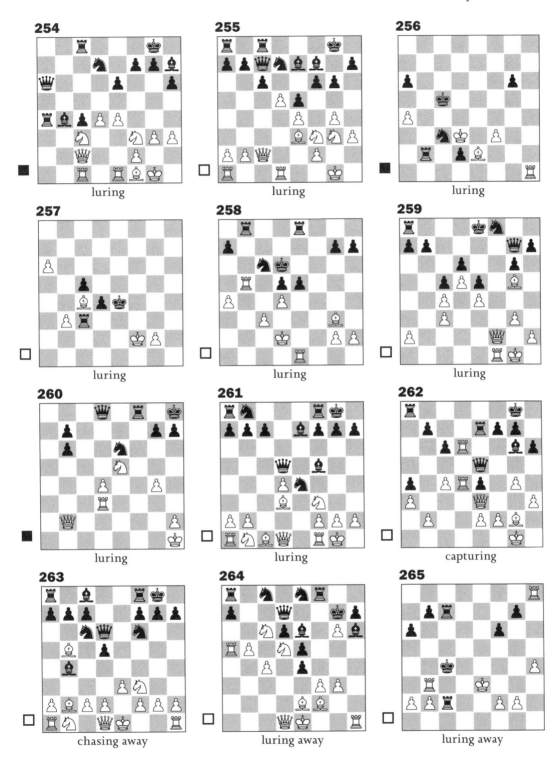

254
luring

255
luring

256
luring

257
luring

258
luring

259
luring

260
luring

261
luring

262
capturing

263
chasing away

264
luring away

265
luring away

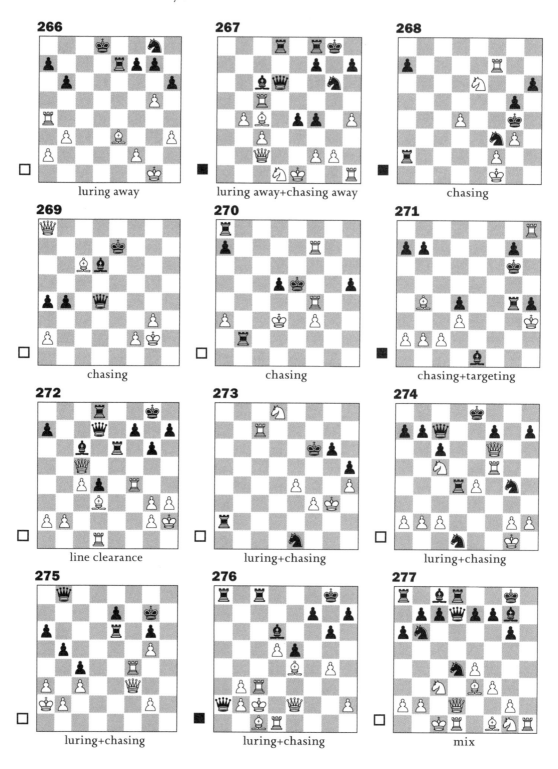

266

luring away

267

luring away+chasing away

268

chasing

269

chasing

270

chasing

271

chasing+targeting

272

line clearance

273

luring+chasing

274

luring+chasing

275

luring+chasing

276

luring+chasing

277

mix

CHAPTER 5

Pin

A pin is a situation in which a piece attacks an enemy piece and indirectly threatens a more valuable enemy piece or square behind it. The difference with a skewer is that with a pin, the most important target (king, (mating) square, or more valuable piece) is *behind* the piece of less value. This means in the case of an 'absolute pin' (where the hindmost piece is the enemy king) that the pinned piece is not allowed to move (because this will put the king in check), or, in case of a 'relative pin', that in most cases it is not smart to move the pinned piece as this will result in either material loss or mate.

All in all, this makes a pinned piece vulnerable.

Fabiano Caruana	2782
Etienne Bacrot	2688

Paris rapid 2017 (6)

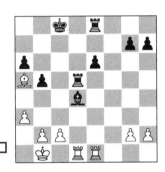

30.罝f4!
Pinning the bishop. 30.奧d3 was played in the game, but the text move is winning. The only way for Black not to lose material at once is to protect the bishop with
30...h5
as 30...exf4 leads to 31.豐xg7#. **A pinned piece is a bad defender!** But now with
31.h3+−
White wins the bishop by **attacking the pinned piece**.

In the next example, White can again win material by *attacking a pinned piece*, but accuracy is required:

Arkadij Naiditsch	2716
Maxime Vachier-Lagrave	2731

France tt 2011 (9)

The black bishop is pinned as it is protected by a rook that is, in turn, only defended by a pinned pawn. In the previous exercise we already saw that *a pinned piece is a bad defender*. White can attack the pinned bishop in four ways, but there is only one that leads to material gain.
25.奧b6!
25.奧c3? fails, as after 25...奧xc3 the rook on e1 is hanging: 26.罝xd5?? 奧xe1−+. After 25.罝e4 or 25.c3 Black can close off the e-file, after which the e6-pawn is no longer pinned: 25...奧e5=. After 26.罝xd5 exd5, now the black bishop is pinned

on the e-file, but White lacks time to exploit this. On the next move Black will play ...♔d7, and then the bishop can move again as the rook on e8 is protected.

25...e5

Compared to 25.c3, now 25...♗e5 does not work as after 26.♖xd5 exd5 White has time to *attack the pinned bishop* with 27.♗d4; 25...♗xb6 26.♖xd5+−.

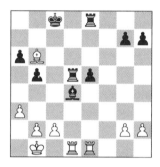

26.♖xd4! 1-0

26...♖xd4 27.♗xd4+−.

26.♗xd4 would be a bad mistake, as after 26...♖ed8!= it is Black's turn to pin a bishop!

After 26.c3 (attacking the pinned bishop) Black could limit the damage with 26...♔b7 27.♗a5 (27.♗xd4 ♖ed8!) 27...♗f2!. Black uses a discovered attack as a counterattack! If the back piece of a pin is a bishop, rook or queen, you always have to be wary of moves by the front piece that attack a more important target (or, in this case, an equally valuable piece).

In Chapter 11 you will find some exercises on this topic.

In the previous chapters you may have noticed pins contributing to execute a winning tactic, see for instance Exercises 10 (Demchenko-Brokken, Elimination of the Defence), 32

(Nijboer-Leenhouts in Elimination of the Defence), 87 (Timman-Fries Nielsen in Elimination of the Defence), and 134 (Werle-Graf in Double Attack). In the current chapter, a winning pin or the attack or capture of a pinned piece is the end of a combination. Thanks to one or more preparatory moves, this main goal can be achieved.

Tigran L Petrosian	2660
Erwin l'Ami	2648

Antalya Ech tt 2013 (8)

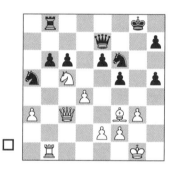

29.♕xa5! 1-0

Black resigned due to 29...bxa5 30.♖xb8+, *chasing the king* (or *luring the knight:* 30...♘e8 31.♗xh5, *attacking the pinned piece*), 30...♔f7 31.♖b7 and compared to the previous examples now the pin itself wins material!

29...♕d8, to protect both the b6-pawn and the rook, thus keeping the fork on a5 and c5 alive, is a clever attempt, but no more than that. White has several ways to defend, e.g. 30.♕a7 and Black can still not capture the knight as the b-pawn is pinned; 30...♖a8 31.♕xb6+−.

Thus, if there is no pin yet, you can create one. In the next example, by using a series of *forcing moves*, Black lures a front and a back piece into position:

Soumya Thakurta   2215
Gevorg Harutjunyan   2455

Mumbai 2013 (5)

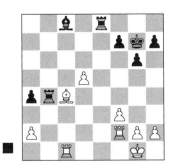

24...♖xc4! 0-1
After 25.♖xc4 ♖e1+ 26.♖f1 ♖xf1+
27.♔xf1, White's rook and bishop are
on the same line (here diagonal), so
27...♗a6 wins a rook and the game.

One piece can also be pinned in two
ways. We are talking about a **cross-pin**:

Francois Godart   2279
Stefan Beukema   2222

Bruges ch-BEL U20 2012 (5)

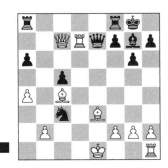

19...♖ad8!
This is called a Maltese Cross: a vertical
and a horizontal pin!
20.♗xf7+
A smart intermediate check!

Capturing the queen runs into
20...♖d1#, while 20.♖xd8 loses a queen:
20...♕xc7. Even 20...♖xd8 is possible,
with the double threat 21...♕xc7 and
21...♖d1#, so here Black wins a queen as
well.
20...♔h8
20...♖xf7? is of course a bad idea as the
d8-rook is en prise: 21.♖/♕xd8+.
20...♕xf7? may be tempting, but
now White has 21.♕xd8!. If 21...♖xd8
22.♖xd8+ ♗f8 23.bxc3 Black has to
look for a perpetual check as otherwise
White has the better chances with two
rooks against the queen.
21.♗e6 ♖xd7 22.♕xd7
22.♗xd7 ♕e4! (threatening 23...♕b1+)
23.0-0 ♘e2+! (forcing the king to
abandon the defence of the rook) 24.♔h1
♕xe3–+, the pinned f2-pawn is a bad
defender!

22...♖d8!
Again, pinning a piece on d7 by putting
a rook on d8!
23.♕xd8+
23.♕xe7 ♖d1#.
23...♕xd8 24.bxc3 ♕d3 0-1

More cross-pins, like the **St Andrew's
Cross** and the **Oblique Cross**, can be
found in the exercises. Please check out
the Solutions to find out more about
these variants!

Exercises

Except for a few exercises concerning the cross-pin, in all the other exercises you will need to find preparatory moves to execute the winning tactic.

However, in the exercises with the hint 'a pinned piece is a bad defender' the required combinations may sometimes be only 3 ply deep. This is because the back piece of a pin is the king, and so taking back with the 'bad defender' is not allowed.

In all the exercises in this chapter, winning material is the main goal. Pins with mate as a motif can be found elsewhere in this book. Some exceptions are Exercises No. 332 (Halfhide-M.Senders) and 335 (Marinkovic-Abramovic) in this chapter, as here the pin does not lead to a forced mate, but the mate threat serves as a means to win material.

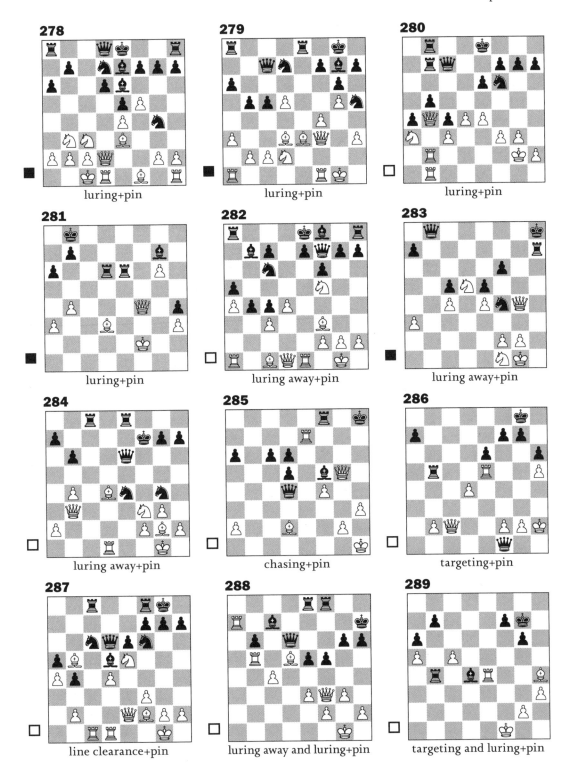

278

luring+pin

279

luring+pin

280

luring+pin

281

luring+pin

282

luring away+pin

283

luring away+pin

284

luring away+pin

285

chasing+pin

286

targeting+pin

287

line clearance+pin

288

luring away and luring+pin

289

targeting and luring+pin

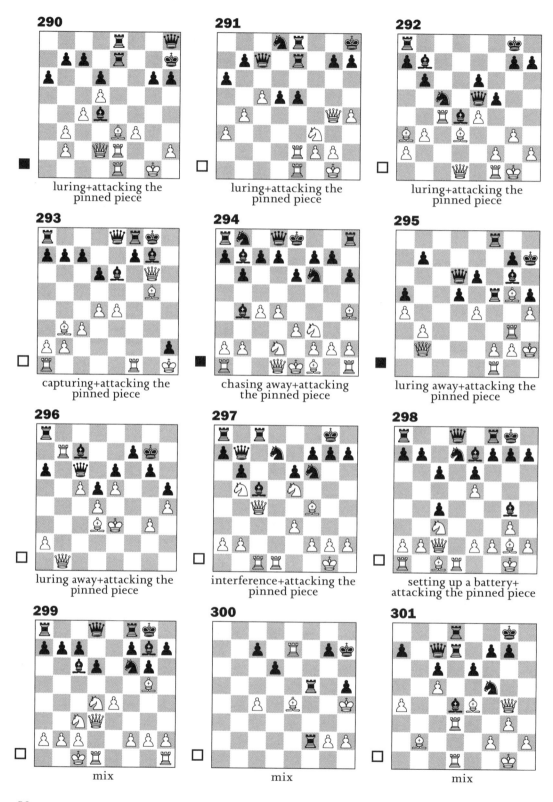

290

luring+attacking the
pinned piece

291

luring+attacking the
pinned piece

292

luring+attacking the
pinned piece

293

capturing+attacking the
pinned piece

294

chasing away+attacking
the pinned piece

295

luring away+attacking the
pinned piece

296

luring away+attacking the
pinned piece

297

interference+attacking the
pinned piece

298

setting up a battery+
attacking the pinned piece

299

mix

300

mix

301

mix

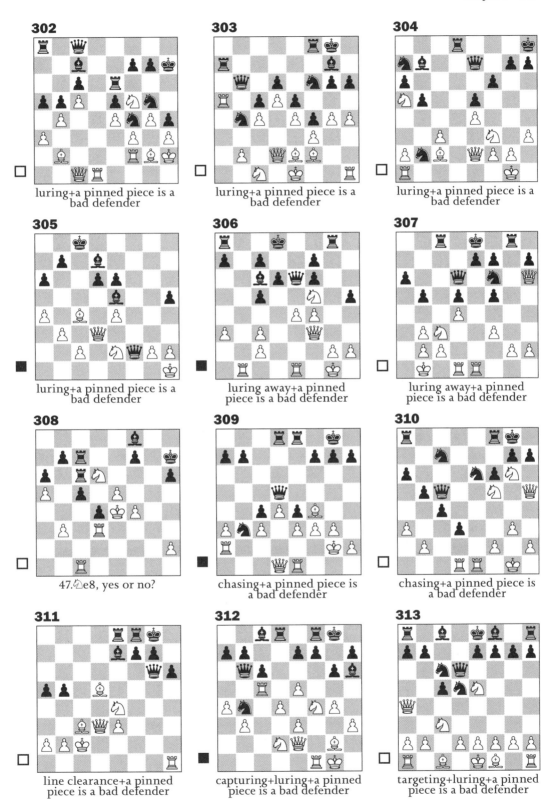

302

luring+a pinned piece is a bad defender

303

luring+a pinned piece is a bad defender

304

luring+a pinned piece is a bad defender

305

luring+a pinned piece is a bad defender

306

luring away+a pinned piece is a bad defender

307

luring away+a pinned piece is a bad defender

308

47.♘e8, yes or no?

309

chasing+a pinned piece is a bad defender

310

chasing+a pinned piece is a bad defender

311

line clearance+a pinned piece is a bad defender

312

capturing+luring+a pinned piece is a bad defender

313

targeting+luring+a pinned piece is a bad defender

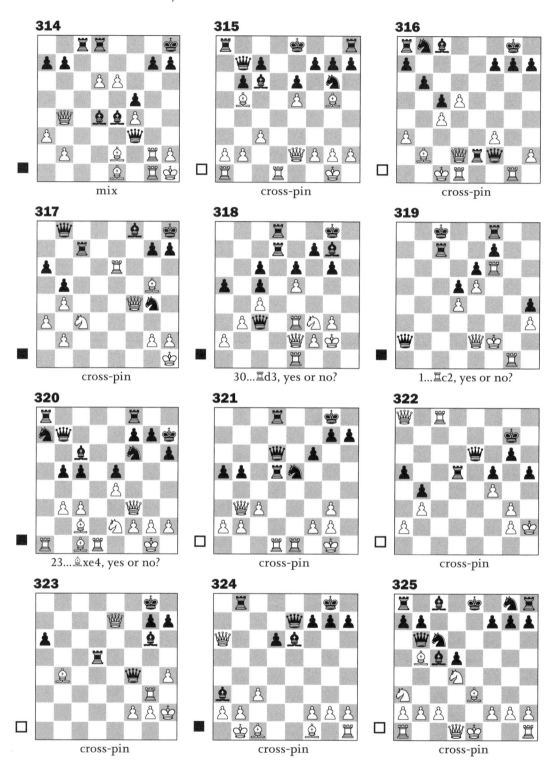

314

mix

315

cross-pin

316

cross-pin

317

cross-pin

318

30...♖d3, yes or no?

319

1...♖c2, yes or no?

320

23...♗xe4, yes or no?

321

cross-pin

322

cross-pin

323

cross-pin

324

cross-pin

325

cross-pin

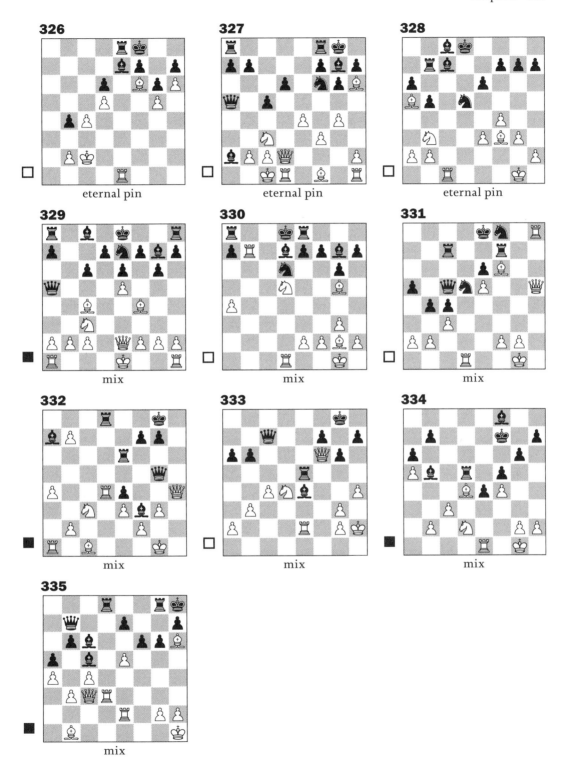

326

eternal pin

327

eternal pin

328

eternal pin

329

mix

330

mix

331

mix

332

mix

333

mix

334

mix

335

mix

CHAPTER 6

Trapping a piece

If a piece is limited in its mobility, it runs the risk of being trapped. Naturally, a piece can be trapped on any square on the board, but on the *edge* or in a *corner* of the board a piece may more easily run low on squares.

Arthur Pijpers   2448
Liam Vrolijk   2427

Wijk aan Zee 2018 (6)

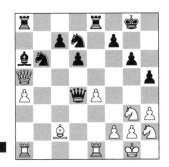

The white queen is in danger. The black pieces control many escape squares and some of White's own pieces (♖e1, ♙a4) are in the queen's way.

The only safe square available to the queen is g5, but...

29...♖e5!

... not anymore! It looks like White can resign now, but he comes up with a smart reply.

30.♘f3

A counterattack, forking the queen and the attacking rook! Now if Black captures the queen, White will capture Black's and he is still in the game. Of course Black had foreseen the text, and he came up with an in-between move:

30...♕xa1!

If you have to give up your queen anyway, then it's better to grab some material for it! After 31.♖xa1 ♖xa5 it is of course game over, but chess is not checkers! Capturing is not mandatory (31.♘xe5 ♕xe5–+):

31.♕b4

White sells his life dearly. Now it's the black queen in the corner that is in danger! The rook on e5 blocks the escape route for her majesty, while most of the other escape squares are covered by the white pieces. Only a2 is available. However, the white queen is exposed as well, so, like White on move 30, Black goes for a counterattack:

31...♘d5!

Black is a rook up, so he can afford to give back a knight. Another important point is that this move creates an escape square for the queen if White chooses not to capture the knight: 32.♕b3 ♕c3–+.

A counterattack with 31...c5 would also do: 32.♕b3 c4 33.♕b4 ♕a2–+. Of course the queen does not make a good impression on the edge of the board, but White is not able to exploit this, and besides, Black is still a piece up, even if White takes the exchange on e5.

31...♕a2 is less good, and risky. After 32.♗b3 ♕b2? Black loses the queen by a discovered attack: 33.♗xf7++–. So this means that Black has to find 32...c5!, but then it would have been much better to play this one move earlier: 33.♕c3 ♘xa4! (33...♕a3 34.♗xf7+ and again Black loses the queen by a discovered attack) 34.♕e3 ♕b2 (finally the queen can move!) 35.♗xa4 ♘f6 36.♘xe5 ♕xe5 and after many complications Black is 'only' one pawn up, although his position must be winning.

32.exd5 ♖xe1+ 33.♘xe1

33.♕xe1 ♕xe1+ 34.♘xe1 ♗c4 is hopeless as well.

33...♖e8 34.♗b1 ♖b8 0-1

In the next example, a queen is again in trouble on the edge of the board. With the help of some, by now well-known, preparatory moves, White is able to trap the queen:

Lucas van Foreest	2453
Eric Lobron	2528

Amsterdam 2017 (2)

117.♖c5+!

Targeting! The rook is on its way to c1 with gain of tempo.

117...♔d6 118.♖c6+

118.♖c1 at once was just as good.

118...♔e7 119.♖c1

Chasing the queen to h2: 119...♕h2 120.♖h1 and the queen is trapped. The game continued with

119...♕xc1 120.♘xc1

and White won.

We have seen plenty of forcing moves so far, but sometimes a quiet move can work as well:

Sahaj Grover	2532
Matthew Sadler	2660

Wijk aan Zee 2012 (13)

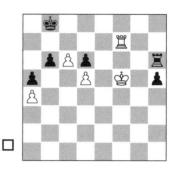

54.♖f8+!

Depriving the black rook of access to the back rank. This motif is called **shutting off**. 54.♔g5 was played in the game.

54...♔c7

The black rook is running out of squares, but going after it immediately is not the key to success: 55.♔g5 ♖h7 56.♔g6 (56.♖e8 ♖f7) 56...♖e7. 55.♖a8, with the idea to control the h7-square tactically as there is a skewer in the air, is a nice idea, but it does not work: 55...h4 56.♔g5? h3 57.♔xh6 h2, and this is the topic of the next chapter! However, the **quiet move**

55.♖e8!

comes to the rescue! White first has to take away the e7-square from the black rook before going after it! White has time to do this, as Black has no way to flee:

55...h4 56.♔g5 ♖h7 57.♔g6

And now, compared to the 55.♖a8 line, another important point is that on e8 the rook is in time to stop the passed pawn:

57...h3 58.♔xh7 h2 59.♖e1+−

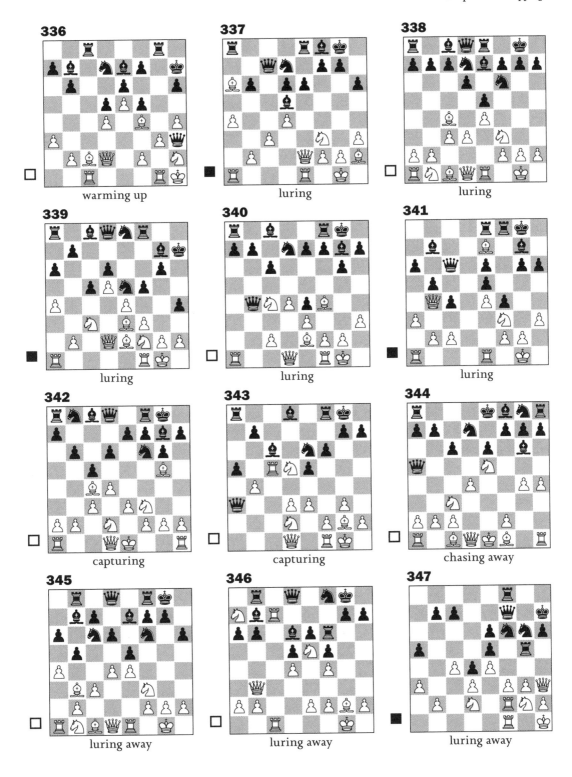

336 warming up

337 luring

338 luring

339 luring

340 luring

341 luring

342 capturing

343 capturing

344 chasing away

345 luring away

346 luring away

347 luring away

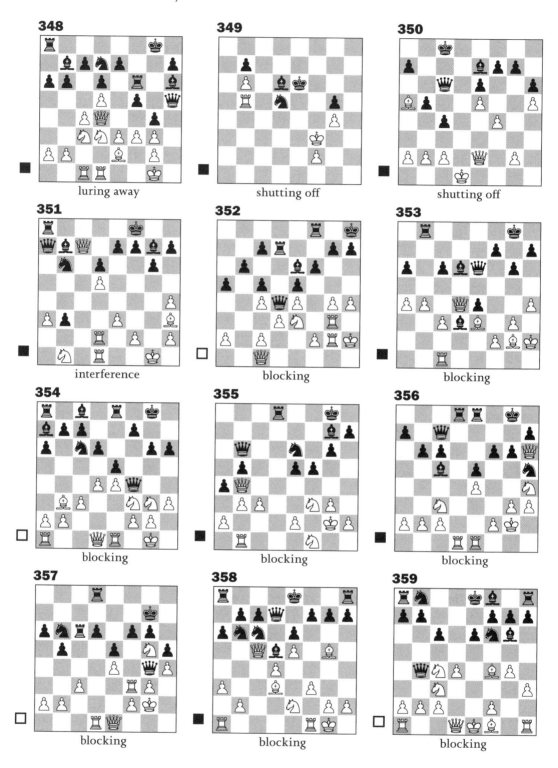

348

luring away

349

shutting off

350

shutting off

351

interference

352

blocking

353

blocking

354

blocking

355

blocking

356

blocking

357

blocking

358

blocking

359

blocking

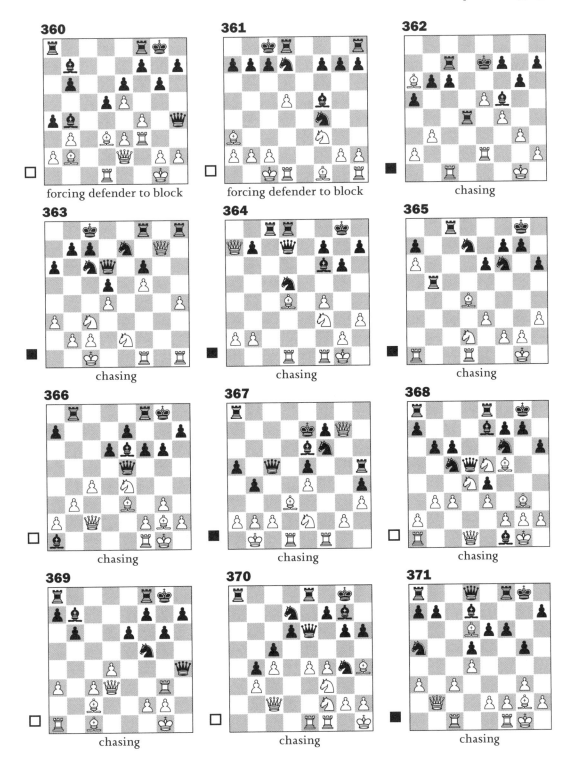

360

forcing defender to block

361

forcing defender to block

362

chasing

363

chasing

364

chasing

365

chasing

366

chasing

367

chasing

368

chasing

369

chasing

370

chasing

371

chasing

372

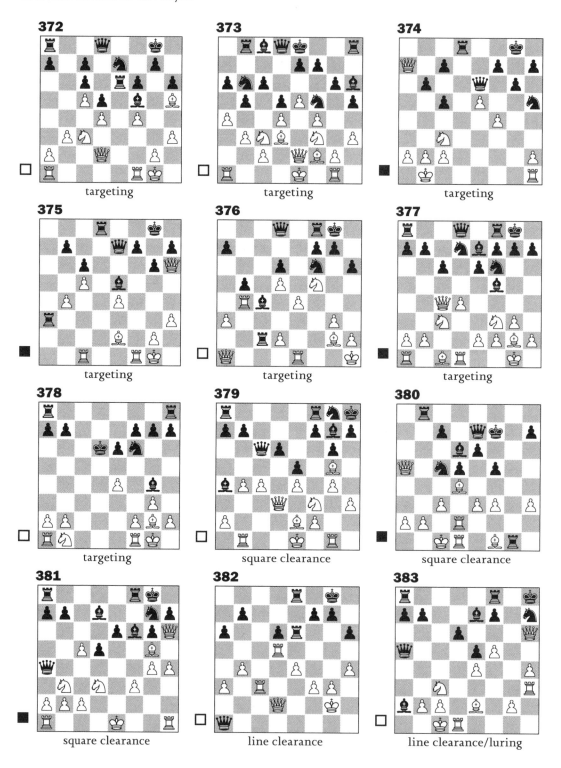

targeting

373

targeting

374

targeting

375

targeting

376

targeting

377

targeting

378

targeting

379

square clearance

380

square clearance

381

square clearance

382

line clearance

383

line clearance/luring

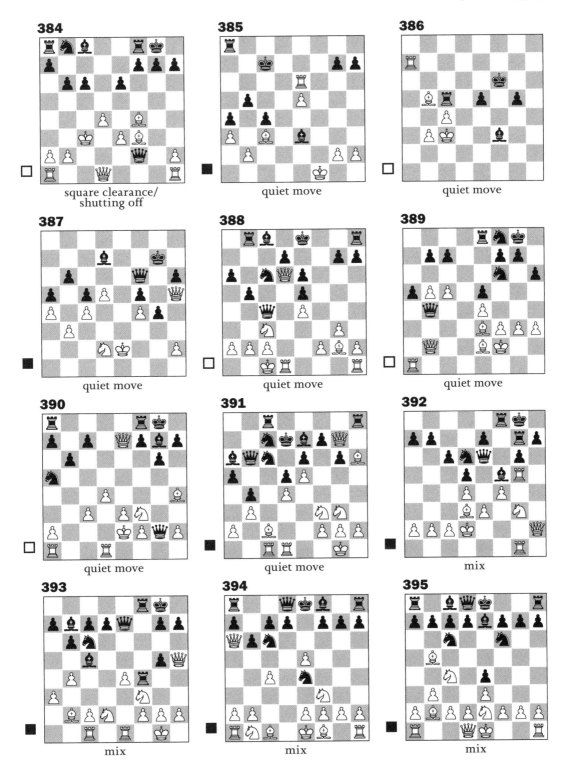

384

square clearance/
shutting off

385

quiet move

386

quiet move

387

quiet move

388

quiet move

389

quiet move

390

quiet move

391

quiet move

392

mix

393

mix

394

mix

395

mix

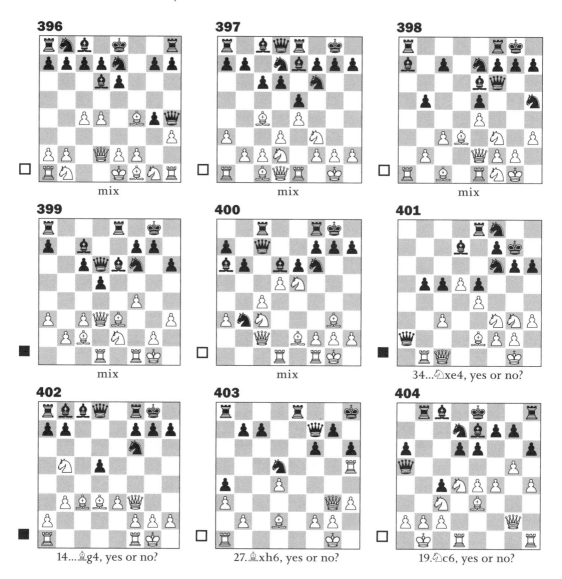

396

mix

397

mix

398

mix

399

mix

400

mix

401

34...♘xe4, yes or no?

402

14...♗g4, yes or no?

403

27.♗xh6, yes or no?

404

19.♘c6, yes or no?

CHAPTER 7

Promotion

In the previous chapters we have already witnessed the power of a passed pawn. In Exercises 62, 69, 72, 80, 96, 101 and 105 of Chapter 1, a passed pawn was involved in the mating process, while in Exercise 12 (Langeveld-Van Rooden) the pawn contributed to Black's material gain by eliminating a defender. In Exercises 123 (Duijker-E.Hansen), 136 (Zamarbide Ibarrea-Kononenko), 137 (Edouard-Ernst) and 178 (Hayrapetyan-Khairullin) the pawn helped setting up a double attack, while in Exercises 256 (Navara-Bacrot) and 257 (Ramirez-Kaidanov), the pawn promotion served as a preparatory move for a skewer.

In this chapter we will fully concentrate on methods to get the pawn promoted or to win material thanks to the promotion of a pawn – the latter being the case if the new queen (or another piece in case of an *underpromotion*) can be captured but the attacker can recapture it.

Pawn promotions preluding another tactic, like the promotion with a skewer in Exercises 252 (Karjakin-Gelfand) and 253 (Van Malder-Hilwerda) in the Skewer chapter, or pawn promotions connected with a mate attack, are not included in this chapter and can be found elsewhere in this book. The only exception is Exercise 414 (Cs.Balogh-Van Dooren). Here, after the better alternative 18...♗e6 instead of 18...cxd5, White would still have obtained a winning advantage with 19.exf8♕+.

To exploit a passed pawn, elimination of the defence is often a good method.

Deimante Cornette   2462
Alexander Donchenko   2610

Douglas 2018 (2)

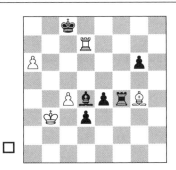

White's *back* piece is under attack, but that does not stop White from capturing the bishop with a discovered check:
64.♖xd4+ ♔b8
64...♖xg4 is of course what Black wants to play, but in that case, eliminating the defender of the rook's pawn, i.e. the black king, by luring it *away* ensures pawn promotion: 65.♖d8+! ♔xd8 66.a7 and the pawn is unstoppable.
65.♗d7?
Black is a piece down and now 65.♖d8+ ♔a7 66.♗c8 would be the easiest way to win for White. However, after the text Black is back in business again!

65...e3!

Very often, **two connected passed pawns on the sixth rank are stronger than a rook** – and this situation is no exception! After 66.♖xf4 e2 the rook cannot prevent at least one of the pawns from queening, while the white king is just too far removed to stop the march of the pawn(s). However, White could still have made a draw here with 67.♖f7 e1♕ 68.♗c6. White threatens a6-a7-a8, so Black has to go for some checks: 68...♕b1+ 69.♔a4 (69.♔c3 ♕a1+ 70.♔xd3 ♕xa6 should also be a draw, but Black can still try a little) 69...♕a2+ 70.♔b5 and as now the queen controls the rook's pawn, Black has the possibility to advance his trump: 70...d2.

analysis diagram

However, now White can force the draw with a funny line: 71.a7+ ♕xa7 (71...♔c8 72.♖f8+ ♔c7 73.♖f7+= ♔d6? 74.♖d7+ ♔e6 75.a8♕ ♕xa8 76.♗xa8 ♔xd7 77.♗f3+–) 72.♖f8+ ♔c7 73.♖f7+
  A) 73...♔c/b8 74.♖f8+=;
  B) 73...♔d8 74.♖xa7 d1♕ 75.♖d7+ ♕xd7 76.♗xd7 ♔xd7 77.♔c5=;
  C) Avoiding a draw is not a good idea: 73...♔d6? 74.♖xa7 d1♕ 75.♖d7+ ♔e6 76.♖xd1+–.
Of course, all these lines are not easy to see, especially not at the end of a long game, and certainly not when you were winning just one move ago! White decided to wipe one of the passed pawns off the board, but after

66.♖xd3 e2 67.♖e3

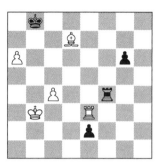

67...♖f3!
White still cannot prevent Black from queening. Again we see that luring away an important defender can be a great help when the goal is to promote a pawn!
68.♖xf3 e1♕
Mission accomplished, although objectively the position is still level. However, White did not manage to hold a draw and had to lay down her king on move 103. Chess can be cruel!

In the next example, thanks to some preparatory moves Black manages to victoriously push through his passed pawn.
Here again, eliminating an important defender plays a crucial role:

Alexey Shirov   2639
Jakov Loxine   2393
Germany Bundesliga 2018/19 (3)

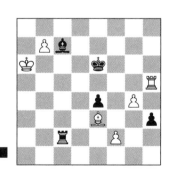

44...♖a2+!
Chasing the king to b5 in order to skewer the king and the rook on the next move.
45.♔b5 ♖a5+
And White resigned because of 46.♔c6 ♖xh5 (*capturing the defender*) 47.♔xc7 (47. gxh5 ♗b8 (*no hurry!*) 48.h6 h2 49.h7 h1♕; promoting, while covering White's h-pawn) 47...♖h7+ 48.♔c6

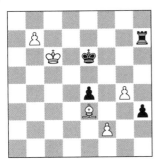

analysis diagram

48...♖xb7! (48...♖h8 49.♗f4 and White wins!) 49.♔xb7 (49.♗f4 ♖f7–+) 49...h2–+.

A passed pawn can also be destructive in the middlegame.

Miguel Santos Ruiz   2072
Carlos Matamoros Franco   2519
Navalmoral de la Mata 2012 (1)

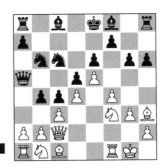

14...b3! 15.♕e2 ♕xa2!
Luring the rook.
16.♖xa2 bxa2 0-1
A double attack, although 17...a1♕ is unstoppable anyway.

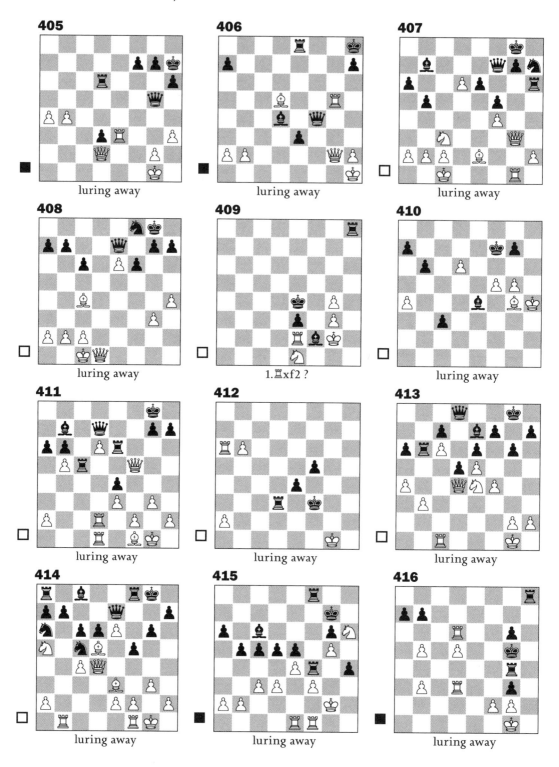

405

luring away

406

luring away

407

luring away

408

luring away

409

1.♖xf2 ?

410

luring away

411

luring away

412

luring away

413

luring away

414

luring away

415

luring away

416

luring away

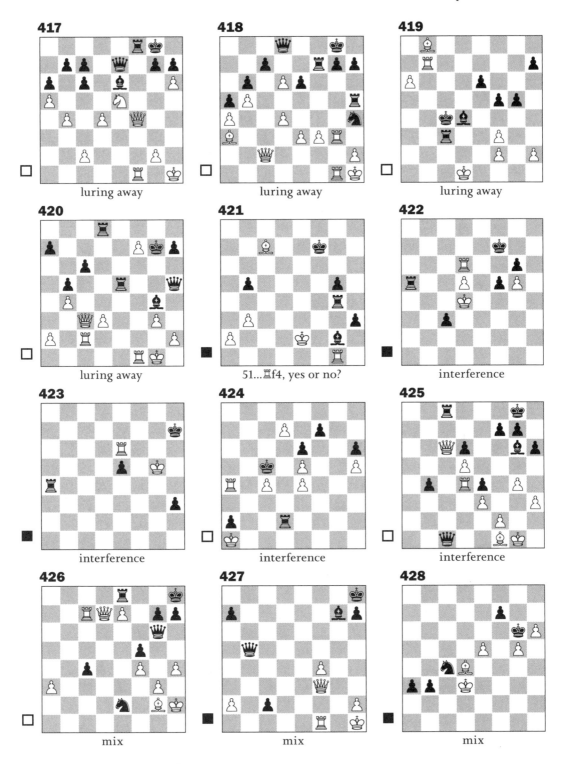

417

luring away

418

luring away

419

luring away

420

luring away

421

51...♖f4, yes or no?

422

interference

423

interference

424

interference

425

interference

426

mix

427

mix

428

mix

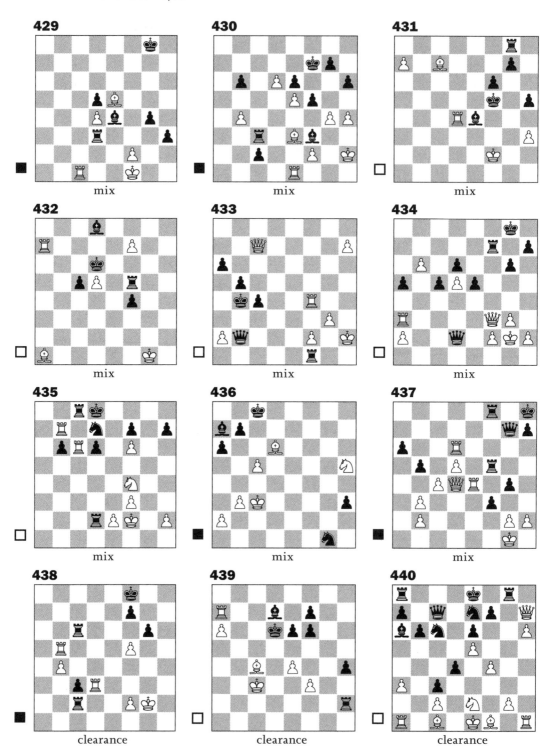

429

mix

430

mix

431

mix

432

mix

433

mix

434

mix

435

mix

436

mix

437

mix

438

clearance

439

clearance

440

clearance

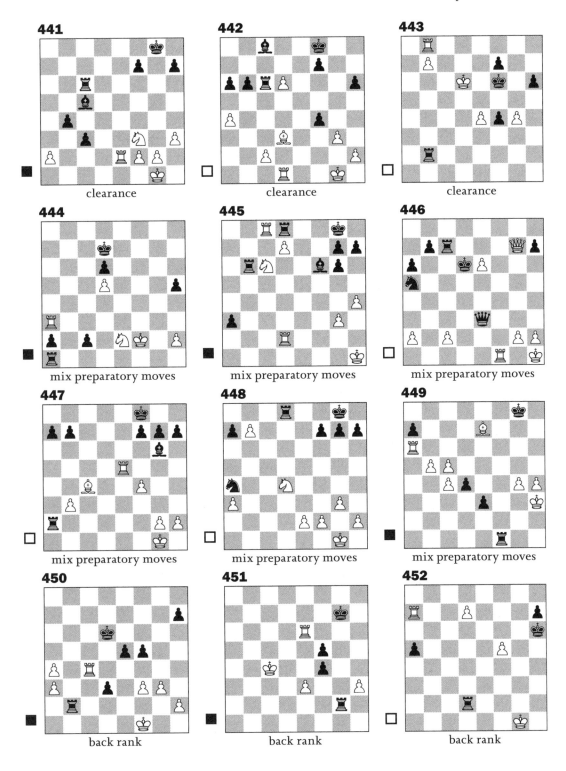

441

clearance

442

clearance

443

clearance

444

mix preparatory moves

445

mix preparatory moves

446

mix preparatory moves

447

mix preparatory moves

448

mix preparatory moves

449

mix preparatory moves

450

back rank

451

back rank

452

back rank

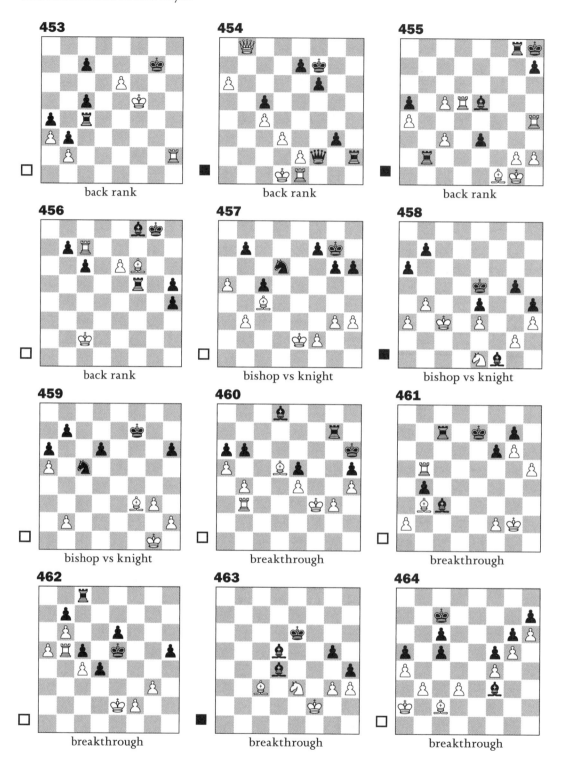

453

back rank

454

back rank

455

back rank

456

back rank

457

bishop vs knight

458

bishop vs knight

459

bishop vs knight

460

breakthrough

461

breakthrough

462

breakthrough

463

breakthrough

464

breakthrough

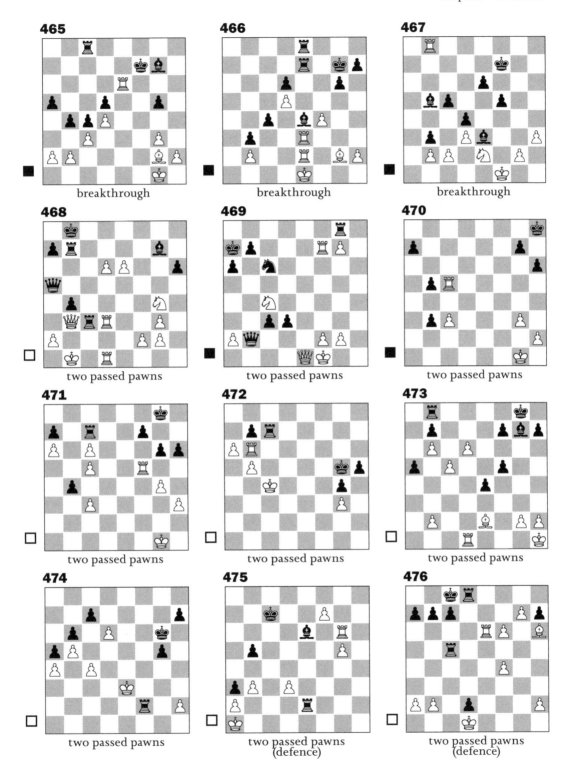

465

breakthrough

466

breakthrough

467

breakthrough

468

two passed pawns

469

two passed pawns

470

two passed pawns

471

two passed pawns

472

two passed pawns

473

two passed pawns

474

two passed pawns

475

two passed pawns
(defence)

476

two passed pawns
(defence)

477

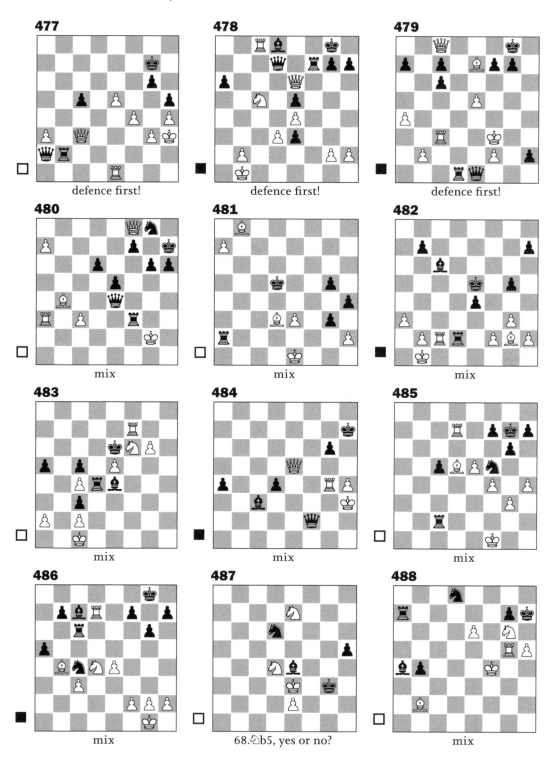

defence first!

478

defence first!

479

defence first!

480

mix

481

mix

482

mix

483

mix

484

mix

485

mix

486

mix

487

68.♘b5, yes or no?

488

mix

489

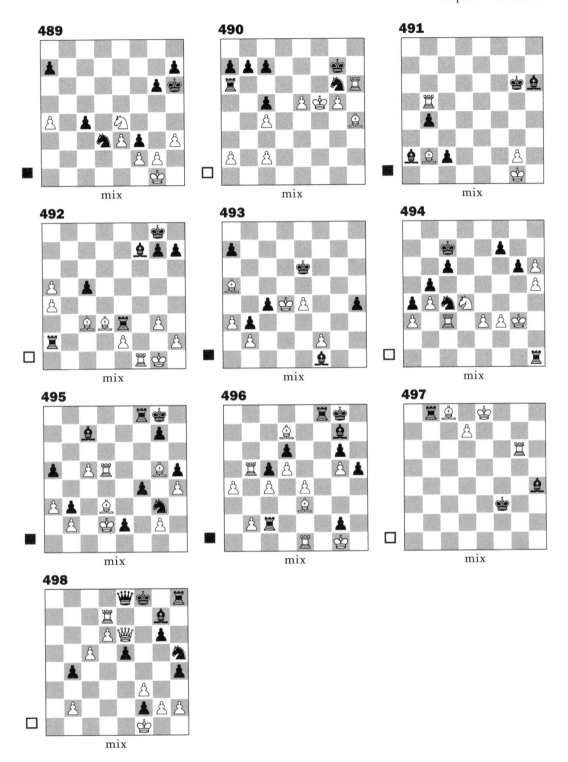

mix

490

mix

491

mix

492

mix

493

mix

494

mix

495

mix

496

mix

497

mix

498

mix

CHAPTER 8

Draw

There are several ways to draw a game. In this chapter we will focus on the following methods:
– Repetition of moves by perpetual check or a perpetual attack;
– Stalemate;
– Liquidation to a theoretically drawn endgame.

A good reason for securing a draw is because otherwise you are simply lost. In such cases a draw can feel like a victory.

Vadim Moiseenko   2548
Evgeny Alekseev   2607
Sochi 2017 (4)

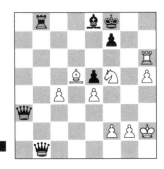

Black is two queens up and it is his move, but he still cannot prevent White from making a draw!

44...♕g1+
44...♔g8 (White was threatening 45.♖h8#) 45.♖g6+ ♔h8 46.♖h6+ ♔g8 47.♖g6+ with perpetual check.
45.♔xg1 ♕c1+ 46.♔h2 ♕f4+ 47.g3!
Now Black has to move away the queen. 47.♔h3? ♔g8 (47...♖b3+ 48.g3 ♔g8 transposes) 48.g3 ♖b3!. The black queen has to stay on f4, because here it controls everything (48...♕g5? 49.♖g6++−; 48...♕c1 49.♘e7+ ♔f8 50.♘f5 ♔g8 51.♘e7+=).

Remarkably, White is in a kind of *zugzwang* here.
Firstly, White has no perpetual with ♖h6-g6-h6, as the queen covers the h6-square: 49.♖g6+ ♔h7 50.♖h6+ ♕xh6.
Secondly, after 49.♘e7+ ♔g7 50.♘f5 Black can give back material to avoid a draw: 50...♕xf5+.
Thirdly, moving the king is not an option for White either as he will be too exposed after 49.♔g2 ♕f3+ 50.♔h3 ♕xf2 51.♖g6+ ♔f8 52.♖h6 ♖xg3+!! 53.♘xg3 ♗d7+ 54.♔h4 ♕f4#.
Fourthly, after 49.c5 the black bishop comes into play: 49...♗b5!.
All in all this means White has to move his rook, after which the drawing mechanism is no longer available.
47...♕xf2+ 48.♔h3 ♔g8 49.♖g6+ ♔f8 50.♖h6 ♕f1+
Black decides he wants to force a draw by perpetual check!
51.♔h4 ♕h1+ 52.♔g4 ♕d1+ 53.♔h4 ♕h1+ ½-½

In the next example, another kind of repetition of moves comes to the rescue, but here liquidation to a theoretically drawn endgame also plays an important role:

75

L. Silaev, 1978

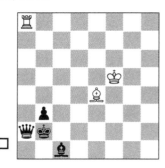

6.♗d5!
Threatening to liquidate into a theoretically drawn ♔+♗ vs. ♚ ending. Moreover, this move prevents Black playing 6...♚c3, after which he would be able to move the queen.
6...♛b1+
6...♚a1 7.♖xa2+ bxa2 8.♗xa2 ♚xa2=.
7.♗e4! ♛a2 8.♗d5
with a perpetual pursuit.

When there are few pieces left on the board and your king has not much space, for instance if it is on the edge of the board, you always have to be alert that sacrificing the last piece (a so-called **'rampant' piece**) can lead to stalemate:

Sergey Grigoriants 2626
Magnus Carlsen 2939
St Petersburg Wch blitz 2018 (2)

67...♛e3+! 68.♛g3+

68.♔g4 ♛e4+ 69.♔g3 ♛g2+ 70.♔f4 ♛xb7=.
68...♔h1! 69.♛xe3 ½-½
White could have tried 69.b8♛, after which it is not that easy to find a way to a draw, certainly not in a blitz game. By combining perpetual check with stalemate tricks, White can succeed: 69...♛e6+! 70.♛g4 (if 70.♔h4 Black has the beautiful 70...♛g4+!. After 71.♛xg4 the g3-queen has cleared the way for the other queen, which means that the h2-square is still covered: stalemate!) 70...♛e3+! 71.♔h4 ♛f2+! 72.♔h5 (72.♔g5 ♛f6+ 73.♔h5 ♛h6+ 74.♔xh6, stalemate!) 72...♛f7+! 73.♛g6 (73.♔h6 ♛g6+ 74.♛/♔xg6, stalemate!; 73.♔g5 ♛f6+ 74.♔h5 ♛h6+ 75.♔xh6, stalemate!) 73...♛f3+!. And now 74.♛g4 ♛f7+ transposes to 72...♛f7+, but the other options lead to stalemate: 74.♔g5 ♛g3+!; 74.♔h6 ♛f4+!; or 74.♔h4 ♛f4+.

Of course, there are ways to avoid stalemate:

Grigory Serper 2450
Catalin Navrotescu 2280
Oakham 1988

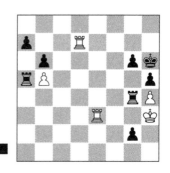

46...g1♖! 0-1
A funny way to finish a game. Five rooks on the board is quite rare! Underpromotion to a knight would

also do the trick, but after queening, 46...g1♕?, White could bail out with 47.♖h7+! ♔xh7 48.♖e7+ ♔g8 49.♖g7+! with a **rampant rook**. Capturing leads to stalemate because the white king cannot move to h2, while there is no way for Black to escape from the checks if the rook stays on the seventh rank: 49...♔f8 50.♖f7+ ♔e8 51.♖e7+ and so on. Here we have a minor promotion that specifically serves to prevent stalemate.

In the previous example we saw that in the case of promotion to a queen, eventually the black king could not escape stalemate or perpetual check. But sometimes it is possible to walk out of a series of checks. In the next example Black had a difficult choice.

Henrik Westerweele	1917
Willem Hajenius	1893

Netherlands tt 2014/15 (5) (analysis)

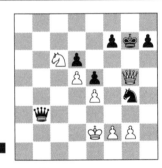

37...♔f8! 38.♕xg4

Here the queen blocks the escape route from the white king, as becomes clear after

38...♕c2+

and now 39.♔f3? ♕d3#. Therefore, White has to settle for a draw:

39.♔e1 ♕c3+ 40.♔f1 ♕c1+

40.♔d1 ♕d3+=.

41.♔e2 ♕c2+

Losing is 37...♔h8. Now, 38.♕xg4? is similar to 37...♔f8, but 38.♘e7! is an important intermediate move: 38...♕c2+ (if 38...♕b8, 39.♔f3 (39.♕xg4? ♕b2+=) is strong, e.g. 39...♘h2+ 40.♔g3 ♘f1+ 41.♔h3 ♕f8 42.♘f5 f6 43.♕c1+–) 39.♔f3 ♕xf2+.

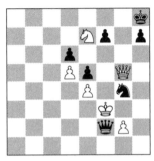

analysis diagram

Now the g4-square is accessible for the king: 40.♔xg4 ♕xg2+ 41.♔h5 ♕h3+ 42.♕h4 ♕f3+ 43.♕g4 ♕h1+ 44.♔g5 ♕c1+ 45.♔f6 ♕h6+ 46.♔xf7 and here there is neither a perpetual check nor a way to force stalemate, as moving the queen means that Black clears the path for the h-pawn.

499

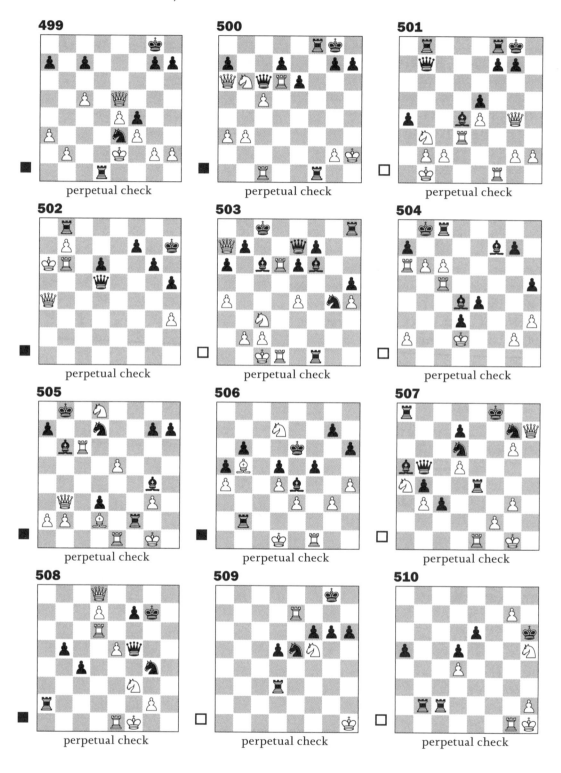

perpetual check

500

perpetual check

501

perpetual check

502

perpetual check

503

perpetual check

504

perpetual check

505

perpetual check

506

perpetual check

507

perpetual check

508

perpetual check

509

perpetual check

510

perpetual check

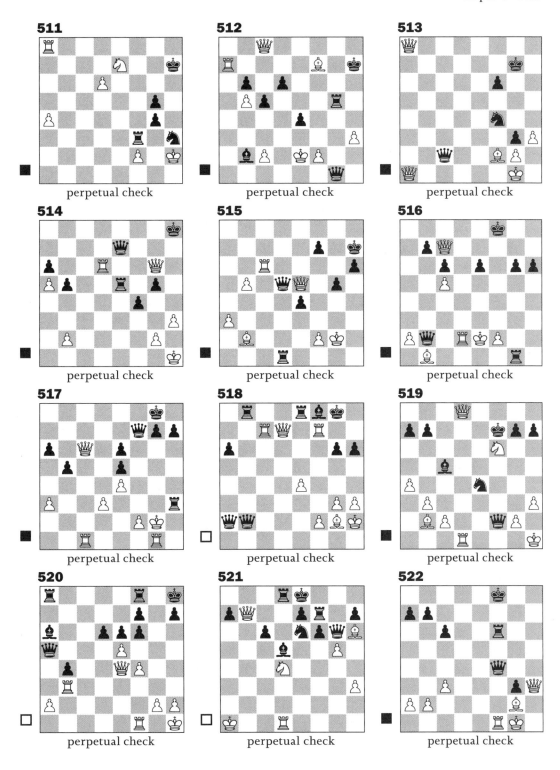

511

perpetual check

512

perpetual check

513

perpetual check

514

perpetual check

515

perpetual check

516

perpetual check

517

perpetual check

518

perpetual check

519

perpetual check

520

perpetual check

521

perpetual check

522

perpetual check

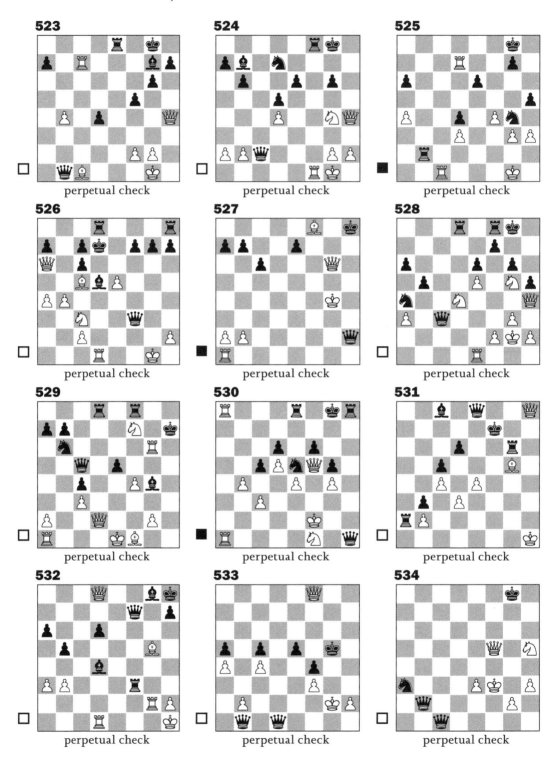

523

perpetual check

524

perpetual check

525

perpetual check

526

perpetual check

527

perpetual check

528

perpetual check

529

perpetual check

530

perpetual check

531

perpetual check

532

perpetual check

533

perpetual check

534

perpetual check

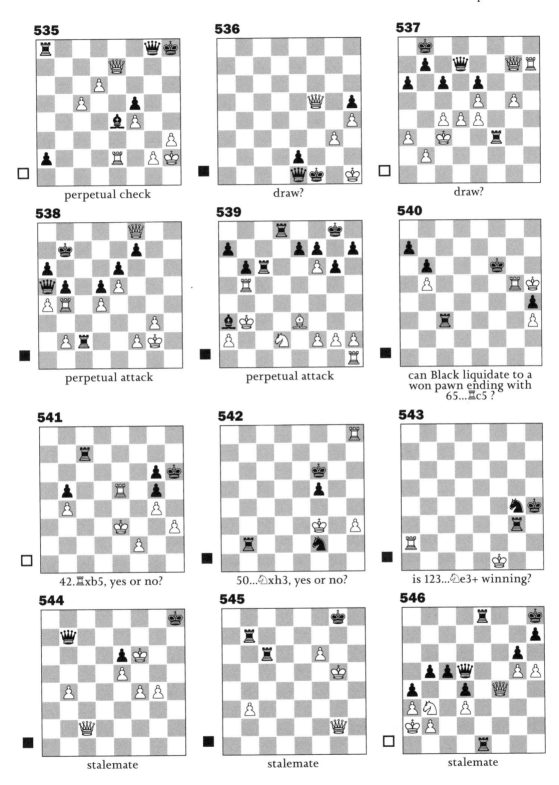

535

perpetual check

536

draw?

537

draw?

538

perpetual attack

539

perpetual attack

540

can Black liquidate to a won pawn ending with 65...♖c5 ?

541

42.♖xb5, yes or no?

542

50...♘xh3, yes or no?

543

is 123...♘e3+ winning?

544

stalemate

545

stalemate

546

stalemate

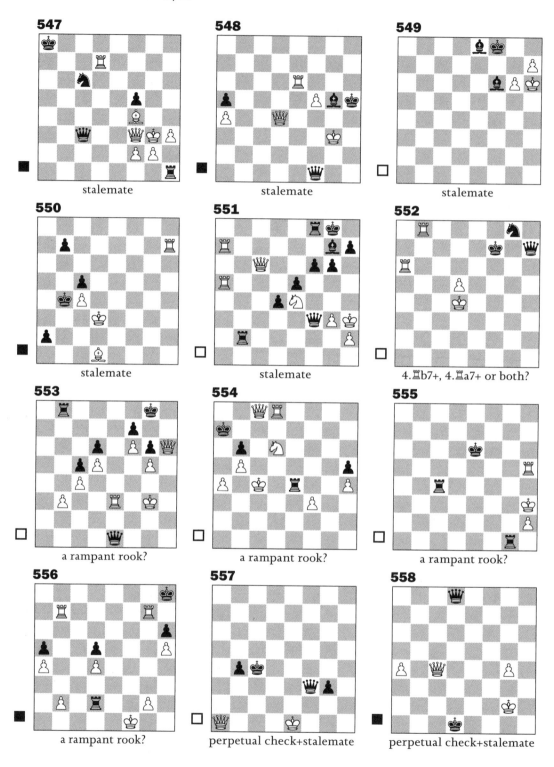

547

stalemate

548

stalemate

549

stalemate

550

stalemate

551

stalemate

552

4.♖b7+, 4.♖a7+ or both?

553

a rampant rook?

554

a rampant rook?

555

a rampant rook?

556

a rampant rook?

557

perpetual check+stalemate

558

perpetual check+stalemate

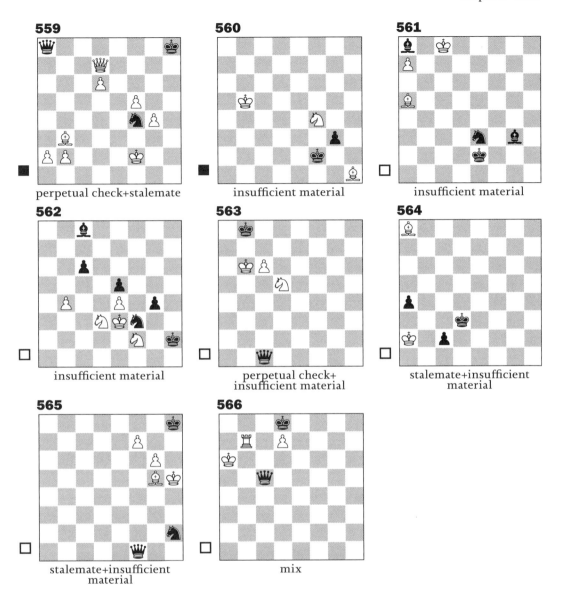

559

perpetual check+stalemate

560

insufficient material

561

insufficient material

562

insufficient material

563

perpetual check+
insufficient material

564

stalemate+insufficient
material

565

stalemate+insufficient
material

566

mix

CHAPTER 9

Mate

There are many ways to checkmate your opponent. One method is to give a series of forcing checks. By doing this, you keep your opponent busy in any case. But in the following example, the checks even lead to mate by force! Black simply gets no time to put up a defence.

Robert Fontaine	2567
Maxime Vachier-Lagrave	2595

Aix-les-Bains ch-FRA 2007 (10)

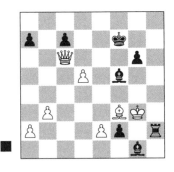

35...f1♘+!
An underpromotion as a prelude to checkmate.
35...f1♕? 36.♕xc7+ leads to a perpetual, e.g. 36...♔f6 37.♕d6+ ♔g5 38.♕f4+ ♔f6 39.♕d6+ ♔g7 40.♕e7+=.
36.♔f4 ♖h4+ 37.♔g5
37.♔e5 ♗d4# or 37...♗h2#; 37.♗g4 ♖xg4+ 38.♔f3 ♘h2# or 38...♘d2#.

37...♗e3+ 38.♔xh4 g5+ 39.♔h5 ♘g3+ 0-1
40.♔h6 g4#.

In the previous example, the white king was chased all across the kingside. Sometimes a sacrifice has to be made to get the king out of its castle (**gaining access**) and force it to enter unsafe territory. Get ready for the **magnet** sacrifice!

Peter Svidler	2737
Dmitry Andreikin	2719

St Petersburg Wch rapid 2018 (10)

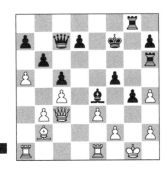

25...♕xh2+!
Black **attracts** the king into the open.
26.♔xh2
Refusing the sacrifice does not help: 26.♔f1 ♗f3, **taking away the escape route** from the white king; ...♕g2# or ...♕h1# cannot be averted. Sometimes **quiet moves** can be even more powerful

than a series of forcing moves/checks. Mark my words!

26...♖xh4+ 27.♔g3

27.♔g1 ♖h1#.

27...♖h3+ 28.♔f4 ♖f3+ 29.♔e5

29...♖g6! 0-1

With a queen down, Black just goes for a **quiet move**! However, since he has now taken away the d6-square from White, the game is over as the white king is caught in a **mating net**! There is nothing White can do against either 30...♖e6# or 30...d6#.

The defender does not always have to accept the sacrifice, but this may mean he will lose material (Exercises 690-695, 'gaining access; mate or material').

There are also other ways to make a breach in the defensive wall of the enemy king. It is not always necessary to start a mating attack with a check:

Alexander Alekhine
Supico

Lisbon simul blindfold 1941

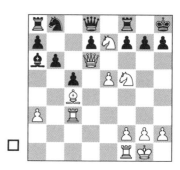

20.♕g6!

Black resigned, as after 20...fxg6 21.♘xg6+ hxg6, both the f- and h-pawn have been lured away, and now after 22.♖h3+ ♕h4 23.♖xh4, **Greco's Mate** appears on the board.

Another **mating pattern** emerges after 20...hxg6 21.♖h3# or 20...♖g8 21.♕xh7+ (yet another *magnet sacrifice!*) 21...♔xh7 22.♖h3#. In both cases we see **Anastasia's Mate**.

Alekhine's move cannot exactly be called 'quiet', but as it is not with check we will use this term within quotation marks in the hints on the Exercises pages.

In the Solutions you will find the names of many more mating patterns!

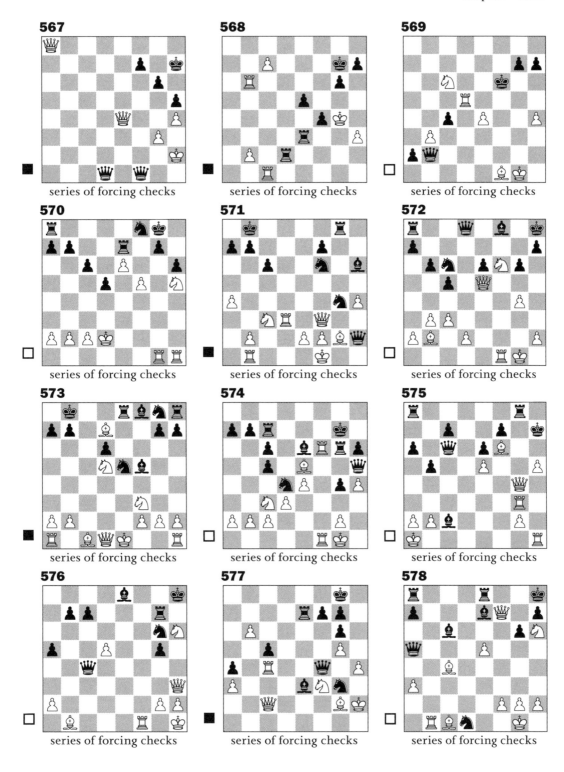

567

series of forcing checks

568

series of forcing checks

569

series of forcing checks

570

series of forcing checks

571

series of forcing checks

572

series of forcing checks

573

series of forcing checks

574

series of forcing checks

575

series of forcing checks

576

series of forcing checks

577

series of forcing checks

578

series of forcing checks

579

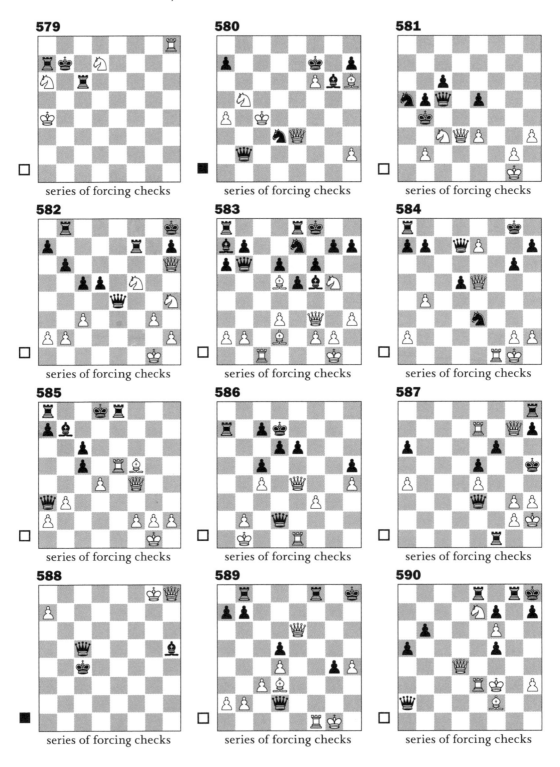

series of forcing checks

580

series of forcing checks

581

series of forcing checks

582

series of forcing checks

583

series of forcing checks

584

series of forcing checks

585

series of forcing checks

586

series of forcing checks

587

series of forcing checks

588

series of forcing checks

589

series of forcing checks

590

series of forcing checks

591

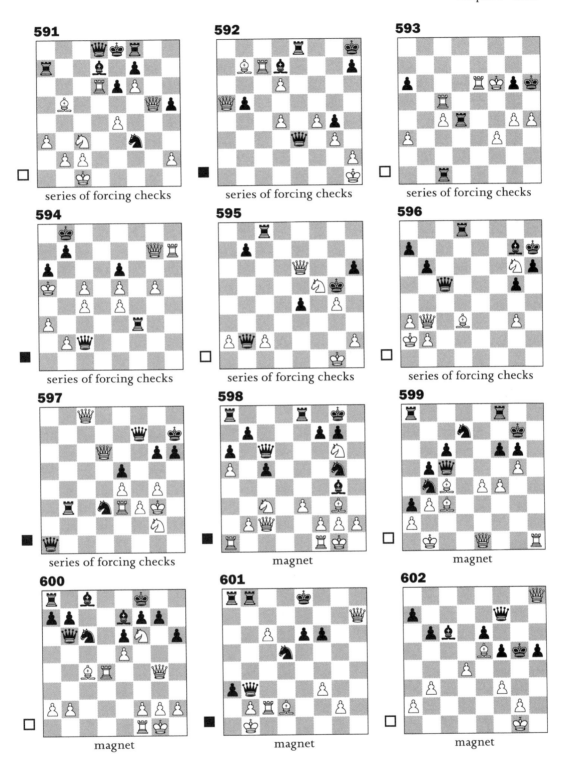

series of forcing checks

592

series of forcing checks

593

series of forcing checks

594

series of forcing checks

595

series of forcing checks

596

series of forcing checks

597

series of forcing checks

598

magnet

599

magnet

600

magnet

601

magnet

602

magnet

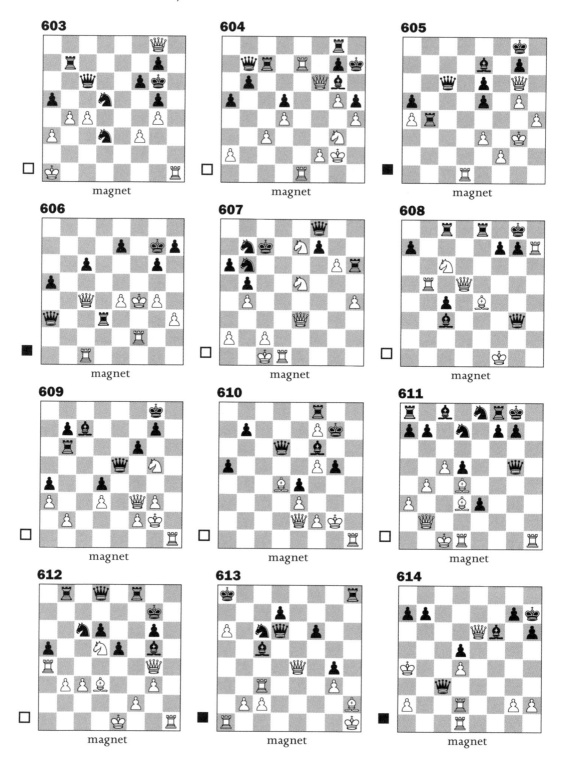

603

magnet

604

magnet

605

magnet

606

magnet

607

magnet

608

magnet

609

magnet

610

magnet

611

magnet

612

magnet

613

magnet

614

magnet

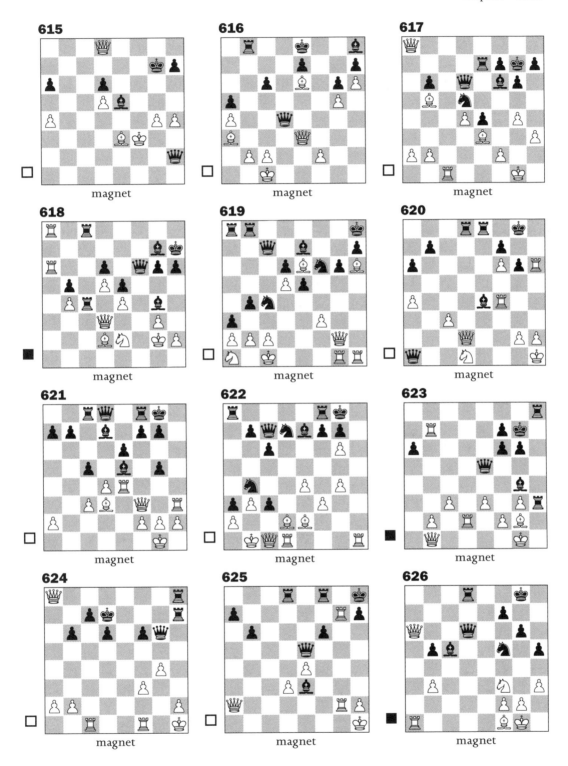

615

magnet

616

magnet

617

magnet

618

magnet

619

magnet

620

magnet

621

magnet

622

magnet

623

magnet

624

magnet

625

magnet

626

magnet

627

628

629

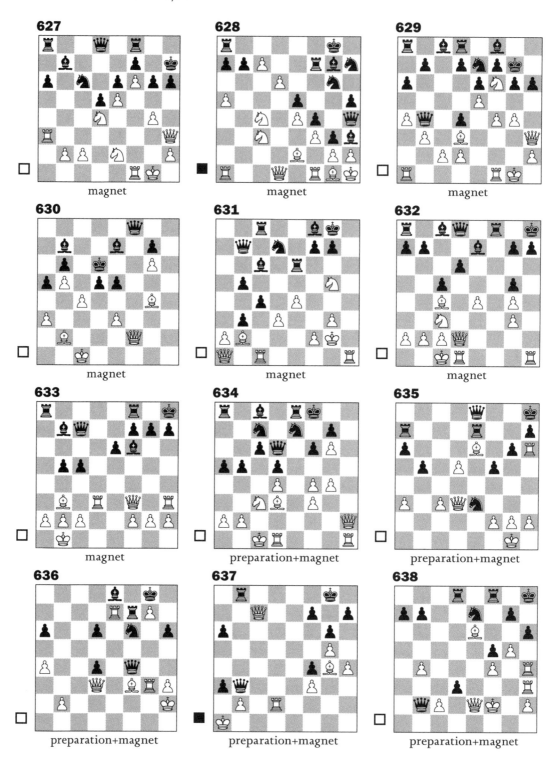

magnet

magnet

magnet

630

631

632

magnet

magnet

magnet

633

634

635

magnet

preparation+magnet

preparation+magnet

636

637

638

preparation+magnet

preparation+magnet

preparation+magnet

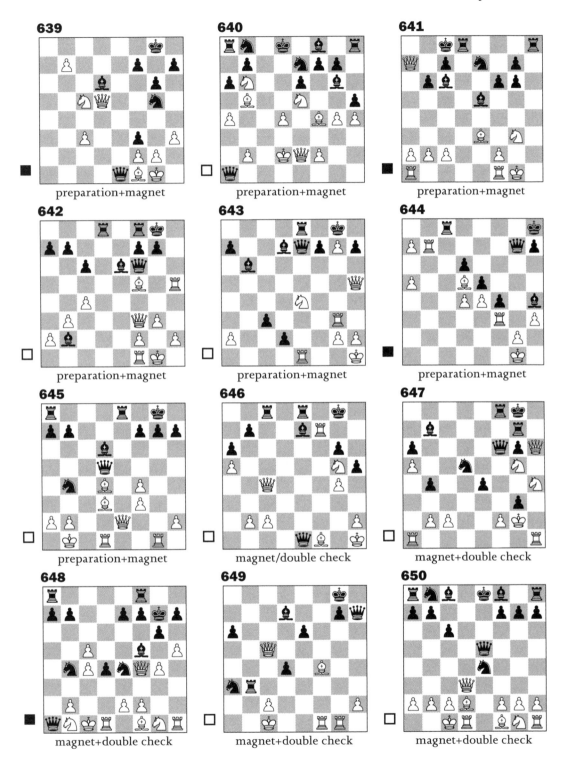

639

preparation+magnet

640

preparation+magnet

641

preparation+magnet

642

preparation+magnet

643

preparation+magnet

644

preparation+magnet

645

preparation+magnet

646

magnet/double check

647

magnet+double check

648

magnet+double check

649

magnet+double check

650

magnet+double check

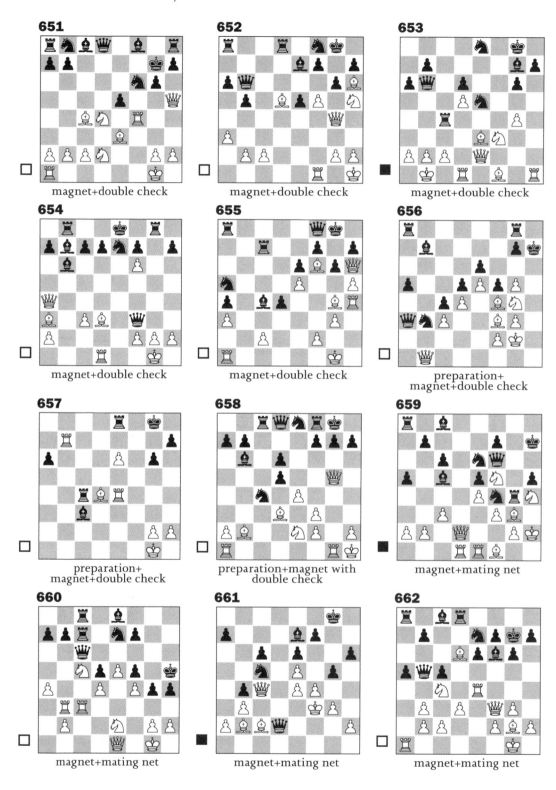

651

magnet+double check

652

magnet+double check

653

magnet+double check

654

magnet+double check

655

magnet+double check

656

preparation+
magnet+double check

657

preparation+
magnet+double check

658

preparation+magnet with
double check

659

magnet+mating net

660

magnet+mating net

661

magnet+mating net

662

magnet+mating net

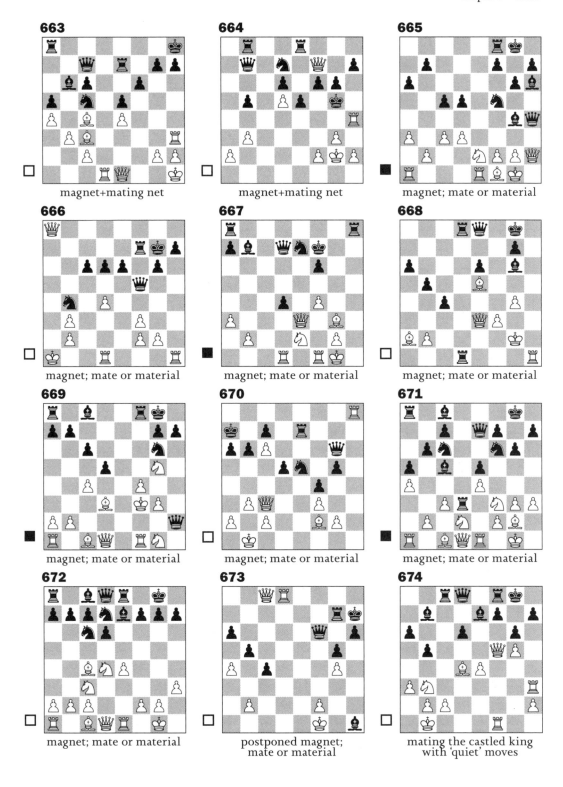

663

magnet+mating net

664

magnet+mating net

665

magnet; mate or material

666

magnet; mate or material

667

magnet; mate or material

668

magnet; mate or material

669

magnet; mate or material

670

magnet; mate or material

671

magnet; mate or material

672

magnet; mate or material

673

postponed magnet;
mate or material

674

mating the castled king
with 'quiet' moves

675

676

677

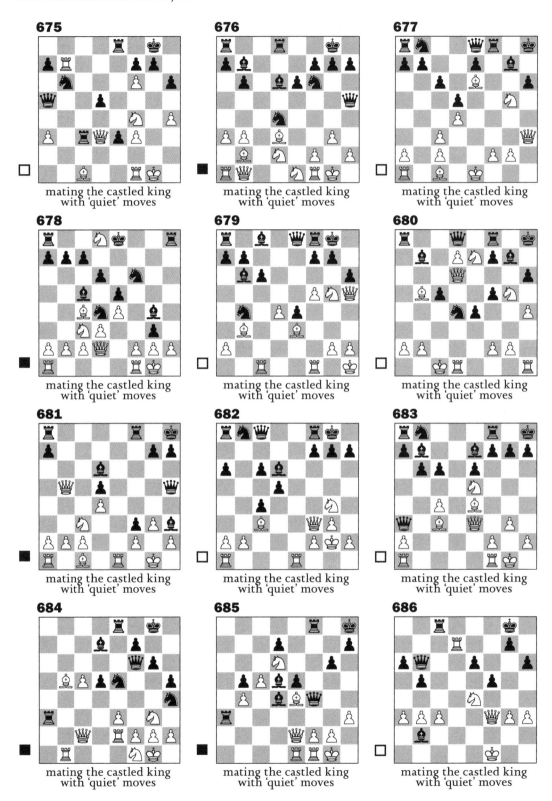

mating the castled king
with 'quiet' moves

mating the castled king
with 'quiet' moves

mating the castled king
with 'quiet' moves

678

679

680

mating the castled king
with 'quiet' moves

mating the castled king
with 'quiet' moves

mating the castled king
with 'quiet' moves

681

682

683

mating the castled king
with 'quiet' moves

mating the castled king
with 'quiet' moves

mating the castled king
with 'quiet' moves

684

685

686

mating the castled king
with 'quiet' moves

mating the castled king
with 'quiet' moves

mating the castled king
with 'quiet' moves

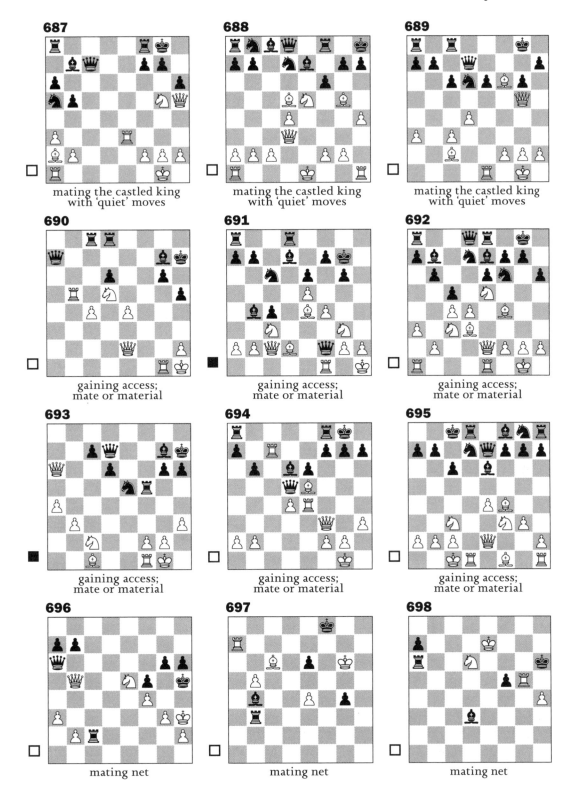

687

mating the castled king
with 'quiet' moves

688

mating the castled king
with 'quiet' moves

689

mating the castled king
with 'quiet' moves

690

gaining access;
mate or material

691

gaining access;
mate or material

692

gaining access;
mate or material

693

gaining access;
mate or material

694

gaining access;
mate or material

695

gaining access;
mate or material

696

mating net

697

mating net

698

mating net

699

700

701

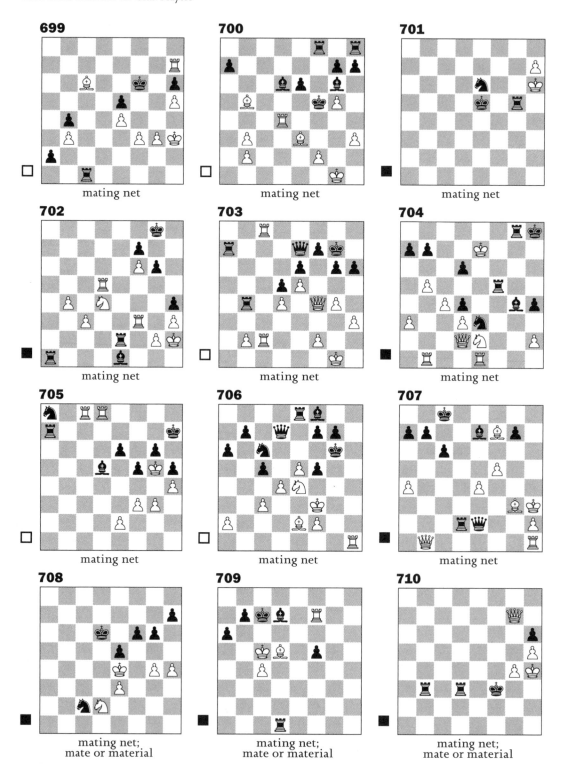

mating net

mating net

mating net

702

703

704

mating net

mating net

mating net

705

706

707

mating net

mating net

mating net

708

709

710

mating net;
mate or material

mating net;
mate or material

mating net;
mate or material

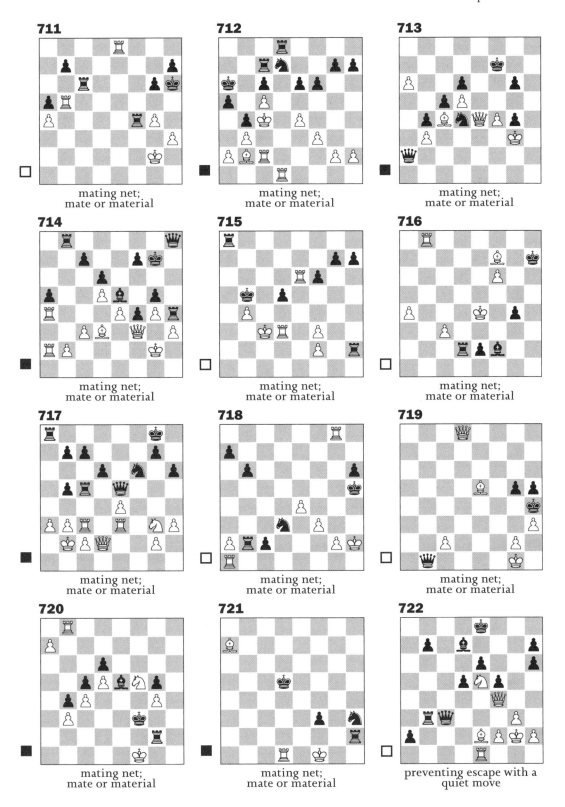

711

mating net;
mate or material

712

mating net;
mate or material

713

mating net;
mate or material

714

mating net;
mate or material

715

mating net;
mate or material

716

mating net;
mate or material

717

mating net;
mate or material

718

mating net;
mate or material

719

mating net;
mate or material

720

mating net;
mate or material

721

mating net;
mate or material

722

preventing escape with a
quiet move

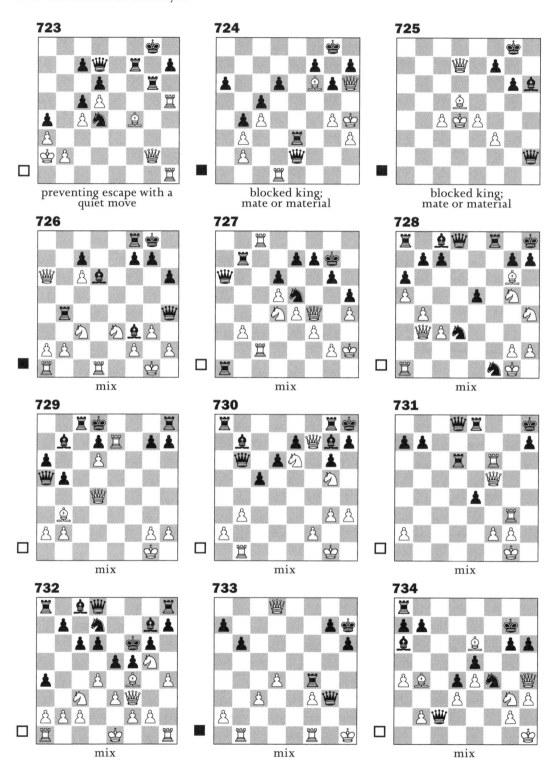

723

preventing escape with a
quiet move

724

blocked king;
mate or material

725

blocked king;
mate or material

726

mix

727

mix

728

mix

729

mix

730

mix

731

mix

732

mix

733

mix

734

mix

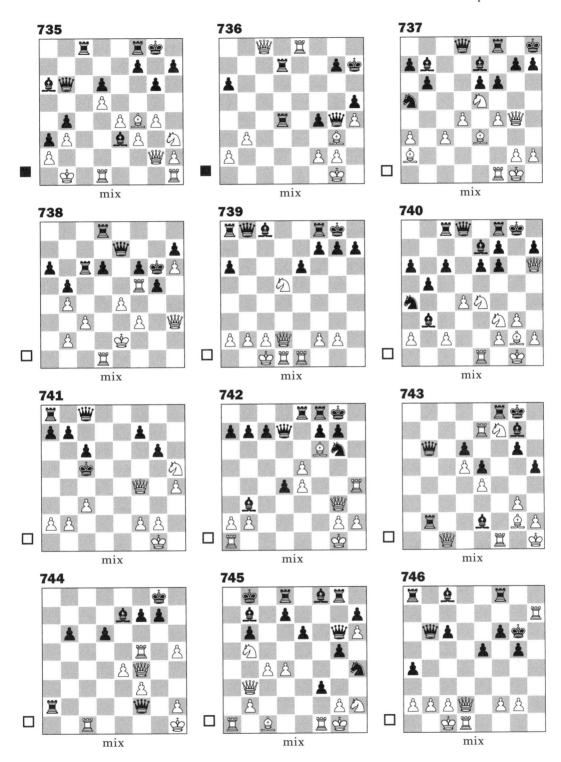

735

mix

736

mix

737

mix

738

mix

739

mix

740

mix

741

mix

742

mix

743

mix

744

mix

745

mix

746

mix

CHAPTER 10

Defending

Now that you are equipped with several tactical weapons, it is time to learn how to defend against them! All the topics from the previous chapters are covered in the exercises of this chapter, with the difference that here you have to arm yourself against them.

In the following example, both players are required to find an 'only' move so as not to lose the game.

Jan van Mechelen   2194
Robert Ris   2394
Belgium tt 2012/13 (1)

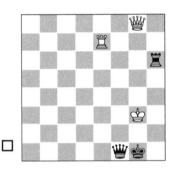

Both sides have just queened and now White, to play, seems to be in danger. The most obvious threat is 89...♕g2+, skewering the white king and queen, but in addition there are some mating attacks in the air.

Moving away the queen or protecting the queen with the rook to defend against the skewer threat does not help, e.g.

A) 89.♕f7 ♖h3+ 90.♔g4 ♕g2+ 91.♔f5 ♖f3+–+;

B) 89.♕d5/♕a2 ♖g6+ 90.♔h4 ♕f4+ and mate next move;

C) 89.♖e8 ♕f2+ 90.♔g4 ♖h4+ 91.♔g5 ♕f4+ 92.♔g6 ♖h6+ 93.♔g7 ♕f6#.

However, when you are looking for tactics, it is important to notice that it's not only the white queen and king who are standing on the same line!

89.♖e1!

And suddenly Black seems to be in danger! The black queen is pinned, and after 89...♕xe1+ White can move his king with a discovered check while keeping the f2-square covered: 90.♔f3+ ♔h2 91.♕g2#.

89...♖h3+!

An intermediate check comes to the rescue!

90.♔g4

90...♕xe1

Another remarkable, but rather contrived defence was 90...♔g2 91.♕a2+ (91.♖xf1 ♖g3+=; 91.♕a8+ ♕f3+=) 91...♕f2 92.♖e2 ♖g3+ 93.♔h5 ♖h3+ 94.♔g5 ♖g3+ with a perpetual.

91.♔xh3+

And now, with the white king on h3 instead of f3, the black king has enough breathing space.

91...♔f2 92.♕g3+

92.♕g2+ ♔e3 and the king walks away.

92...♔e2 93.♕xe1+ ½-½

Arkadij Naiditsch	2682
Julio Granda Zuniga	2667

Douglas 2015 (5) (analysis)

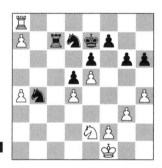

White threatens to promote to a queen with 42.♖e8+, clearing the a8-square with gain of tempo. Black can prevent this by playing 41...♘b6, but after 42.♖b8 ♖xa7 43.♖xb6 White has won back his piece and the game is equal. Of course, a draw is better than a loss, as we have learned in Chapter 8, but defending is not always about equalizing. Black can win by letting White execute his threat!

41...♘c6! 42.♖e8+ ♔xe8 43.a8♕+ ♘db8!

44...♖a7 is next, and the queen is trapped!

Teimour Radjabov	2717
Krishnan Sasikiran	2680

Bilbao tt 2014 (4) (analysis)

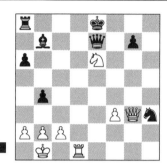

With the king in the middle, the knight on h3 hanging and threats all over the place (27.♘c7+, 27.♖e1, 27.♕g6+ followed by ♘xg7+), Black is forced to take the white knight, as running away with the king does not solve his problems: 26...♔f7 27.♕xg7+ ♔e6 28.♖e1++−.

26...♕xe6 27.♖e1

Pinning the queen. After 27...♕xe1+ 28.♕xe1+ ♔f7 29.♕xb4 Black's loose pieces do not make a good impression, but isn't this the best Black can hope for? No, he has a big surprise in store. He can unpin the queen without losing material:

27...0-0-0!

And White cannot capture Black's queen in view of 28...♖d1#. Black is two pieces up.

Instead of 27.♖e1, better is 27.♕xg7, but after 27...♗d5 28.♕h8+ ♔e7 29.♕h4+ ♔d7 30.♕c4 ♔e8 31.♕xd5 ♕xd5 32.♖xd5 White is the one who must fight for a draw.

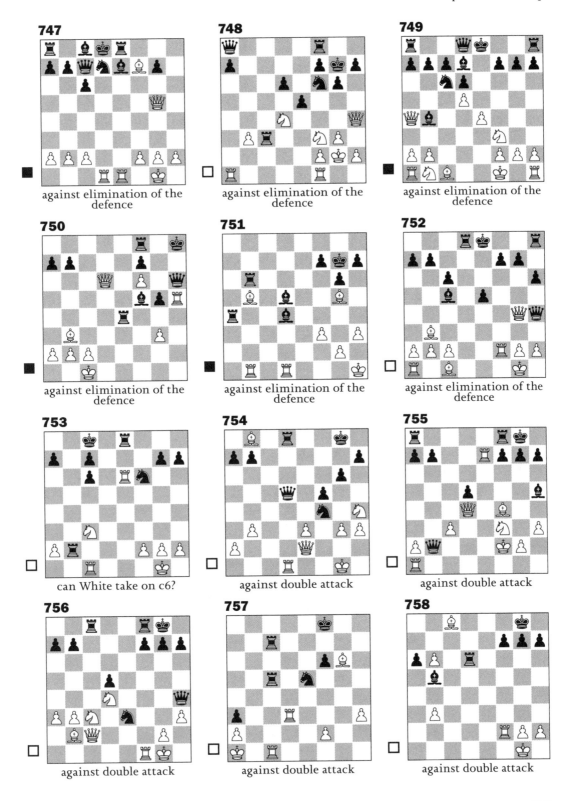

747

against elimination of the defence

748

against elimination of the defence

749

against elimination of the defence

750

against elimination of the defence

751

against elimination of the defence

752

against elimination of the defence

753

can White take on c6?

754

against double attack

755

against double attack

756

against double attack

757

against double attack

758

against double attack

759

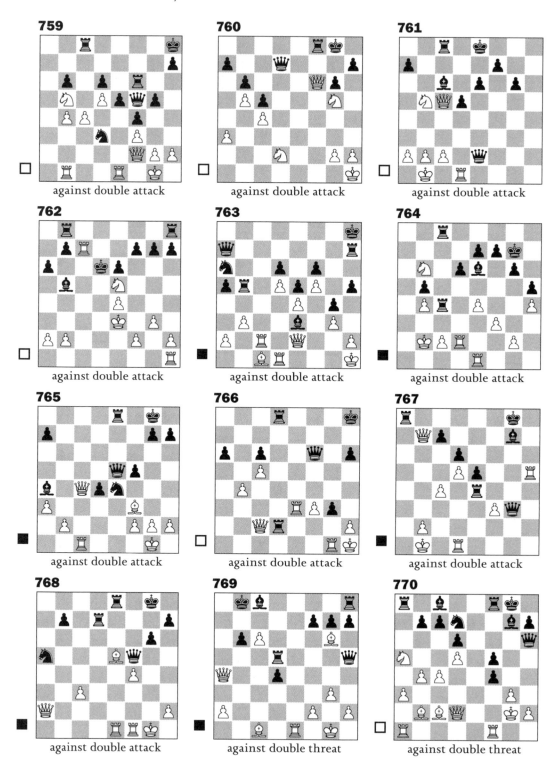

against double attack

760

against double attack

761

against double attack

762

against double attack

763

against double attack

764

against double attack

765

against double attack

766

against double attack

767

against double attack

768

against double attack

769

against double threat

770

against double threat

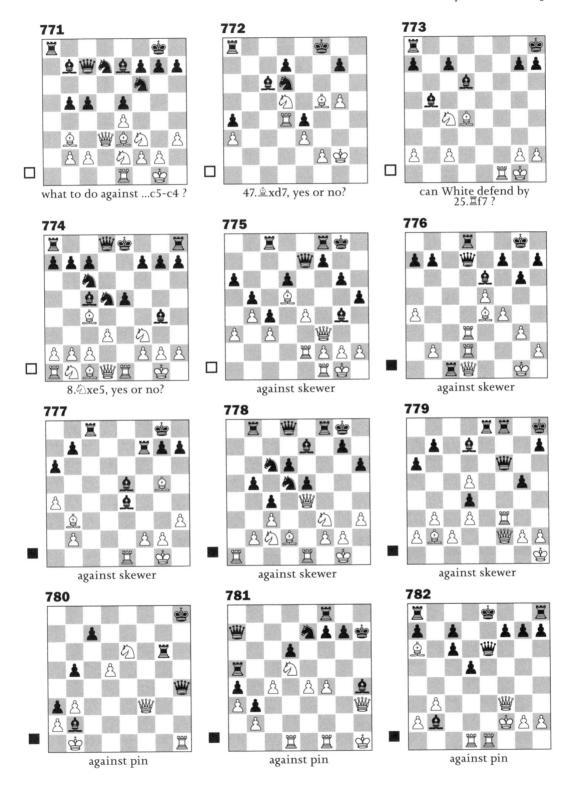

771

what to do against ...c5-c4 ?

772

47.♗xd7, yes or no?

773

can White defend by
25.♖f7 ?

774

8.♘xe5, yes or no?

775

against skewer

776

against skewer

777

against skewer

778

against skewer

779

against skewer

780

against pin

781

against pin

782

against pin

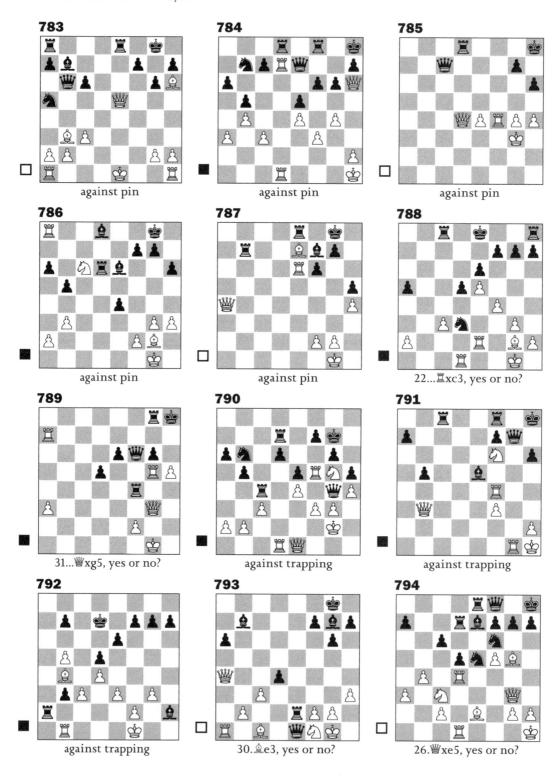

783

against pin

784

against pin

785

against pin

786

against pin

787

against pin

788

22...♖xc3, yes or no?

789

31...♕xg5, yes or no?

790

against trapping

791

against trapping

792

against trapping

793

30.♗e3, yes or no?

794

26.♕xe5, yes or no?

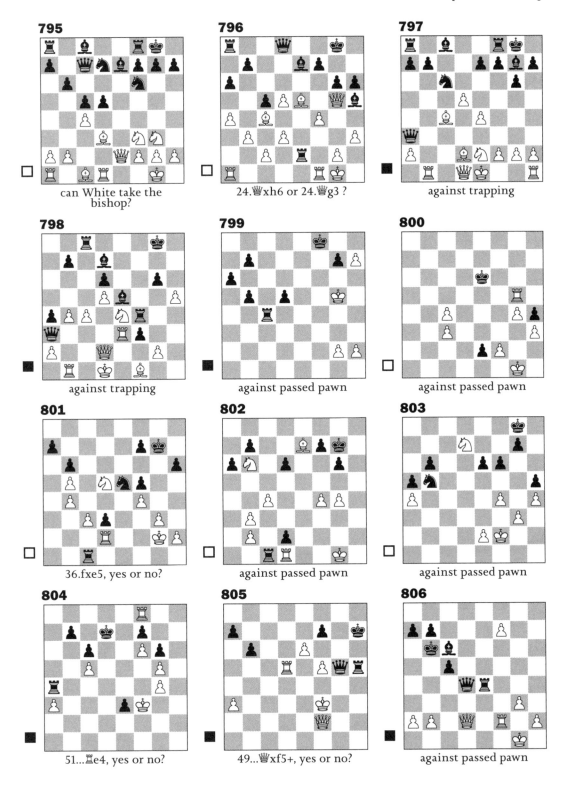

795

can White take the bishop?

796

24.♕xh6 or 24.♕g3 ?

797

against trapping

798

against trapping

799

against passed pawn

800

against passed pawn

801

36.fxe5, yes or no?

802

against passed pawn

803

against passed pawn

804

51...♖e4, yes or no?

805

49...♕xf5+, yes or no?

806

against passed pawn

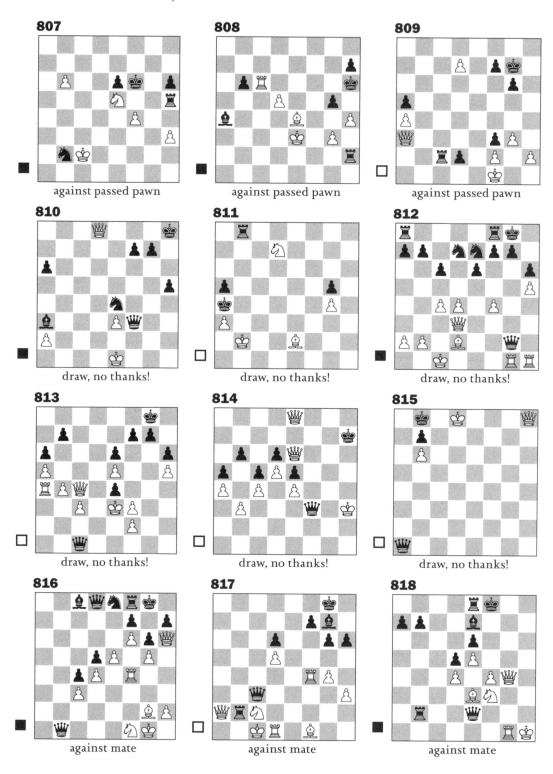

807

against passed pawn

808

against passed pawn

809

against passed pawn

810

draw, no thanks!

811

draw, no thanks!

812

draw, no thanks!

813

draw, no thanks!

814

draw, no thanks!

815

draw, no thanks!

816

against mate

817

against mate

818

against mate

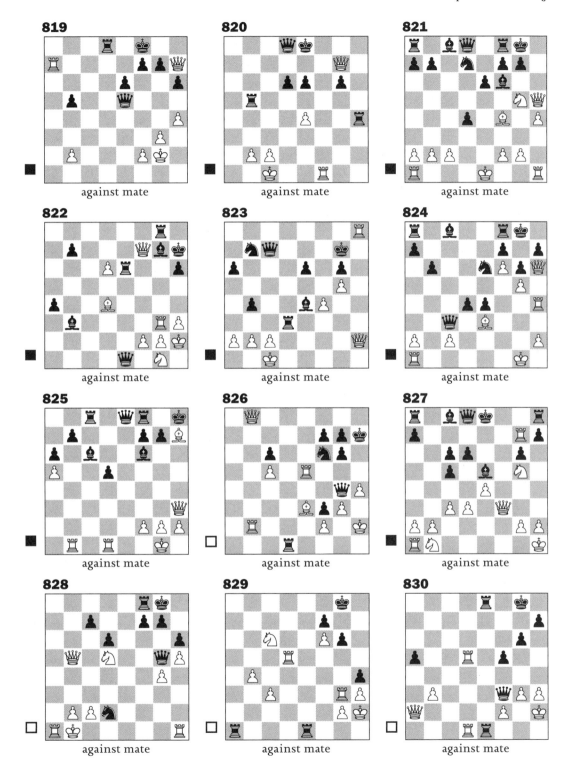

819

against mate

820

against mate

821

against mate

822

against mate

823

against mate

824

against mate

825

against mate

826

against mate

827

against mate

828

against mate

829

against mate

830

against mate

831

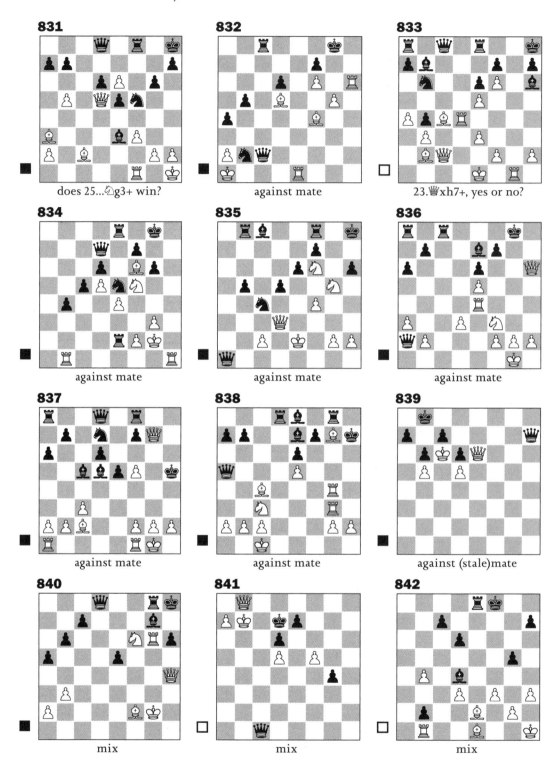

does 25...♘g3+ win?

832

against mate

833

23.♕xh7+, yes or no?

834

against mate

835

against mate

836

against mate

837

against mate

838

against mate

839

against (stale)mate

840

mix

841

mix

842

mix

843

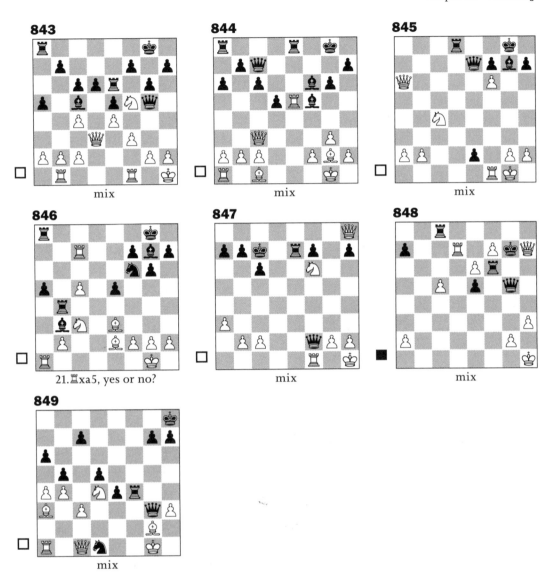

mix

844

mix

845

mix

846

21.♖xa5, yes or no?

847

mix

848

mix

849

mix

CHAPTER 11

Mix

It is time for a review of all the previous topics. Each of the exercises in this chapter contains several tactical themes, and there are no hints below the diagrams. It's just like playing a real game!

Before we start, here is just one example to warm up.

Bassem Amin	2686
Robert Baskin	2348

Hoogeveen 2018 (2)

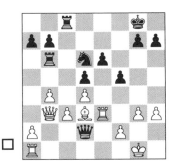

Would you play 25.♗e2 or 25.♗c2 ? Both moves intend to **trap** the black queen with 26.♖d1, but only one of them should lead to victory.

25.♗c2 was played in the game. Possibly White wanted to prevent the knight leap to e4, as after 25...♘e4 26.♗xe4 fxe4 27.♖d1, White's plan of trapping the queen has succeeded. However, on c2 the bishop is vulnerable. Black can **defend** with 25...♖bc6! 26.♖d1 ♕xe3! (*removing a defender*) 27.fxe3 ♖xc3 (**double attack**). With a rook and a knight for the queen Black is still alive.
Winning is
25.♗e2!
and now 25...♖bc6 is not as powerful as in the 25.♗c2 line. White keeps his bishop after 26.♖d1 ♕xe3 (26...♖xc3 27.♖xd2 ♖xb3 28.axb3+−) 27.fxe3 ♖xc3 28.♕a4+−.
A better attempt is
25...♘e4,
which makes more sense here than in the 25.♗c2 line, but still it does not work in view of
26.♖d1 ♖xc3 27.♕a4!,
threatening **mate** on e8 while the black queen is still under attack. White is winning!

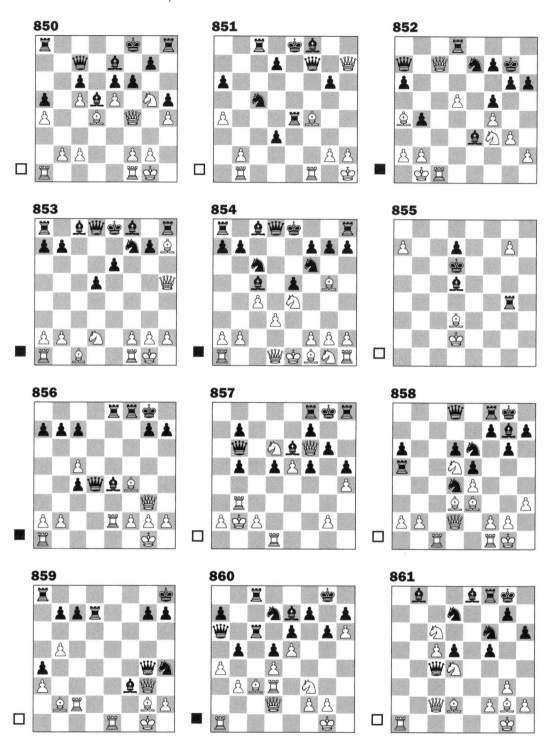

850

851

852

853

854

855

856

857

858

859

860

861

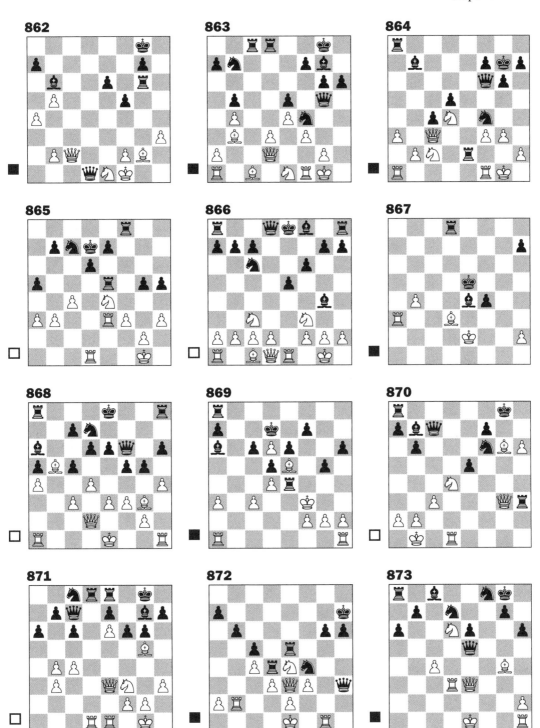

862

863

864

865

866

867

868

869

870

871

872

873

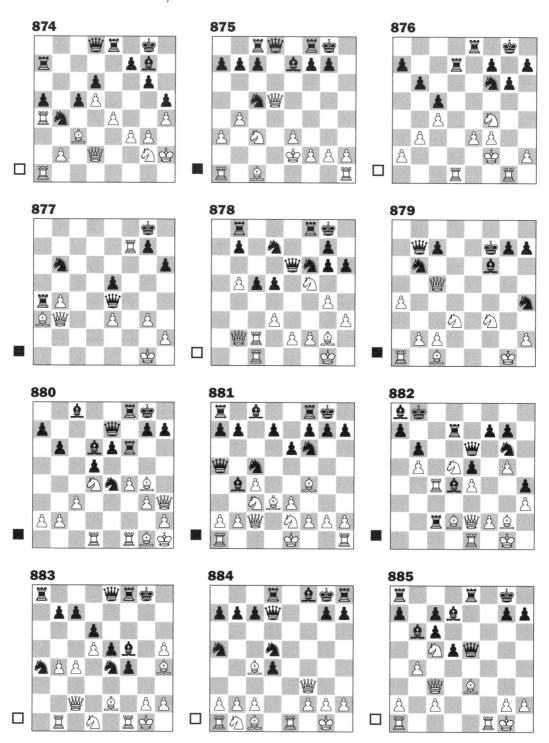

874

875

876

877

878

879

880

881

882

883

884

885

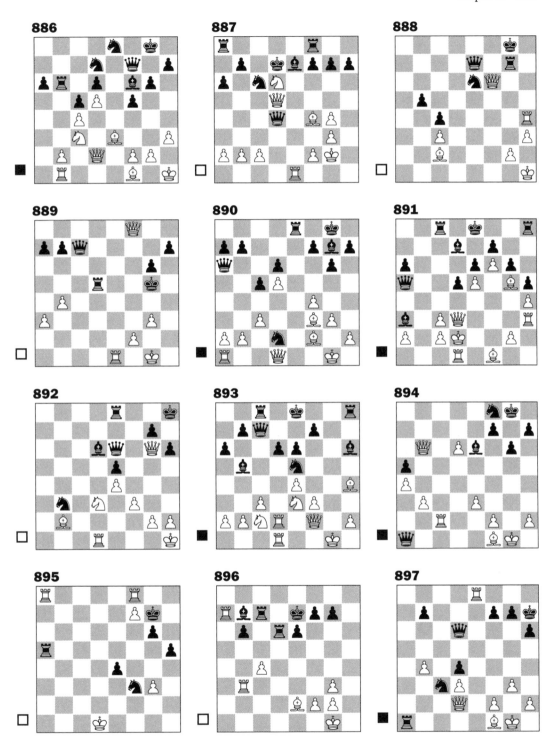

886

887

888

889

890

891

892

893

894

895

896

897

898

899

900

20.♕f5, yes or no?

901

902

903

904

905

906

907

908

909

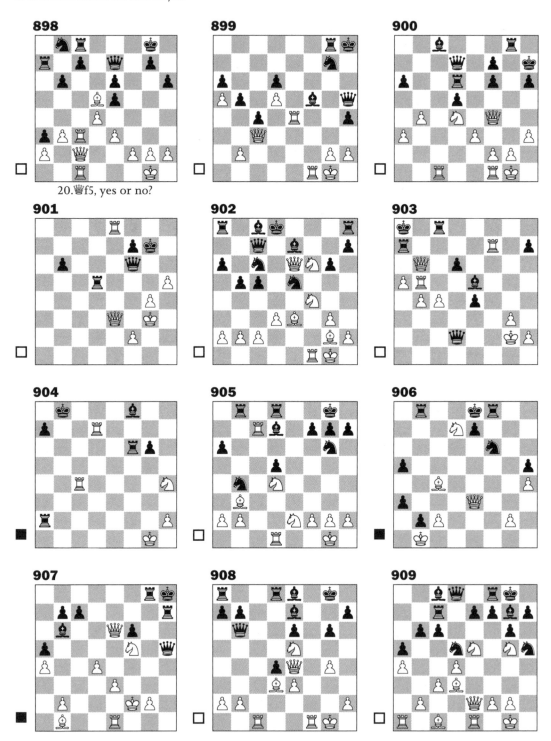

910

911

912

913

914

915

916

34...♗b4, yes or no?

917

918

919

920

921

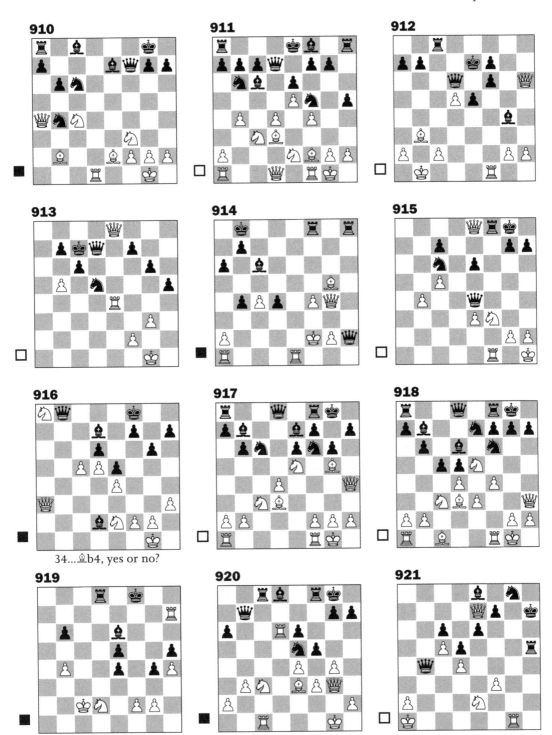

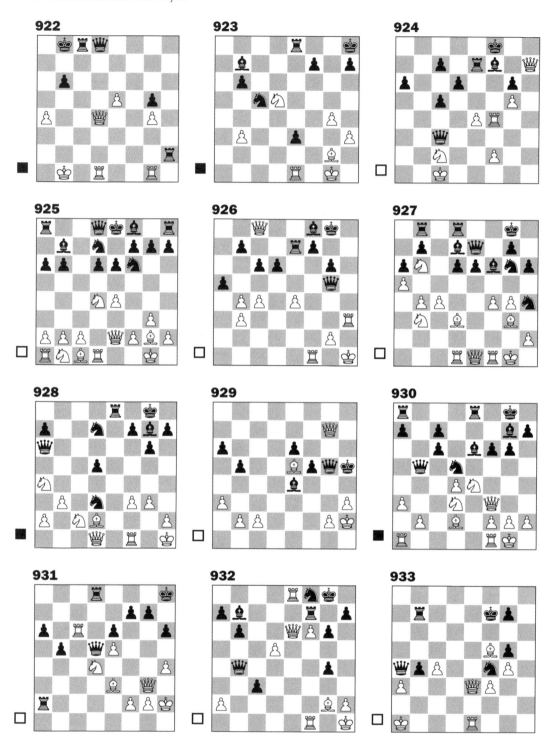

922

923

924

925

926

927

928

929

930

931

932

933

934

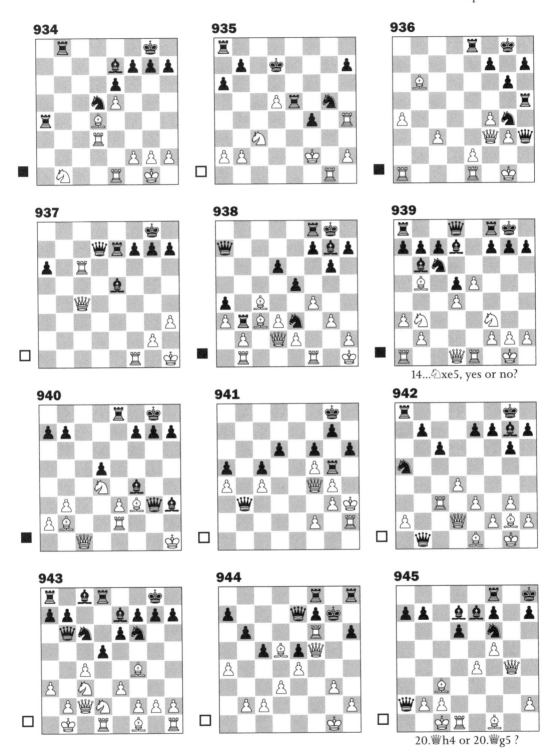

935

936

937

938

939

14...♘xe5, yes or no?

940

941

942

943

944

945

20.♕h4 or 20.♕g5 ?

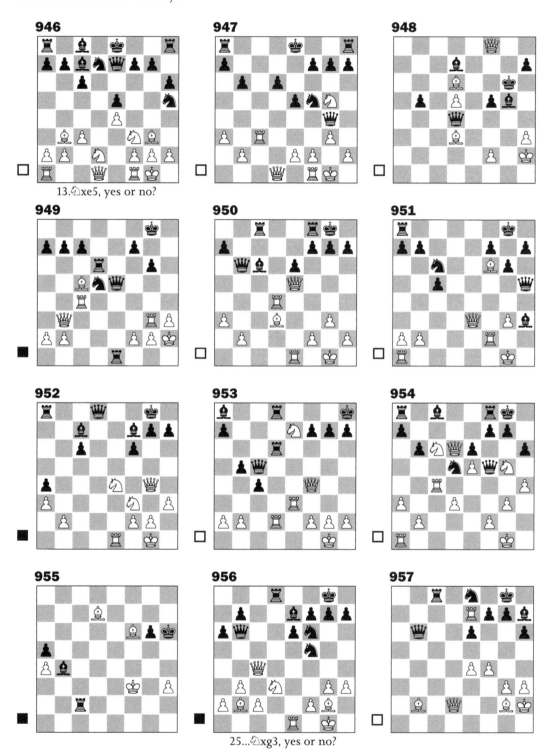

946

13.♘xe5, yes or no?

947

948

949

950

951

952

953

954

955

956

25...♘xg3, yes or no?

957

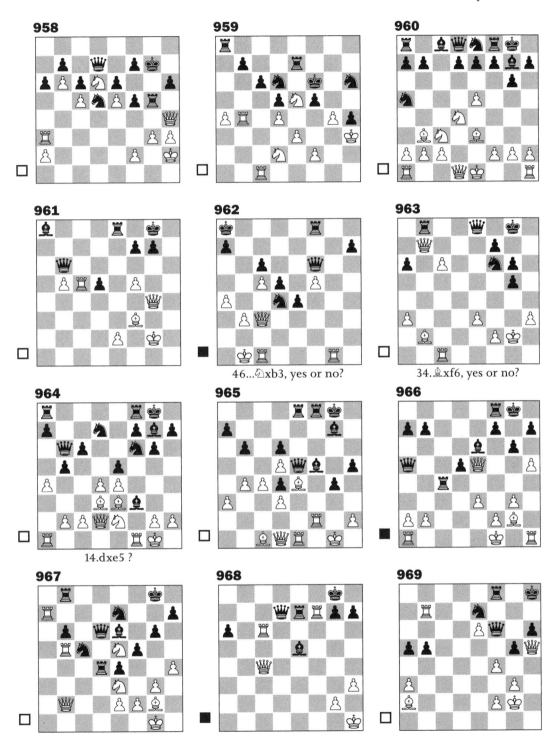

958

959

960

961

962

46...♞xb3, yes or no?

963

34.♗xf6, yes or no?

964

14.dxe5 ?

965

966

967

968

969

970

971

972

973

974

975

31.♘xd5, yes or no?

976

977

978

979

980

981

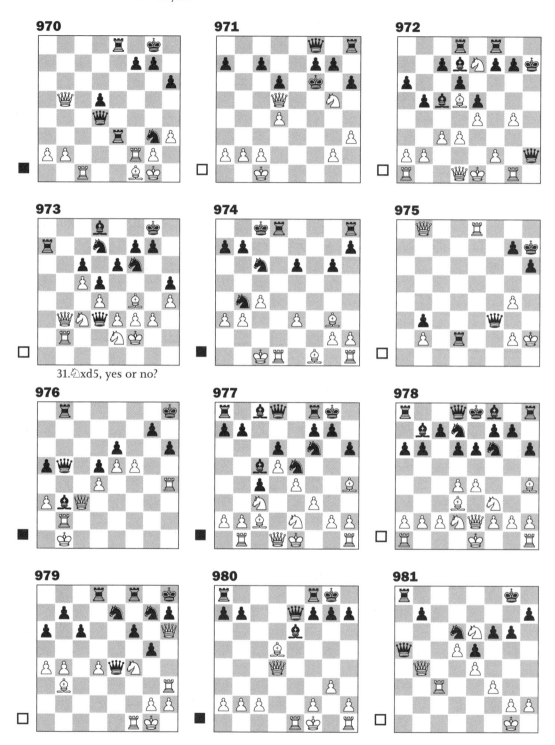

982

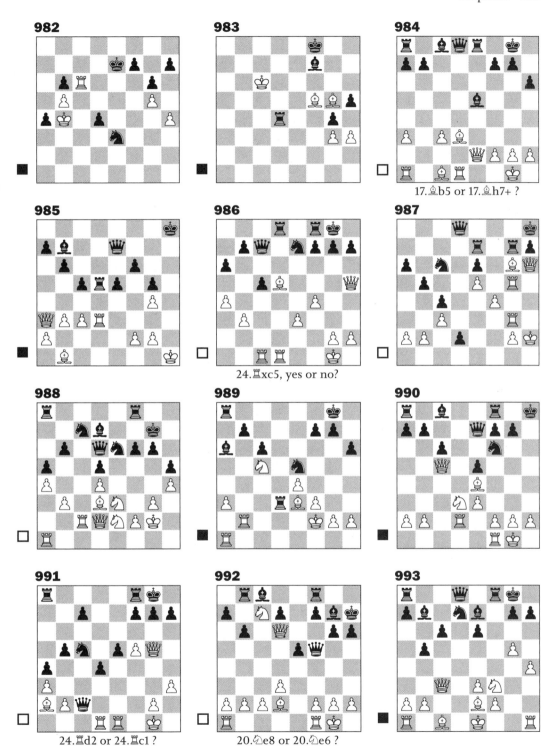

983

984

17.♗b5 or 17.♗h7+ ?

985

986

24.♖xc5, yes or no?

987

988

989

990

991

24.♖d2 or 24.♖c1 ?

992

20.♘e8 or 20.♘e6 ?

993

994

995

996

997

998

49.♗e4, yes or no?

999

1000

38...♕xb4 or 38...♖xb4 ?

1001

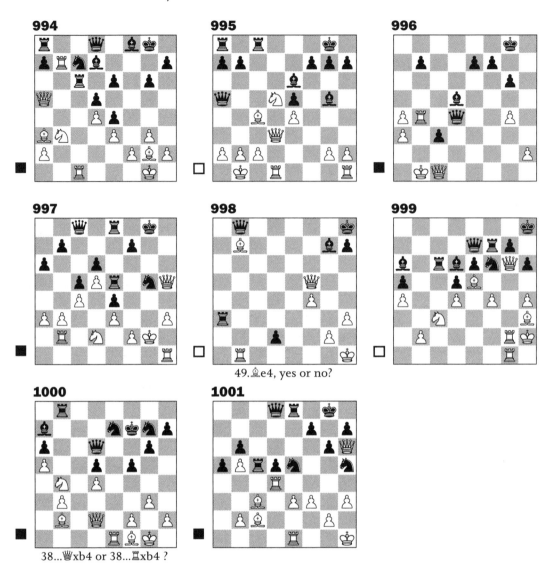

CHAPTER 12

Solutions

1   **24.♖xa7+!** 1-0 Maletin-Vidit, Moscow 2013; 24...♔xa7 25.♖xa5+ bxa5 26.♕xb3+–.

2   **24.♘f6+! gxf6 25.♖xd8+** 1-0 Ris-Van Heirzeele, Belgium tt 2012/13; 25...♖xd8? 26.♕xc6+–.

3   **18...♗xd4! 19.♕xd4 ♖xb5!** and Black won, Parligras-P.H.Nielsen, Khanty-Mansiysk playoff rapid 2011.

4   **21.♖xe4! dxe4** 21...♕xe3+ 22.♖xe3+–. **22.♖d8+!** Removing the guard. This particular tactic is also known als the 'Hook and Ladder trick'. If the bottom falls (the black rook), the top goes with it (the black queen)! **22...♖xd8 23.♕xc5+–** Solberg-Tari, Norway tt 2012/13.

5   **13.♘xf6+!** Clearing the e4-square for the bishop. **13...♗xf6 14.♗e4 e5** 1-0 Grigorov-Veselinov, Borovec 2002; 15.♕xd8 ♖xd8 16.♗xa8+–; 14...♖a7 15.♕xd8 ♖xd8 16.♗xb8+–.

6   **32.♗e4! ♘xe4 33.♖h8+!** 1-0 Giri-Sethuraman, Tbilisi playoff rapid 2017; 33...♔xh8 34.♕xg6+–.

7   **17...♘xe4!** △ **18.♕xe4 d5!**, chasing away the defender of the knight on h4. Black wins a pawn, Jongste-Hilwerda, Leiderdorp 2018 (analysis).

8   **30.♘f5+! gxf5 31.♖g1+ ♔f8 32.♕xf6–+** Vrolijk-I.Sokolov, Amsterdam 2018 (analysis).

9   **44.♘xf4+! exf4 45.♕xe6+ ♖xe6 46.♖xc8** and White won, S.Zhigalko-Vavulin, Katowice Ech rapid 2017.

10   **24.♕a2!** 1-0 Demchenko-Brokken, Skopje 2017. After 24...♔f7 the black king is overloaded as it has to protect both the rook and the bishop: 25.♗xf8 △ 25...♔xf8 26.♕xe6.

11   **45.f3!** 45.♖d6 was played in the game. **45...♖xe3 46.♖h8+ ♔xh8 47.♕xg6+–** Karpov-Timman, Groningen m 2013.

12   **36...hxg4!** 36...♖g6 was played in the game Langeveld-Van Rooden, Rijswijk ch-NED jr W 2012. **37.fxg5 gxh3+ 38.♔xh3 ♖xf1–+**

13   **39.c4+! dxc3 40.♘e3+ ♔e6 41.♔xe4** and White won, Van de Fliert-Ondersteijn, Utrecht 2016.

14   **31...♕e5! 32.♕xe5** 32.♕d2 ♖xc1+ 33.♕xc1 ♕xd4+–+. **32...♖xc1+ 33.♔f2 ♖xe5 34.♘xf6 ♔xf6 35.♖xd7 ♖e7–+** Jonkman Inza-K.Arnold, Assen ch-NED jr W 2018 (analysis).

15   **12.g4! ♗g6** 12...♗xg4 13.♗xd7+ ♘xd7 14.♘xg4+–. **13.g5** 1-0 Mammadov-Jovancevic, Maribor Wch jr 2012.

16   **24.♕h8+! ♕d8 25.♖xb7!** 1-0 Warmerdam-Sieglen, Karlsruhe 2016; 25...♕xh8 26.♖b8#; 25...♖xb7 26.♕xd8–+.

17   **34...♖xg2+!** 34...♖g8 was played in the game. **35.♔xg2 ♖xf2+** Deflecting the rook. **36.♖xf2** If White does not take the rook, he will get mated: 36.♔g1 ♕g3+ 37.♔h1 ♕g2#/♕h2#; 36.♔h1 ♕xh3+ 37.♔g1 ♕g2#/♕h2#. **36...♕xe7–+** J.van Foreest-Lorparizangeneh, Moscow 2017.

18   **34.♖b4! ♗c3 35.♖b8 ♖xb8** 35...♔f7 36.♖xe8 ♔xe8 37.♗xe6+–. **36.♗xe6+** and White won, Sandipan-Laarhoven, Vlissingen 2012.

19   **35...♖xc1+! 36.♘xc1 ♖g8!** 0-1 T.Dijkhuis-Ris, Netherlands tt 2014/15; 37.♗xd4 ♖xg3–+; 37.♘e2 ♖xg3 38.♘xg3 (38.♗xd4 ♖xg2+–+) 38...♗xe3+–+; 37.♖xg8 ♗xe3+ 38.♔f1 ♔xg8–+.

20   **22...e5!** 0-1 Strating-F.Erwich, Haarlem 1998; 23.dxe6 ♘xe6 24.♕xd6 ♘c8 (or 24...♖d8 25.♕e7 ♘c8–+; 25...♖a7–+; 25...♖d7–+).

21   **17...♗b4! 18.♕d4 e5! 19.♕b6 ♕xb6 20.♗xb6 ♗xd2** 0-1 Luttikhuis-Moerman, Borne jr 2015.

22   32.♗xf6+! ♕xf6 33.♘xh5+! 1-0
Christensen-Lauber, Rogaska Slatina tt 2011;
33...gxh5 34.♖g3+ ♔h7 35.♕xf6+–.

23   31.bxc6! After 31.♖xd4 ♕xd4
32.bxc6 ♕xc3 33.♖xc3, Black can defend
against the double attack with 33...♖d1+.
31...♖xd2 32.♖xg5+! 1-0 Moiseenko-
Huzman, Jerusalem Ech 2015; 32...hxg5
33.h6++–.

24   46...♗g5+! 47.♔b1 ♖d2 0-1 E.de
Boer-Nijboer, Hilversum 2018; 48.♖f2+ ♔g3
49.♖f3+ ♔g2–+; 48.♖e3+ ♔f4 49.♖f3+ ♔xe4
50.♖f2 ♔e3–+.

25   40.h5! ♘xh5 41.♘xg6 ♕xg6
42.♖h8+ ♔g7 43.♖g8+ ♔xg8 44.♕xg6+
♘g7 45.♕xh6 and White won, Ernst-Illner,
Amsterdam 2012.

26   37.♘f6+! 1-0 Agdestein-Predojevic,
Norway tt 2014/15; 37...gxf6 38.♕xf7+!
(38.♖h8+ ♔xh8 39.♕xh6+ ♔g8 and Black
is still in the game) 38...♕g7 39.♕h5+ ♕h6
40.♖c7+ (40.♖h8+ ♔xh8 41.♕xh6+ ♔g8
42.♕g6+ ♔f8 43.♕xf6+ etc. wins as well,
but 40.♖c7 leads to a quick mate – and gains
more material) 40...♔g8 41.♕xh6, mating.

27   40.♖b6! ♖c6 41.♖axa6! bxa6
41...♖xd6 42.♖xa7+ ♔xa7 43.♖xd6+–;
41...♖xb6 42.♖xa7+ ♔xa7 43.♕a3++–.
42.♖xc6 ♖b8 43.c3 1-0 Caruana-Vitiugov,
Reggio Emilia 2012.

28   33.f4+! ♕xf4 34.♖e1+ ♕e4 35.♕c7+!
Luring away the bishop from the g7-square.
35...♗d6 35...♔f5 36.g4+, chasing away the
defender of the queen. **36.♕g7+ ♔f5** 36...♔d5
37.c4+!. **37.g4+!+–** Karpov-Topalov, Dos
Hermanas 1994 (analysis).

29   31...♗d3+! 32.♔a1 32.♕xd3 ♖c1+
33.♖xc1 ♕xd3+ 34.♔a1 ♕xd4–+. **32...♕xd4**
0-1 Giroyan-Fang Yan, Maribor Wch jr 2012;
33.♕xd3 ♖c1+ (the Hook and Ladder trick,
see also Exercise 4, Solberg-Tari) 34.♖xc1
♕xd3–+.

30   27...♗e2! 28.♗xd8 28.♖xe2 ♖xg2+
29.♔f1 (29.♔h1 ♖xh2#) 29...♖g1#; 28.g3
♖xe7 (or 28...♕xe7–+). **28...♖xg2+ 29.♔h1
♖xh2#** Anand-Ganguly, Kolkata rapid 2018
(analysis).

31   33...♗g5+! 34.♔xh5 34.♘xg5
♕xe2–+. **34...♗e3+** 0-1 Tjurin-Shanava,
Pardubice 2012; 35.♔h4 ♕xe4+–+.

32   54.♗c4! Pinning the knight. 54.f5
was played in the game Nijboer-Leenhouts,
Delft rapid 2017. **54...♖d7** 54...♔e6 55.f5++–,
see the main line. **55.♗d6!** Interference!
55...♔e6 56.f5+ Chasing away the defender!
Or 56.♗xd5+ ♗xd5 57.f5+ ♔f6 58.♗xd5+–.
56...♔f6 57.♗xd5+–

33   18...b4! 19.cxb4 axb4 20.♕xb4
c5! 21.dxc5 ♔g6 and Black won, Vogel-
Vocaturo, Groningen 2014.

34   47...♕xc3! 47...fxg6 48.♖c7+ ♔h6
(48...♖d7 49.♕xd2) 49.♕g7+ ♔g5 50.♕e7+!
♔f4 (50...♖f6? 51.h4+! ♔f5 (51...♔xh4
52.♕xf6+–) 52.♕e4#; 50...♔h6 51.♕g7+=)
51.♕e4+ ♔g5 52.♕e7+=; 47...♖d1+ 48.♖g1.
48.♖h6+ ♔g7 49.bxc3 f6! 0-1 Bruzon Batista-
Wang, Danzhou 2015.

35   26.♗d2! h4 27.♗f4 ♖3xf4 28.gxf4
and 1-0, Tiviakov-Strikovic, Portugal tt 2011.

36   24...♗e3! 24...♖e3? 25.♖xd4!. **25.fxe3**
25.♖d3 ♕xg3+–+. **25...♕xg3+ 26.♔h1 ♖e5**
0-1 Clancy-Shetty, Washington 2013.

37   24...♗f3! 24...g6? 25.♕e2=. **25.gxf3**
Now the f3-pawn blocks the h5-d1 diagonal,
so after 25.♕xf3 ♖xe5 is winning. **25...
g6** White has no 26.♕e2. **26.♖xe6** 26.♖xc5
gxh5∓; 26.♕h6? ♖xe5–+. **26...fxe6** and Black
won, Holland-Gormally, Sunningdale 2011.

38   25...d1♕+! 0-1 A.Onischuk-Akobian,
St Louis ch-USA 2018; 26.♖xd1 (26.♘xd1
♗xe2–+) 26...♘xc3 27.bxc3 ♗xe2–+.
If instead 25...♘xc3 26.♖xd2.

39   16...♖f8! 17.♕g3 ♖f1+! 18.♔xf1
♘xh2+ 19.♕xh2 19.♔f2 ♘g4+ 20.♔e2
♕xg3–+. **19...♕xh2** 0-1 Adams-Je.Piket, Wijk
aan Zee 1991.

40   23.c5! 23.cxd5 was played in
Carlsen-Giri, Bilbao 2016. **23...bxc5 24.♖a6!**
♕b7 24...♖d8 25.♖xd6 ♕xd6 26.♗xe5 is very
good for White. **25.♖xd6 ♘f7 26.♗e5 ♘xd6
27.♗xd6** White is better.

41   29.♖xe7! ♕xe7 29...♘xe7 30.♕g7#.
30.♘xg6+ 1-0 Kobalia-Cherniaev, Khanty-
Mansiysk Wch blitz 2013; 30...fxg6
31.♕xe7+–.

42   35...♖xe3! 0-1 Shengelia-Sargissian, Porto Carras Ech tt 2011; 36.♖xf7 ♖xg3+ 37.hxg3 ♔xf7–+; 36.fxe3 ♕f1#; 36.♕xe3 ♕xc7–+.

43   35...♖xe4! 36.♕xe4 36.♖xe4 ♕xb1+–+. **36...♕xf2+ 37.♔h1 ♖c2** 0-1 Kuderinov-Iuldachev, Al-Ain tt 2012.

44   29.♗xd5! ♕xd5 29...♘xd5 30.♕g7#; 29...♕xc3 30.♗xe6+ (check!) 30...♔f8 31.♖xc3+–. **30.♕xc8+ ♘e8 31.♕d7** 1-0 J.Polgar-Singh, Hastings 1988/89.

45   26.♘e7+! ♔h8 26...♖xe7 27.♕xg7#; 26...♕xe7 27.♕xc8++–. **27.♕xe6 fxe6 28.♗xg7+ ♔xg7 29.♘xc8+–** F.Erwich-Vavulin, Riga 2014 (analysis).

46   28.♕e3! 1-0 Matlakov-Shomoev, Khanty-Mansiysk 2011; 28...♕e7 (28...♕xe3 29.♖xf8#) 29.♖xf8+ ♕xf8 30.♕xa7+–.

47   34.♘d7+! ♔e8 34...♕xd7 35.♕b4+ ♕e7 (35...♔e8 36.♖xg8#) 36.♖xg8+ ♔xg8 37.♕xe7+–. **35.♖xg8+** and White won, Swinkels-Guramishvili, Netherlands tt 2015/16.

48   25...♖e2! 0-1 Janev-Kesidis, Blagoevgrad 2013; 26.♖xe2 (26.♕xd4 ♖xe1+ 27.♖xe1 ♖xe1#) 26...♕xa1+ 27.♕c1 ♕xc1+ 28.♗xc1 ♖xe2–+.

49   22.♕c3! ♕b4 23.♘e7+ 1-0 Rathnakaran-Karthik, India tt 2016; 23...♕xe7 24.♕xg7#; 23...♘xe7 24.♕xb4+–; 23...♔h7 24.♘xc6+–.

50   7.♘xd4! ♗xd4 7...♘xd4 8.♗xe7+–; 7...0-0 8.♘xc6 bxc6 9.♘xe7++–; 7...f6 8.♘xf6+ ♗xf6 9.♗xf6+–. **8.♕xd4!** See also Andreikin-Karjakin in the introduction to this chapter for the same motif! **8...♘xd4** 8...0-0 9.♘f6+ ♔h8 10.♘g4+ ♘xd4 11.♗f6+ ♔g8 12.♘h6#. **9.♘f6+ ♔f8 10.♗h6#** 1-0 Mashreghi Moghaddam-Ahani, Birjand 2018.

51   25...♗c1! 26.♖xc1 26.♖a4 ♕e1+, mating. **26...♕xa3** and Black won, Kula-Miculka, Frydek-Mistek 2013.

52   29.♘b6+! Chasing the king. White missed this opportunity in the game Hendriks-Galjé, Utrecht 2006. **29...♔a7 30.♘c8+!** Interference and mate. **30...♔a8** Or luring away the rook and winning the queen: 30...♖xc8 31.♕xd4++–. **31.♕b8#**

53   49.♕f8+! ♕f7 50.e5+ dxe5 51.fxe5+ ♔e6 51...♔xe5 52.♕xf7+–. **52.♕d6#** Peerlings-Majhi 2013 (place unknown, analysis).

54   43.♖xf8+! ♔xf8 44.♕h8+ ♕g8 45.♖xe8+ Deflecting the king or luring away the rook, 1-0 Iljin-Tsydypov, St Petersburg 2016; 45...♔xe8 (after 45...♖xe8, now both the queen and the rook are blocking the king: 46.♕f6+ – almost an epaulette mate! – 46...♕f7 47.♕xf7#) 46.♕xg8+ ♔d7 47.♕d5+ ♔e8 (47...♔c8 48.♕f5+ ♔d8 49.♕xc2+–; 47...♔c7 48.♕xc5+ ♔d7 49.♕xc2+–) 48.♕a8+ ♔d7 49.♕a4+ ♔d6 50.♕xc2+–.

55   32.♕xg5! △ 33...hxg5 33.♘f6+ ♔f8 33...♔h8 34.g7# (34.♖h7 is the Arabian Mate). **34.g7#** Perunovic-Sipila, Deizisau 2012.

56   37.♕xe3! 1-0 Ivanchuk-Pijpers, Batumi Ech 2018; 37...♘xe3 38.♖xe8+ ♔f7 39.♖f8#.

57   40...♕xe2! 0-1 Grandelius-Giri, Doha 2015; △ 41.♘xe2 ♘d2+ 42.♔a2 ♖a8+ 43.♕a7 ♖xa7# Anastasia's Mate.

58   38.♖xe8! 38.h4 was played in the game Kevlishvili-Dev, Hoogeveen 2018. **38...♖xe8 39.♖xc6+ ♖xc6 40.♘xb5#**

59   46.♖c7! ♖a1+ 47.♔g2 47.♔h2 is also good. **47...♕d6** 47...♖a8 48.♕b7! △ 48...♕d6 49.♖xh7+ ♘xh7 50.♕xh7#; 47...♕xc7 48.♕xc7+–. **48.♕xf8+!** 1-0 Capablanca-Lasker, Havana Wch m 1921; 48...♕xf8 49.♖xh7#.

60   25...♖xd3! 26.♖xb7+ 26.♖xd3 ♕e1#; 26.♕xd3 ♕xg2#. **26...♔a8!** 0-1 Firat-Kinsiz, Turkey tt 2013. Capturing is not mandatory! 27.♕xd3 (27.♕xe4 ♖d1+ 28.♕e1 ♖xe1#) 27...♕e1+ 28.♕f1 ♗xf2+ 29.♔h1 ♕xf1#. If 26...♕xb7? 27.♕xd3+–.

61   10.♗xf6! Eliminating Black's most important defender! **10...g6** 10...♗xf6 11.♕h5 ♖e8 12.♗h7+! ♔h8 (12...♔f8 13.♕xf7#) 13.♘xf7#. **11.♕h5!** 1-0 Chernyshov-Les, Soviet Union 1969; 11...gxh5 (11...♗xf6 12.♕h7#) 12.♗h7# is Blackburne's Mate.

62   39...♕xd2! 0-1 Kojima-Hou Yifan, Honolulu blitz 2015; 40.♕xd2 f2+ 41.♔g2 f1♕#.

63   28.♖xc6! ♖xc6 28...♕xc6 29.♕xg7#; 28...♕xg3 29.♖xc8#; 28...♖e8 29.♖xg6+–. **29.♕b8+ ♖c8 30.♕xc8#** Bachmann-Rychagov, Cappelle-la-Grande 2015 (analysis).

64 33...♗c3+! 33...♕e1+ was played in the game De Jong-Muhren-Paulet, Amsterdam ch-NED W 2015, after which Black did not find anything better than a repetition of moves: 34.♔d3 ♕f1+ 35.♔d2 ♕e1+ 36.♔d3 ♕f1+ 37.♔d2 ♕e1+ 38.♔d3 ♕f1+ 39.♔d2 ♕e1+ ½-½. **34.bxc3** 34.♔d3 ♕f1+ (or 34...♕a6+ 35.♖b5 ♕xb5#) 35.♕e2 ♕xe2#. **34...♕e1+ 35.♔d3 ♕xc3#**

65 24.♖xd4! 24.♖e7 was played in the game Goni Osacar-Boix Pons, Gijon tt 2011. **24...♕xd4 25.♖xd4 ♖xd4 26.♖e8+ ♖f8 27.♖xf8#**

66 30.♕xd7! ♖xd7 31.♖e8+ ♔h7 **32.♖cc8** Both the g6-pawn and the queen are blocking the escape route of the king, so Black has to sacrifice the queen not to get mated. **32...♖d8 33.♖exd8** (33.♖cxd8? ♕c1+! 34.♔g2 g5! and the black king has luft) 1-0 Alekhine-Colle, Paris 1925; 33...♕xd8 34.♖xd8+−.

67 28.♖f8! ♔xf8 28...♕xf8 29.♕xg6+ ♔h8 30.♕h7#. **29.♗xg6 ♕xg6** 29...♕c8 30.♕f7#. **30.♕xg6+−** F.Erwich-Sanders, Leiden 2012 (analysis).

68 23.♗g8! ♖xg8 23...♖e7 24.♗xe7 and mate on h7 follows soon. **24.♗f6+ ♖g7** A pinned piece is a bad defender! **25.♕xh7#** J.Zwirs-Warmerdam, Netherlands tt jr 2014 (analysis).

69 34...♕a1! 35.♖cxd2 35.♖xa1 d1♕+ 36.♖xd1 ♖xd1#; 35.h3 ♕xd1+ 36.♔h2 ♕b1−+. **35...♕xd1+ 36.♖xd1 ♖xd1#** Kortchnoi-Spassky, Belgrade ct 1977 (analysis).

70 37.♗xg7! 1-0 Moiseenko-Alekseenko, Moscow 2014; 37...♖xg7 (37...♕xg7 38.♕c6#; 37...♖e6 38.♗xf8+−) 38.♗xd5+ c6 39.♗xc6+ ♖b7 40.♗xb7+ ♔xb7 41.a8♕#.

71 20.♕h5! 1-0 Tal-NN, Berlin (East) simul 1975; 20...♕xh5 (20...♕xf5 21.♕h8#) 21.♘e7+ ♔h7 22.♖xh5# Anastasia's Mate.

72 37.♕xd8! ♖xd8 38.♖e8+ ♕f8 **39.♖he5** and 40.♖xd8 followed by 41.♖e8+ cannot be averted. The game continued 39.♖xf8+ ♖xf8 40.♖f5 (40.♖e5? ♖f1#) 40...♖d8 41.♖e5 and Black resigned, R.Dimitrov-Petrov, Sunny Beach 2012.

73 27.♖d7! (27.♗b2+ e5 28.♖d7?! (28.♖de1+−) 28...♖f1+) Luring away the queen, so that ...e6-e5 is no longer a defence after ♗b2+. Moreover, White threatens to give mate on g7 or h7. Black resigned in Iv.Saric-Bosiocic, Batumi Ech 2018; 27...♕xd7 28.♗b2+ e5 (28...♕d4 29.♗xd4+ cxd4 30.♕g7#) 29.♗xe5+ ♖8f6 30.♕f8+ ♗g8 31.♕xg8#.

74 20.♕b4! and Black resigned in Rahman-Chatterjee, Mumbai 2012; 20...c5 (20...♕xb4 21.♖xd8#) 21.♖xd8+ ♔c7 (21...♕xd8 22.♕xb7#) 22.♕xb7+ ♔xd8 23.♕b8+ ♔d7 24.♕xa7++−.

75 18.♘d5! 1-0 Smirin-Kunche, Arlington 2015; 18...♕xc2 (18...♕xa5 19.♕c5!+− △ 19...♕xc5 20.♘c7+ ♔f8 21.♖d8+ ♗e8 22.♖xe8#; 18...exd5 19.♕xc5+−) 19.♘c7+ ♔f8 20.♖d8+ ♗e8 21.♖xe8#.

76 25...♗e4! Clearing the f-file, while attacking White's bishop. **26.♗xe4** 26.♘g3 ♗xb7−+ (26...♕xf2+? 27.♖xf2 ♖d1+ 28.♘f1+−). **26...♕xf2+!** 0-1 Abdullatif-Martins, Maribor Wch jr 2012; 27.♖xf2 ♖d1+ 28.♕e1 ♖xe1#.

77 31...♖f1! (31...♕d1 32.♕e5+ ♔g8 33.a4 ♕xc1+ 34.♔a2 and although Black is a rook up, he is losing due to his unsafe king) 0-1 Brenninkmeijer-Jens, Netherlands tt 2017/18; 32.♘f4 ♖xc1+ 33.♔xc1 ♕d1#; 32.♖xf1 ♕d1+ 33.♖xd1 ♖xd1#; 32.♖xh6 ♖xc1+ 33.♔xc1 ♕d1#; 32.a4 ♖xc1+ 33.♔a2 ♕d5+−+; 32.b3 ♖xc1+ 33.♔b2 ♖b1+ 34.♔xb1 ♕d1+ 35.♔b2 ♗c1+ 36.♔c3 (36.♔b1 ♗a3#) 36...♖c8+ 37.♔b4 ♕d2+ 38.♔a4 ♕a5#.

78 22.♘xf6+! ♗xf6 23.♕xe5! 1-0 Cornette-Warman, London 2011; 23...♗xe5 24.♖d8+ ♖f8 25.♖dxf8#.

79 25.♖xc7! 25.g4 was played in the game Gashimov-Navara, Wijk aan Zee 2012. **25...♕xc7 26.♕g5 g6** 26...♖g6 27.♕xg6 – the pinned f7-pawn is a bad defender. **27.♕xh6 gxh5 28.♕g5+ ♔h8 29.♖xh5+ ♖h6 30.♖xh6#**

80 29...♖xf1+! 30.♖xf1 ♕f4! (30...♕e1? 31.♗f6++−) 0-1 Kolosowski-Tomczak, Legnica 2011; 31.♖xf4 d1♕+ 32.♖f1 ♕xf1#.

81 **29.♖f2!** 29.♕xh7+? ♔xh7 30.♖h3+ ♕h6−+. **29...♗g2** 29...♕xf2 30.♕xh7+! ♔xh7 31.♖h3+ ♔g8 32.♖h8#. **30.♖xf4** 30.♖xg2 is also good. **30...♗xh3 31.♖xh3** and White won in Munguntuul-Nguyen Thi Thanh An, Mashhad Ach W 2011.

82 **45.♕c1! ♕xc1** 45...♔h7 46.♕xh6+ ♔xh6 47.♖xf8+−; 45...g5 46.♕xg5 ♕xg5 47.♖xf8+ ♔h7 48.hxg5+−. **46.♖xf8+ ♔h7 47.♖xf7+ ♔h8** 47...♔h6 48.♘g8#. **48.♘xg6+ ♔g8 49.♖g7#** Gopal-Howell, Gibraltar 2016.

83 **16.♗d8+! ♔xd8 17.♘g5** 1-0 Rossolimo-Romanenko, Bad Gastein 1948; the only way to defend against 18.♘xf7# is to move the knight, but after 17...♘h6 the defender of the e7-square is gone: 18.♕e7#.

84 **31...♕a5! 32.♖ad1** 32.♖xa5 ♖f1+ 33.♕g1 ♖f/gxg1#. **32...♕xd2! 33.♕xd2** 33.♖xd2 ♖f1+ 34.♕g1 ♖f/gxg1#. **33...♘f2+ 34.♕xf2 ♖xf2** 0-1 A.l'Ami-Merry, Douglas 2015.

85 **31.♖a8!** See also Exercise 77, Brenninkmeijer-Jens, in which a similar motif shows up! **31...♕b6** 31...♖xa8 32.♕d8+ ♖xd8 33.♖xd8#; 31...g6 32.♖xf8+ ♔xf8 33.♕h8+ ♔e7 34.♕d8#; 31...h6 32.♖xf8+ ♔xf8 33.♕d8#. **32.♕xb6 ♖xb6 33.♖dd8! ♖b1+ 34.♗f1 g6** 34...♖xd8 35.♖xd8#. **35.♖xf8+** and White has won a rook, although he still has some work to do, Tukhaev-Carlsen, St Petersburg Wch rapid 2018 (analysis).

86 **19.♗xh6! ♘xh6** 19...gxh6 20.♕xf7#. **20.♕h8+ ♘hg8** 20...♘eg8 21.♘g6#. **21.♕xg8+ ♘xg8 22.♘g6#** 1-0 Tal-Myagmarsuren, Nice ol 1974 (adjusted).

87 **31...♖d2! 32.♗xd2** 32.♕xd2 ♕xg3+ 33.♕g2 ♕xg2#; 32.♕e1 ♕h2# (32...♖g2#); 32.♗xf3 ♖xf2 33.♔xf2 gxf3−+. **32...♗d4! 33.♗xf3 gxf3** 0-1 Timman-Fries Nielsen, Helsingor 2014; 34.♕xd4 ♕xg3+ 35.♔h1 ♕g2#.

88 **23...♖e1+! 24.♖xe1** 24.♕xe1 ♕g2#. **24...♗xd4 25.♕xd4** 25.♖e4 ♗xf2+−+. **25...♕g2#** R.Byrne-Fischer, New York ch-USA 1963 (analysis).

89 **22...♖e2!** 0-1 Draskovic-Romanishin, Porto San Giorgio 2013; 23.♖xe2 (23.♕xe2 ♘xg3#) 23...♘xg3+ 24.♕xg3 ♕xf1+ 25.♕g1 ♕xg1#.

90 **18...♘c3+! 19.♗xc3 ♕xf2! 20.♖xd7** 20.♕xf2 ♖d1+ 21.♖xd1 ♖xd1#; 20.♖de1 ♕xe2 21.♖xe2 ♖d1+ 22.♖xd1 ♖xd1#. **20...♕xe2** and Black won in Bologan-Naiditsch, Chisinau rapid 2012.

91 **28.♗f4! ♗xf4 29.♕xb6!** Deflecting the second defender of the d8-square; 1-0 Cordova-Hevia Alejano, Havana 2015; 29...♖xb6 30.♖d8#; 29...♗c1 30.♖d8+ ♖xd8 31.♕xd8#.

92 **26...♕a5+!** 26...♘f3+ was played in the game Svidler-Vitiugov, Moscow ch-RUS 2012. **27.b4** 27.♗d2 ♘f3+ 28.♔d1 ♕xd2#; 27.♕c3 ♕xc3+ 28.bxc3 ♘c2+ 29.♔e2 f3#. **27...♕xb5 28.♕xb5** 28.♔d3 ♘f3+ 29.♔e2 ♖xd3−+. **28...♘c2+ 29.♔e2 f3#**

93 **32.♖a4! ♖d2** 32...♔g8 33.♕xg8! (clearing the fourth rank for the a4-rook) 33...♘xg8 34.♖h4+ ♕h5 35.♖g6+! (chasing away the defender; note that the queen is pinned, so there is no 35...♕xg6) 35...♔h7 36.♖xh5+ ♘h6 37.♖hxh6#; 32...♔h7 (to defend against 33.♕g7+ ♕xg7 34.♖h4#) 33.♕h4+ (33.♕g8+? ♘xg8 34.♖h4+ ♘h6−+) 33...♕h5 34.♕xh5#. **33.♕g7+!** 1-0 Socko-Brunello, Italy tt 2015; 33...♕xg7 34.♖h4#.

94 **39.♖e7! ♕xe7** 39...♔b8 40.♗a6+−; 39...♗e8 40.♖xe8 ♕xe8 41.♕xe8+−. **40.♗a6! ♔xa6 41.♕a8#** 1-0 Caruana-Ponomariov, Dortmund 2014.

95 **26...♖e4!** 0-1 Kuznetsov-Boiskov, USSR cr 1972; 27.♕g3 (27.♕xe4 ♕xh2#; 27.♕xc7 ♖h4−+; 27.♕xf3 ♕xf3+−+) 27...♖g4! (luring away either the rook or the knight!) 28.♘xg4 (28.♕xg4 ♕xh2#; 28.♕xc7 ♖g1#) 28...♕f1+ 29.♕g1 ♕xg1#.

96 **21.♕f4!** Luring away the queen from the e7-square. **21...♕xf4** 21...f5 22.♕xh4 ♘xh4 23.♘f6+ ♔f7 24.♘xe8+−. **22.♘e7+! ♖xe7 23.♗xh7+ ♔xh7 24.g8♕+ ♔h6 25.♕h8#** Kasparov-Yurtaev, St Petersburg m 1981 (analysis).

97 **17.♘f6+! ♔h8 18.♘h5 ♖g8** 18...g6 19.♕e5+ f6 20.♕xf6+ ♖xf6 21.♖d8+, mating. **19.♖d8** and Black resigned in Safarli-Donchenko, Basel 2017; if 19...♗d7 (19...♖xd8 20.♕xg7#) 20.♕xg7#.

98   34...♗g3! 35.gxf5 35.fxg3 ♕xg4+
36.♔h2 hxg3+ 37.♖xg3 ♕h4+ 38.♔g1 ♕xg3+
39.♔f1 ♕g2+ 40.♔e1 ♕e2#; 35.♖xg3 hxg3
36.gxf5 ♕xf5+ 37.♔xg3 ♖d6 38.♖h4 ♖g6+
39.♔h2 ♕g5−+. **35...♕xf5#** Lai-Van Wessel,
Netherlands tt 2015/16.

99   22...♗e1 22...♗xf1 was played in
the game Wantola-Schoorl, Haarlem 2012.
23.♕xd3 23.fxg4 ♕xf1#; 23.♖xe1 ♖xe1
24.♖xe1 ♖c2−+. **23...♗f2#**

100   17.♘c6! ♗d6 17...dxc6 18.♕c7#;
17...♕xa5 18.♘a7#. **18.♗xd6** Also good is
18.♘a7+! ♕xa7 (18...♕b8 19.♕xc5 − the pinned
bishop is a bad defender!) 19.♗xd6 ♗d5
20.♖d4 followed by 21.♖xb4 with threats
like ♕xa6+ or ♕c5+ (luring the queen away
from b8) and/or ♖e3 with ♖c3 next. Black
is defenceless. **18...♕xd6 19.♘xd8 ♖xd8
20.dxe6** and White won in Haddouche-
Bouaziz, Tunis 2013.

101   23.d6! ♕b7 24.d7 1-0 Bourgonjen-
Noordenbos, Borne jr 2015; △ 24...♗xd7
25.♕xg7#.

102   33.♖1e5! ♘xe5 33...♕d6 34.♖h5#;
33...♕xe5 34.♖xe5+−. **34.♘f6+!** 1-0 Sutovsky-
Grigoriants, Plovdiv Ech 2012; 34...gxf6
(34...♔h6 35.♘g8+ ♔g5 (35...♔h7 36.♕h5#)
36.♖xe5+ ♕xe5 37.♕g4#) 35.♕h5+ (the
pinned g-pawn is a bad defender) 35...♔g7
36.♕h8#.

103   33.♘d8! ♖xd8 33...♗xd8 34.♕xe8#.
34.♖d7! 1-0 Jobava-Timman, Hoogeveen m
2014; 34...♕xd7 (34...♕b6 35.♕f7#; 34...♖xd7
35.♕xe8#) 35.cxd7 ♖e5 36.♖xe5 ♗xe5
37.dxe8♕+ ♖xe8 38.♕f5+ ♗f6 (38...♔g8
39.♕d7+−) 39.♕xh7+−.

104   34.♗e5! A Novotny interference!
The bishop can be taken by three different
pieces, but whichever way Black makes the
capture, this will interfere with the other
captures. Moreover, this is not only an
attacking, but also a defending move (Black
threatened 34...♗xb2+ followed by 35...♕c2#).
1-0 Miles-Pritchett, London 1982; 34...♖8xe5
or 34...♖2xe5 35.♕xg7#; 34...♕xd1+ 35.♖xd1
♖2xe5 (35...♗xe5 36.♕xe8++−) 36.bxc3+−;
34...♗xe5 35.♕xe8+ ♔h7 36.♕g6+ ♔g8
37.♖d8+ ♕e8 38.♖xe8#.

105   36.♖c6! Combining the Novotny
interference (the white rook cannot be taken
either way because the c6-square intersects
the lines of the rook, which guards the
e6-square, and the bishop, which guards the
d5-square) with the fact that the black queen
cannot move! 1-0 Navara-Dergatschova-
Daus, Mainz rapid 2007; 36...♖xc6 37.♕d5+
♖e6 38.♕xe6#; 36...♖xc6 37.e8♕+ ♕xe8
38.♕xe8#; 36...♗xc6 37.♕e6#.

106   31.♗c7! A Plachutta interference.
The bishop can be captured by two similarly
moving pieces (in this case the queen and the
rook) moving along different lines (in this
case the c-file and the 7th rank). Whichever
way Black takes, it will interfere with the
range of the other piece. 1-0 Tarrasch-Allies,
Napoli 1914; 31...♖xc7 (31...♕xc7 32.♖xc5+
♕xc5 33.♕b7+ ♔xa5 34.♖a1#) 32.♕b7+!
♖xb7 (32...♔xa5 33.♖a1/a2+ ♔a4 34.♖xa4#)
33.♖xc5#.

107   28...♘f3+! Interference! **29.♔h1**
29.♖xf3 ♕xg2#. **29...♕g3!** 0-1 Bartell-Brooks,
St Louis 2012; 30.gxf3 (30.♕xf3 ♖xf3−+)
30...♕xh3+ (blocking!) 31.♖h2 ♕xf1#.

108   42.♖e7! 42.f6 was played in the game
Piasetski-Van Kampen, Hoogeveen 2012,
and after 42...♕d7+ 43.♔g2 ♕d5+ 44.♔h3
♕d7+ the players agreed a draw. **42...♘f7
43.♕xg8+ ♔xg8 44.♖e8#**

109   31...b4! 31...♕b1+? 32.♔a3 ♕a1+
33.♔xb4+−. **32.♕d1** 32.♕xb4 ♕b1+ 33.♔a3
♕a1#. **32...♕xd1** 0-1 Etchevest-Conde,
Buenos Aires 2013.

110   22...♘e2+! 23.♖xe2 23.♔f1 ♘xg3+
24.fxg3 ♕xg3 (24...♖h1+ 25.♔f2 ♖xa1
or 24...♖f8 are also winning for Black);
23.♘xe2 ♖h1#. **23...♖h1+!** 0-1 Berenboym-
Hovhannisyan, Jerusalem Ech jr 2015;
24.♘xh1 ♕h2+ 25.♔f1 ♕xh1#.

111   22...♖xe5! 23.fxe5 ♗h6+ 24.♖d2
24.♘d2 ♕a1#. **24...♘xd2** 0-1 Foo-Chigaev,
Maribor Wch jr 2012; 25.♘xd2 ♕a1#.

112   25...♘e1! 26.♘e7+ ♔f8 27.♘g6+
♔e8 0-1 Holt-Nakamura, St Louis ch-USA
2015; 28.♗xf7+ (28.♖h8+ ♗xh8 29.♘h4
prevents mate, but leaves White a rook down)
28...♔xf7 29.♘h4 ♕g2+! 30.♘xg2 ♘f3#.

113 **27.♖d7!** Blocking the king's escape route. If Black removes the attacker with **27...♗xd7**, it turns out that the bishop occupies an important escape square for its king: **28.♕h8+ ♔e7 29.♕f6+ ♔f8 30.♖h8#** 1-0 Leko-Vachier-Lagrave, Beijing rapid 2013.

114 **27...♖8xf4!** 27...♘c3 was played in the game Carlsen-Aronian, Bilbao 2012. **28.gxf4** What else? **28...♘xf4 29.♖a8+ ♗f8** This backward bishop move is what Aronian had missed. 29...♔f7 or 29...♔h7 loses the queen due to the knight fork 30.♘g5+. **30.♖g1 ♕xh2+ 31.♔xh2 ♖h3#**

115 **29...♕c3+! 30.♔f1 ♕h3+!** 30...♕xa1+? 31.♔g2=. **31.♔e1** 31.♗g2/31.♕g2 blocks the g2-square for the king: 31...♕d3+ 32.♔e1 ♕e2#; 31.♖g2 shuts off the a8-h1 diagonal: 31...♕xh1+ 32.♖g1 ♗d3+ (32...♕xd5–+) 33.♔e1 ♕xg1+ 34.♔d2 ♕xf2+ 35.♔xd3 ♕e2+ (35...♕c2+ 36.♔e3 ♕e2#) 36.♔c3 ♕c2#. **31...♕d3** 0-1 Nenezic-Popovic, Serbia tt 2017. There's no escaping 32...♕e2# without losing big material: 32.♕xd4 ♕xd4 33.♖c1 ♕b2 34.♔d2 ♗a4+ 35.♔e3 ♕xa3+. Black has a queen and four pawns (b5 will fall as well) against two uncoordinated rooks, and moreover White's king lacks safety. Black is winning.

116 **12...♗f3!** 12...♕xh4 13.f4 is the reason why Black has to block the f2-pawn first. **13.♗c1** 13.exf3 ♕xh4 and now the white king can only flee by giving lots of material, e.g. 14.f4 (14.h3 ♕f4–+) 14...♕xf4 (14...♗xf4? 15.h3+–) 15.f3 ♕xh2+ 16.♔f2 ♗g3+ 17.♔e3 ♗xe1–+. **13...♕xh4 14.h3 ♘f4!** **15.♗xf3** 15.exf3 ♘xh3+ 16.♗xh3 (16.♔h1 ♘xf2+ 17.♔g1 ♗h2#) 16...♕xh3 17.f4 ♕g4+ 18.♔h2 0-0-0 followed by 19...♖h8, mating. **15...♕xh3** 0-1 Gomez Sanchez-Otero Acosta, Santa Clara 2017; 16.♕d2 (16.♗xf4 ♗xf4 17.♗g2 ♕h2#) 16...♘e2+ (clearing the b8-h2 diagonal) 17.♕xe2 ♕h2#.

117 **12.♗f6!** A move that is remindful of Fischer's 19.♖f6 in his game against Pal Benko, New York ch-USA 1963. If you don't know this game, I advise you to take a look at it! Moreover, the same motif showed up in the previous exercise. However, with the knight not standing on the c-file, here the attacker has to find another brilliant move to finish off the defender. 12.♕xh5 f5! was played in the game Köhler-Antal, Amsterdam 2012. **12...♘d7** 12...exf6 13.♕xh5 f5 14.♕xf5 f6 15.♕xh7+ ♔f7 16.♗g6+ ♔e6 17.♗xe8+–. **13.♗xh7+!** 13.♕xh5? ♘xf6 is an important difference with the previous exercise. **13...♔xh7 14.♕xh5+ ♔g8 15.♗xg7 ♔xg7** After a move like 15...f5 or 15...f6 White already wins back the invested material, while the attack is still going on. A sample line to show how bad Black's position is: 15...f6 16.♕h8+ ♔f7 17.♕h7 (threatening amongst others 18.♗xf8+ ♔xf8 19.♘g6+) 17...♖g8 (17...♔e6 18.d5+! (again, blocking!) 18...♗xd5 (18...♔xd5 19.♕e4#) 19.♘g6, threatening amongst others 20.♘f4+ ♔e5 21.g4 and soon ♕f5#) 18.♕g6+ ♔e6 19.♕g4+ ♔f7 20.♘f5+–. **16.♕g5+ ♔h7 17.♘f5 ♖g8 18.♕h6#**

118 **43.♗f4!** Threatening 44.♗h6+. **43...♘xf4** 43...♗xe2 44.♗h6+ ♘g7 45.♗xg7+ ♔g8 46.♗h6+ ♔h8 47.f7 ♕c7+ 48.f4, mating; 43...♕f7 44.♗d6+ ♔e8 45.♖xe6+ ♔d8 46.♕xf7+–. **44.♖e8+ ♕xe8 45.♕g7#** G.Jones-Hawkins, North Shields ch-GBR 2012.

119 **19.♕xd5!** Luring the e-pawn away. This is the first step: the e-file is opened. **19...exd5** 19...♕xd5 20.♖xd5 △ 20...exd5 21.♘f6+ gxf6 22.exf6+ ♗e7 23.♖xe7+ ♔f8 24.♖e4+/e3+ ♔g8 25.♖g4/g3#. **20.♘f6+! gxf6 21.exf6+** Mission accomplished! **21...♗e7 22.♖xe7+ ♔f8 23.♖e8+!** A magnet sacrifice with double check! A little appetizer for Chapter 9. 1-0 Bartel-G.Szabo, Hungary tt 2016/17; 23...♔xe8 24.♖e1#.

120 **27...♖xb3! 28.axb3** 28.♖e4 ♕xe4 (28...♕xa2–+) 29.fxe4 (29.♖xe4 ♖d1+ 30.♖e1 ♖bb1–+) 29...♖xg3+; 28.♖xe2 ♖b1+ (28...♖d1+ transposes) 29.♖e1 (29.♕e1 ♖dd1 30.♖ce4 ♗d2!–+) 29...♖dd1 30.♖ce4 ♗d2!–+. **28...♖d1 29.♖e4** 29.♖xd1 ♕xd1+ 30.♕e1 ♕xe1#. **29...♕f1+!** and mate; 0-1 Vegh-Feher, Hungary t 1996/97.

121 **25.0-0-0! ♘xe5 26.♔xb2±** and White won in Gelfand-Adams, London rapid 2013.

122 **14...♗xa1 15.♗xh8 0-0-0!–+** Fischer-Smyslov, Monaco 1967 (analysis).

123 50...♘f3! 51.♖xe2 51.♖c1 e1♕–+.
51...♘g1+ 0-1 Duijker-E.Hansen, Wijk aan Zee 2015.

124 46...♗e7! 0-1 Riemersma-Mollema, Amsterdam 2017; 47.♘c5 (47.♘a5 ♖d5+ 48.♔e4 ♖xa5–+) 47...♖d5+ 48.♔e4 ♖xc5–+.

125 18...♘ec4! 18...♘ed7 was a better idea, although White has a very comfortable position. 19.♘xc4 ♘xc4 20.♕a4 and White won material, Van Haastert-Hill, Gallipoli 2016.

126 12.♗xb7! ♖xb7 13.♕e4 and White won, Bai-Socko, London 2014.

127 19...♗xc5! 20.♗xc5 ♕b5 0-1 Omota-Emans, Borne jr 2015.

128 24.♖xa8+! ♗xa8 25.♕a2 1-0 Zelbel-Tjiam, Belgium tt 2011/12.

129 26.♗xf7+ ♔xf7 26...♔xf7 27.♘d6+ ♔e7 28.♘xe8+–. 27.♘h6+ ♔g7 28.♘xf7+– Brekelmans-Ansems, Goirle 2013 (analysis).

130 55...♘xc3! 56.♘e5+ 56.♕xc3 ♗xd4+–+. 56...♗xe5 57.♖xe5 ♕xb4 and Black won in Ducarmon-Ris, Netherlands tt 2017/18.

131 28.♗xe7! ♖xe7 29.♕e4 1-0 Iv.Saric-Smeets, Germany Bundesliga 2016/17; 29...♖xe5 30.♕a8#; 29...♕xd4 30.♕xd4 (or 30.♕a8+ ♔d7 31.♖d5++–) 30...♖xd4 31.♖xe7+–.

132 40.♖xh7+! 1-0 Carlsen-Rapport, Wijk aan Zee 2019; 40...♕xh7 (40...♔g8 41.♖h8+ ♔g7 42.♕h6/7#) 41.♕xh7+ ♔xh7 42.♘xf6+ ♔h6 (42...♔g7) 43.♘xe8+–. 40.♘xf6 ♘xh4 is not clear at all.

133 19...♖xb1+ 20.♖xb1 ♗xf3 21.♗xf3 ♕f5 22.♖b7 ♕xf3 23.♖xe7 ♘xe7 24.♕xe7 ♖b8 0-1 Korotkevych-T.Willemze, Germany tt 2011/12.

134 29.♕xd3! cxd3 29...♖xb2 30.♕d1+– was played in the game Werle-Graf, Fagernes 2015. 30.♖xc8+ ♔g7 31.♖c7 Decoying the queen by means of a pin. Here the pin is a preparatory move to create a double attack. In Chapter 5 it is the other way around: there, preparatory moves serve to create a pin, winning material. 31...♕xc7 32.♘e6+ ♔f7 33.♘xc7+–

135 39.♖d6! 39.♕xg4+? ♔f7 (or 39...♔h7, pinning the queen); 39.♘xg4? ♕b6+ with a double attack. 39...♕xd6 40.♕xg4+ ♔f6 41.♕xg7+ ♔xg7 42.♘f5+ Réti-Tartakower, New York 1924 (analysis).

136 34.♖f8+! 34.♕g5 was played in the game Zamarbide Ibarrea-Kononenko, Pamplona 2006. 34...♖xf8 35.♕h7+ ♔xh7 36.gxf8♘+ ♔h6 37.♘xd7=

137 42...♕xf4+! 43.♖xf4 d2 43...♘c4 44.♖f1 transposes to the game; 44.e5 d2 45.♖d4 ♘e3 46.e6 ♔g6 47.♖xd2 ♘f1+ 48.♔g1 ♘xd2–+. 44.♖f1 ♘c4! 45.♖d1 ♘e3 0-1 Edouard-Ernst, Wijk aan Zee 2013; 46.♖xd2 ♘f1+ 47.♔g1 ♘xd2–+.

138 21.♖xd4! and White won in the game Beerdsen-Ernst, Hoogeveen 2017. 21...cxd4 22.♘f6+ ♔c6 (if 22...♔d8 23.♘xe8+ White takes the rook with a discovered check!) 23.♘xe8.

139 32...♖xd2! 0-1 Biti-Zecevic, Croatia tt 2013; 33.♖xd2 ♘e3+ 34.♔e2 ♘xc4–+.

140 21.♗xe5! 1-0 Rapport-A.Onischuk, Tromsø ol 2014; 21...fxe5 22.♕c4++–.

141 28.♖xe6! 1-0 Adhiban-Cheparinov, Zagreb 2018; 28...fxe6 29.♕f7+ ♔h8 30.♕xe8++–.

142 25.♖xc4! 0-1 Brzezinski-Antic, Paleros 2012; 26.♘xc4 ♘e2+ 27.♔f2 ♖xc1–+.

143 28.♕xd5! exd5 29.♘f6+ ♔g7 30.♘xd7 1-0 Fragou-Sevastou, Greece tt 2012.

144 27.♖xc5! ♖xc5 28.♘b6! 1-0 Fressinet-Dorfman, France tt 2011.

145 24.♖xd7! ♖xd7 24...♕xd7 25.♘f6++–. 25.♘f6+ 1-0 Kr.Georgiev-Petkov, Plovdiv 2012; 25...♔h8 26.♘xe8+–.

146 22...♖xg3! 0-1 Lintchevski-Kurnosov, Russia tt 2011; 23.hxg3 ♕xe4+ 24.♖e2 ♕xh1+–+. Not 22...♗xg3? 23.fxg3 ♕xe4+? 24.♖e2+–.

147 46...e5+! 0-1 Chapman-Dzagnidze, Gibraltar 2012; 47.dxe6 ♘xe6+–+.

148 25.♕e5! 1-0 Heimann-Moor, Deizisau 2013; 25...f6 26.♕xe6+ ♔h8 27.♕xd5+–.

149 19.♘e3! 1-0 Honkoop-Mensing, Rijswijk ch-NED jr W 2018; 19...♘xe3 (19...♕c6 20.♘xc4/20.♕xc4+–) 20.♗xe6++–.

150 9...b5! 10.cxb5 c4 and Black won in B.Veltkamp-Alekseev, Amsterdam 2016.

151 40...♖xg5! 41.♗e2 41.hxg5 ♖xh3 42.gxh3 ♕xg5+−+. **41...♖f5** and Black won in Goormachtigh-Ro.Duijn, Netherlands tt 2015/16.

152 30...♕xc3! 0-1 J.W.de Jong-Ducarmon, Netherlands tt 2017/18; 31.dxc3 ♖xd1+ 32.♔g2 (32.♖f1 ♗xe3+ 33.♔g2 ♖1/8d2+−+) 32...♖1/8d2+−+.

153 32.♖c8+! ♕e8 32...♕f8 33.♗xd5+ ♔h8 34.♖xf8#. **33.♖xe8+ ♔f7 34.♖a8!!** 1-0 Karjakin-Kosteniuk, Brissago m 2003; 34...♖xa8 35.♗xd5++−.

154 36.♖d8+! ♔g7 37.♘e6+ 1-0 Vachier-Lagrave-Georgiadis, Biel 2018.

155 41...♕e1+! 42.♔h2 ♕h4+ 43.♔g1 ♕xd8 0-1 Bird-Lasker, Newcastle m 1892.

156 54...♕a1+! 0-1 Brink-Beerdsen, Amsterdam 2017; 55.♔h2 ♕e5+−+.

157 29...♖dg2+! 30.♔f1 ♖c2 Both attacking the queen and threatening 31...♖h1#. 0-1 Estremera Panos-Gajewski, Stockholm 2018/19; 31.♕d3 ♖h1#; 31.♕xc2 ♖xc2−+.

158 69...♘e3+ 70.♔h2 70.♔h3 ♖h1#; 70.♔f3 ♖f1#; 70.♔f2 ♖f1#. **70...♘g4+ 71.♔g2 ♘xh6** and Black won in Greenfeld-Swinkels, Amsterdam 2013.

159 37.♘e7+! 1-0 Sipila-Johannessen, Maastricht 2013; 37...♔f8 38.♘f5 (with the double threat 39.♘xd6 and 39.♖h8#) 38...♖h6 39.♘xh6+−.

160 40...fxe5 is no fun for Black, but Noe would still have had to make some good moves to overcome his strong opponent. However, in the game Black played 40...♕xe5? and resigned after 41.♘f8+ as 41...♔h8 runs into 42.♘g6+ with a double attack, Noe-Kasimdzhanov, Karlsruhe 2018.

161 38.♖d8+! 38.♖d6 d2 and White has to work a little longer. **38...♔h7 39.♖d6** 1-0 Ding Liren-Iv.Saric, Batumi ol 2018; 39...♗c4 40.♖h6+ ♔g8 41.♖h8#.

162 31.♕xb5! axb5 32.♘d7! ♖xd7 32...♖fe8 33.♘f6++−. **33.♖xd7** and White won in Nakamura-Aronian, St Louis 2013.

163 52...g3+! 52...♕d4 was played in the game Svetushkin-Cornette, France tt 2012. 53.♔h3 53.♔g1 ♕d4+−+; 53.♔h1 ♕d1+/b1 54.♖f1 ♕xf1#. **53...♕h7+! 54.♔g4** 54.♔xg3 ♕g7+−+. **54...♕e4+ 55.♔xg3 ♕xe7−+**

164 43.♕g7+! ♕f6 43...♔xf4 44.♕g3#. **44.♘g6+ ♔e6 45.♘f8+ ♔e5 46.♘d7+−** F.Erwich-Litwak, Germany tt 2014/15 (analysis).

165 121.♗f7+! ♔h6 121...♔h7 122.♖h2+ ♔g7 123.♘e6++−. **122.♖h2+ ♔g5 123.♘e6+** 1-0 Inarkiev-Chadaev, Olginka ch-RUS rapid 2011.

166 38.♕a3! ♖d2 38...♖e2 39.♕a6!+− with the double threat 40.♖c8+ and 40.♕xe2. **39.♕f8+!** 1-0 Blübaum-Naiditsch, Baden-Baden 2014; 39...♔b7 40.♕b4++−.

167 37...♕g3! 37...a6 was played in the game Ismagambetov-Morozevich, Astana Wch rapid 2012. **38.♖d2 ♕b3+ 39.♔c1 ♕xb5−+**

168 31.♘d7! ♖c8 32.♘f8+ 1-0 Kraus-Rojicek, Czechia tt 2018/19.

169 24...♘e2+! 25.♔f1 ♘c3 26.♕d8+ ♖e8 0-1 Lu Shanglei-Wang Hao, Danzhou 2017.

170 48...♘c5!, with the double threat 49...♘xb7 and 49...♘d3+, wins. 48...♘ed4 was played in the game Matlakov-Mamedyarov, Tromsø playoff rapid 2013.

171 36.♘h4! 36.♖d1 was played in the game Von Popiel-Marco, Monaco 1902, and Black resigned. However, after 36...♗g1 it is White who is on the losing side! **36...♔h7** 36...♕e8 37.e5 g5 38.♖f8+ ♕xf8 39.♘g6++−; 36...♗g1 37.♘g6+ ♔h7 38.♘xe5+−. **37.♘f3** and White wins the bishop.

172 8...♘xc3! 0-1 Mullink-Van Roon, Borne jr 2016; 9.bxc3 ♕d5−+.

173 34.♕g5+! ♔f8 35.♘b5 ♘e2+ 36.♔h1 1-0 Nakamura-Caruana, Moscow blitz 2012.

174 16.♘xd7! 1-0 N.Zwirs-H.Vedder, Netherlands tt 2016/17; 16...♕xd7 17.♕h5 g6 18.♕xa5+−.

175 35...♖c5! 36.♕e2 36.dxc5 ♖xd1+ 37.♔g2 ♕c6+−+. **36...♕c6+ 37.♖g2 ♖xb5** 0-1 Gelfand-Zatonskih, Douglas 2017.

176 13.d5! ♗xd5 14.♘xd6+ 14.♕xd5?
♗b4+ and due to the discovered attack it is
Black who wins material. **14...♕xd6 15.♕e3+
♔d7 16.♕xa7** and White won in Avramidou-
Gunina, Batumi ol 2018.

177 16.♕h5! h6 17.♗xf7+! ♖xf7
18.♕xf7+ Or 18.♘xf7+–. **18...♕xf7 19.♘xf7
♔xf7 20.b4!** 1-0 M.Muzychuk-Skripchenko,
Reykjavik Ech tt W 2015; 20...♘xe4 21.♖d7+
♔e6 22.♖xb7+–.

178 34.♘d6! ♕xc7 35.♖f8+ 1-0
Hayrapetyan-Khairullin, St Petersburg 2014;
35...♔g7 36.♘e8+ ♔xf8 37.♘xc7+–.

179 53...♗xd5! 54.♖xd5 ♘g2+! 0-1
Sukandar-Van Wely, Vlissingen 2016; 55.♔d1
♘e3+–+, defending his own rook while
attacking White's!

180 32...♖g1+! 32...♗xh1 was played in
the game Yu Yangyi-Khismatullin, Moscow
2017. 33.♔xg1 ♘e2+! 34.♔f1 ♘g3+–+

181 37.♕d8+! ♔g7 38.♗h6+! ♔xh6
39.♕d2+ g5 40.♕xc3 f5 41.♕c6+ 1-0
Bachmann-Izquierdo, Montevideo zt 2013.

182 8.♗xf7+! In Praggnanandhaa-So
(Leon rapid 2018) White surprisingly missed
this tactic and went for 8.d3. **8...♔xf7** After
8...♔f8 Black is a pawn and a position down!
**9.♘g5+ ♔g8 10.♘e6 ♕e8 11.♘c7 ♕f7
12.♘xa8** and White won, Arakhamia Grant-
Castillo Pena, Batumi ol W 2018.

183 25.♖xf7! ♔xf7 26.♕d7+ ♔f8 26...♔g6
27.♕d3+ (or 27.♕f5+ ♔f7 28.♕d5++–) 27...♔f7
28.♕d5++–; 26...♔g8 27.♕d5+–+. **27.♕d6+
♔e8 28.♕c6++–** Van Eijk-Ernst, Amsterdam
2014 (analysis).

184 40...♕e3+! 41.♔g2 ♕e4+ 42.♔h3
42.♔f2 ♕d4+–+; 42.♔g1 ♕d4+–+. **42...
g4+ 43.♔h4 ♕e3** Threatening 44...♕g5#;
0-1 Ivanchuk-Mamedyarov, Beijing 2013;
44.♔xg4 ♕d4+–+.

185 59...♖c2+ 60.♔h1 60.♔g1 ♖xh2–+.
60...♖xh2 0-1 Mamedyarov-Topalov, Astana
Wch rapid 2012; 61.♔xh2 ♗e5+ 62.♔g2
♗xb8–+.

186 37...♘d3+! 38.♔f3 ♕xe2+ 39.♔xe2
♘c1+ 40.♔d2 ♘xb3+–+ Wieringa-Cordes,
Den Bosch tt jr 2018 (analysis).

187 25...♗g2! 26.♖he1 ♗xe4+ 27.♖xe4
♖xe4 0-1 Stany-Bogner, Leiden 2014;
28.♔xe4 ♘xc3+.

188 51.♖e5+! ♔d6 52.♘f6 ♗xf4 52...♖e7
53.♘e4++–. **53.♖e4** (53.♖f5 is also winning)
1-0 Fedoseev-Grandelius, Karlsruhe 2017.

189 42.♘c5+! ♔f5 42...♔e7 43.♘d3+–.
43.♕xh5+ ♗g5 44.♕h7+ (44.♔f4 45.♘d3++–)
1-0 Fedorchuk-Ghaem Maghami, Jakarta
2012.

190 24.♘xd5! Clearing the f6-square.
24...cxd5 25.♗f6+! Chasing the king. 1-0
Tiviakov-I.Sokolov, Amsterdam ch-NED
2018; 25...♔g8 26.♗xe7 (luring the queen
away from d5) 26...♕xe7 27.♗xd5+ ♔g7
(27...♗xd5 28.♕xd5+ ♔g7 29.♕xa8+–)
28.♗xb7+–.

191 8.♘b5! Targeting by means of a
discovered attack. **8...♕b6** 8...♕d8 9.♘d6#.
9.♘d6+ ♔d8 10.♘xf5 and White won in
Adams-Merry, Gibraltar 2015.

192 53.♘b6! ♕b7 53...♖xa1 54.♘xc8+,
capturing the queen with check, so Black has
no time to capture White's queen! **54.♖xa7
♕xb6** 54...♖xa7 55.♘c8+ ♔f8 56.♘xa7+–.
55.♕a4 ♔f6 56.♕d7 1-0 Ikonnikov-Bosman,
Netherlands tt 2013/14.

193 37.♖xf5! ♕xf4 37...♖xf5 38.♕xd6+–.
38.♘e6+ 38.♖xf4 ♖xf4 39.♘e6+ is also
good. **38...♔h6 39.♖xf4** 1-0 Van Kampen-
Gullaksen, London 2012.

194 25.♘c1! 1-0 Kortchnoi-Smirin,
Odessa rapid 2007; 25...♖xe1 26.♘xd3+–.

195 18...♗xe2! 19.♕xe2 ♘d4 20.♕d2
20.♖xc8 ♘xe2+–+ (check!). **20...♖xc3**
20...♘e2+ 21.♕xe2 ♖xc3 also wins an
exchange, but the text is more accurate as
after 22.♕d2, Black has no 22...♕c7 because
of the interference with 23.♘c4 and Black
has to give back the exchange. **21.♕xd4**
21.♕xc3? ♘e2+ 22.♔h1 ♘xc3–+. **21...♕c7!–+**
21...♖c6 22.♕xa7 was played in the game
Rakshitta-Tomilova, Hoogeveen 2018.
22.♘c4 ♖c2–+

196 37...♕xf2+! 0-1 Dumitrache-Papp,
Baia Sprie 2012; 38.♔xf2 ♘xe4+ 39.♔e3
♘xg5–+.

197   29.♕xe8+! ♚xe8 30.exd5+ 1-0
N.Guliyev-Goes, Utrecht 2012.

198   16.♖xe5! and after 16...♗e6 White
soon won. If **16...♕xe5**, then **17.♘xc6 ♕c7**
(17...bxc6 18.♕d8#) **18.♕d8+ ♕xd8 19.♖xd8#**
(Köpke-Spiridonov, Sunny Beach 2011).

199   24...♗xc4! 25.♕xc4 ♘e3 26.♗xe3
♖xd1 27.♕xc5? ♘e5! Eliminating the
defender of the rook! **28.♔f1 ♘xf3** 0-1
Schoorl-S.Dijkhuis, Netherlands tt 2014/15.

200   31.♗e7! 1-0 J.van Foreest-E.l'Ami,
Amsterdam ch-NED 2018; 31...♕xe7 32.f6+
♔g8 33.fxe7+–.

201   27.♗c5! ♗xc5 28.dxc5 ♖xd3
28...♕xc5 29.♖xd7+–. **29.♖xd3 ♖xd3** 29...♕xc5
30.♖xd8++–. **30.cxb6** 1-0 Fedorchuk-Bauer,
France tt 2012.

202   28...♕xb6+! 29.axb6 ♗d4+ 30.♔h1
♘f2+ 31.♔g1 ♘d3+ 32.♔h1 ♘xc1 Bianchi-
Dragojlovic, Venice 2011 (adjusted).

203   16.♘g5+! ♔g8 17.♘e6 ♘g4 17...♗xe6
18.dxe6 ♕xe6 19.♗xh6+–. **18.♘xf8+–**
F.Erwich-Wilschut, Voorschoten rapid 2012
(analysis).

204   14.♗xe4 dxe4 15.d5 and White won,
Hinrichs-Timman, Helsingor 2018.

205   13.♗b6! axb6 14.axb6 ♕e7 14...♖xa1
15.bxc7+–. **15.♖xa8** and White won in Sohl-
Gebhardt, Schwäbisch Gmünd 2012.

206   23...♘g4! 0-1 Zufic-Ivekovic, Zagreb
2012; 24.fxg4 f3!–+.

207   37.♗xc5! 37.♖h1 was played in E.de
Groote-Orlov, Netherlands tt 2013/14. **37...dxc5**
37...♖h8 38.♕xe5+!. **38.♕xe5+ fxe5 39.f6+–**

208   37.♖d8+! and after making the move
37...♔f7 Black resigned, because White has
38.♘e5+ with a discovered attack, Acs-
Schneider, Germany Bundesliga 2013/14.

209   27.♘f6+! ♔f8 27...♔g7 28.♘h5+ (or
28.♘e8+ ♔f8 29.♕h8#) 28...♔h7 29.♕g7#;
27...♔h8 28.♘d5++–. **28.♘d5!** 1-0 Nikitinyh-
Bezulenko, St Petersburg 2012; 28...♕d6
29.♕h8#.

210   22...b5! 23.♖d4 23.♖e4 ♗f5 24.♖e5
(24.♖d4 ♘c3–+, see the game) 24...♘xf4
25.♖xf5 ♘e2+–+. **23...♘c3!** 0-1 Banusz-
Timofeev, Warsaw Ech blitz 2011; 24.♖xd8
♘xe2+ 25.♔h1 ♖xd8–+.

211   22.♖g3! ♗xc3 23.bxc3! The queen
on d2 keeps the f4-knight protected. 23.♕xc3
♕xe4 24.♗xb6? ♕xf4+ is the reason why
White has to play 23.bxc3!. **23...♕xe4**
24.♗xb6 ♕c6 25.♘d5 ♔h8 26.♗d4+ 1-0
R.Ratsma-Damen, Borne jr 2016.

212   30...♗f8! 31.♕f6 ♗e7! 32.♕xe5
♗c5+ 33.♔h1 ♖xe5 0-1 Vallejo Pons-
Grischuk, Khanty-Mansiysk Wch blitz 2013.

213   11.c4! 11.d4 was played in the
game Karjakin-Aronian, Wijk aan Zee 2017.
11...♘de7 12.c5 ♗xb3 12...♗xc5 13.♗xe6++–.
13.♕xb3+ ♔h8 14.cxb6+–

214   21...♕xa1! 22.♖xa1 ♗xh2+ 23.♔xh2
♖xa8 0-1 Yamada-T.Willemze, Hoogeveen 2011.

215   20.g6! fxg6 20...exd5 21.♕xh7#.
21.♘xe7+ ♔f7 22.♕xa5+– Afek-Kogan,
Israel rapid 1999 (analysis).

216   35...♖xf1+! 36.♖xf1 ♖f5+ 36.♖xf1 ♖f5+
37.♔g1 ♕xh4–+. **36...♖xg2+! 37.♔xg2 ♕xh4** 0-1
Legaspi-Dimakiling, Ho Chi Minh City 2012.

217   24...♖xf4! 25.♕xf4 The game
Skripka-Buksa, Lviv 2012, continued 25.♘c3
♗f2 26.♕xf4 ♗xe1 and Black soon won.
25...♘d3+! 26.cxd3 ♗e3+–+

218   32...♖c4+! 33.♔a3 33.♔xc4
♖d1+–+; after 33.♔b3, 33...♖xd1 34.♖xd1
♖c1+–+ is the easiest. **33...♖xd1** 0-1 Brito-
Vazquez, Asuncion 2012; 34.♖xd1 ♖c3+–+.

219   47...♖h2+! 48.♔f1 48.♔xh2 ♘xf3+
49.♖gxf3 ♕xb2–+. **48...♖f2+ 49.♔xf2** 49.♔g1
♘xf3+ 50.♖gxf3 ♕xb2–+. **49...♘g4+** 0-1
Hjartarson-Jobava, Helsingor 2018.

220   34...♖d1+ 35.♔g2 35.♗xd1
♕xd1+ 36.♔g2 ♕e2+ 37.♔g1 ♕f2+ 38.♔h1
♕h2/♕f1#. **35...♖g1+** 0-1 Mareco-De
Dovitiis, Montevideo Ach 2018; 36.♔xg1
♗h2+ 37.♔xh2 ♕xd7–+.

221   25...♘f3+! 26.♔h1 26.gxf3 ♖g6+
27.♔h1 ♕xa4–+. **26...♖h6!** 0-1 Saunina-
Fatalibekova, Kamena Vourla Wch sr W
2012; 27.♖xd7 (27.gxf3 ♕xa4–+) 27...♖xh2#.

222   22.♖f4! ♕g5 22...♕h5 23.♖h4+–
♕d5 24.♗xh7+ ♔h8 25.♗e4++–. **23.♘xe6!**
(23.♗xh7+? ♔xh7 24.♖h4+ ♔g6) 1-0
Kotronias-Landa, Cappelle-la-Grande 2015;
23...fxe6 (23...♕d5 24.♘xf8+–) 24.♖xf8+ ♖xf8
25.♕xg5+–.

223 **25.♗f8! ♕xc4** 25...♖xf8 26.♕xc7+−; after 25...♘xh6 White must, of course, first insert 26.♕xc7 (26.♗xh6? ♕xc4−+) 26...♖xc7, and then play 27.♗xh6+−. **26.♗g7#** 1-0 D.Mastrovasilis-Short, Porto Carras Ech tt 2011.

224 **25...♖xe3! 26.♕xf5 ♖xe1+** Check! **27.♘xe1 gxf5** and Black won, Kerkar-Kiran, India tt W 2012.

225 **26.♘xd5!** 26.♕b3 was played in the game Akobian-Liang, St Louis ch-USA 2018. **26...♕xc2** 26...♕xd5 27.♕xc7+−. **27.♘xf6+** Check! **27...gxf6 28.♖xc2** and aside from the fact that White is a pawn up, his position is also much better.

226 **28.♗f8!** 1-0 Meier-Kamsky, Tromsø ol 2014; 28...♕xb3 (28...♖xf8 29.♕xb5) 29.♗xg7+! (check!) 29...♔g8 30.axb3+−.

227 **22.♗d7!** 1-0 Dambacher-M.Erwich, Germany tt 2011/12; 22...♕xb3 23.♗xe6+! (check!) 23...♔f8 24.axb3+−.

228 **13...♘xe4! 14.♗xe7** 14.dxe4 ♗xg5. **14...♘c5! 15.♗d5 ♗xd5 16.♕xd5 ♕xe7** Black is a pawn up and eventually won the game, Caruana-Carlsen, Paris rapid 2016.

229 **12.♘b5!** 12.♘e4 was played in the game Manova-Nikolov, Skopje 2013, but with 12...♕c7 Black saved his bishop. **12...♕xd2** 12...cxb5 13.♕xa5+−; in case of 12...♕c7, the discovered attack has served as a preparatory move for a knight fork (see also the final exercises of the previous chapter): 13.♘d6+ ♔e7 14.♕xa5 ♗xa5 15.♘xb7+−. **13.♘xd6+ ♔e7 14.♘xf5+** Again, check! **14...exf5 15.♗xd2+−**

230 **19.♘xe5!** Luring the queen forward to an unprotected square. **19...♕xe5 20.♘g6 ♕f6** 20...♕xg3 21.♘xe7+ (an important in-between check!) 21...♔h8 22.fxg3+−; 20...♕d6 21.♘xe7+ (or 21.♗f4 e5 22.♘xe7+ ♕xe7 23.♗xe5 g6 24.♗d6+−; 21.♕xf8) 21...♕xe7 22.♗c5+−. In this case the discovered attack served as a preparatory move for a skewer, see also the next chapter. **21.♘xf8 ♗xf8 22.♖c7** and White won, Andreikin-Khenkin, Dortmund 2013.

231 **20.♘c2!** Chasing the queen to a5, where she is loose! **20...♕a5 21.♘d5** 1-0

Edouard-Cacho Reigadas, Spain tt 2016; 21...♕d2 22.♘xf6+ (check!) 22...♔h8 (22...♔g7 23.♘xe8++−, an important in-between check!) 23.♗xd2+−; 21...♕d8 22.♗b6!+−, chasing away the defender, setting up a fork on the next move − see also the previous chapter!

232 **20.♗xc6!** Capturing the defender of the queen. **20...bxc6 21.♘e4! (**21.♘d5? ♕d8 and Black saves the knight) 1-0 Percivaldi-Kumar, Stockholm 2015 (analysis); 21...♕xd2 (21...♘xe4 22.♕xa5) 22.♘xf6+ (check!) ♔h8 (22...♔g7 23.♘xe8++−; an important in-between check!) 23.♗xd2+−.

233 **17.f5!** Luring away the pawn. 17.♘xd5? ♖xd5!, protecting the queen on a5; 17.♘e4 ♕xe1 18.♘xf6+ ♔g7 and Black wins back the piece. **17...gxf5** If 17...♗xf5 18.g4! wins a piece by attacking the pinned bishop; or 18.♘e4 ♕xe1 19.♘xf6+ ♔g7 20.♖axe1 ♔xf6 21.g4!+−. **18.♘e4** 1-0 A.Williams-Morris, Skopje tt 2015; 18...♕xe1 19.♘xf6+ ♔g7 and here it becomes clear why White played 17.f5!. Compared to the 17.♘e4 line, the knight can now safely give an intermediate check on h5 as the pawn on g6 has been moved to f5: 20.♘h5+ ♔g6 21.♘f4+!+− (again, check!). Finally the knight is safe, which means White is a piece up after taking the queen on the next move.

234 **32...♕c1+!** Chasing the king, while setting up a battery. The game Svidler-Kurnosov, Astana Wch rapid 2012, continued 32...♕e1+ 33.♔g2 ♕e4+ 34.♔g1 ♕e1+ 35.♔g2 ♕e4+ 36.♔g1 ♕e1+ and the players agreed a draw. **33.♔g2** 33.♗d1 ♕xd1+ and Black is winning, for example: 34.♔g2 ♘e1+ 35.♔f1 ♘d3+ 36.♔g2 ♘f4+. **33...♘e1++−**

235 **63.♖f6+!** Chasing the king while setting up a battery. 63.♘d4 was played in the game. **63...♔e8** 63...♔g8 64.♘h6+ ♔g7 65.♖xf3+−. **64.♘g7++−** Van Kampen-Smeets, Playchess blitz m 2012.

236 **66.♖g4+! ♔h5 67.♖g5+** Chasing the king while setting up a battery. **67...♔h6** 67...♔h4 68.♘g6#. **68.♘g4+** 1-0 Kazarian-Lanchava, Amsterdam ch-NED W 2015.

237   22.♘xf6+! Eliminating an important defender. **22...♖xf6 23.♕g4 ♖xf5** 23...g6? 24.♘xh6++−. **24.exf5** and White won in Iv.Saric-Toth, Balatonlelle Ech tt jr 2006.

238   24.♕h3 1-0 Nisipeanu-Cornette, Germany Bundesliga 2015/16; 24...♘f6 (24...g6 25.♘h6+ ♗xh6 26.♕xd7+−; 24...♖e6 25.♕xh5 g6 26.♘h6++−) 25.♗xf6 ♖xf6 26.♘h6++−.

239   51...♘xf4+! 51...♕e3 was played in the game Karjakin-Mamedyarov, Moscow blitz 2013. **52.gxf4 ♕e3+ 53.♔h2 ♕xf4+** The battery has been set up. **54.♔h3** 54.♔h1 ♕xh4+ 55.♗h3 ♕xh3#. **54...♕g4+** Chasing the king to a square the bishop can be aimed at. **55.♔h2 ♗e5+** Or 55...♕xh4+ 56.♗h3 ♗e5+−+. **56.♔g1 ♕xc4−+**

240   30...f4! 31.♕xg6+ ♘xg6, again a discovered attack. Both white bishops are under attack (0-1, 70, Tomashevsky-Grischuk, Berlin Wch blitz 2015).

241   22.c4 ♕xd3 22...♗xd2 23.♕xd2+−, again a discovered attack! White wins a piece as both the queen and the knight are under attack. **23.♗xa5+ b6 24.♖xd3** 1-0 H.van Dijk-Polak, Delft 2017.

242   21.♗c3! and there is nothing Black can do about the threat of 22.♗a5. The game So-Anand, Leuven blitz 2017, continued as follows: **21...d4 22.exd4** ≥ 22.♗a5 dxe3 23.♕e1!+−. **22...cxd4** 22...♕c6 △ 23.♗a5 ♖d4! should have been tried, but after a move like 23.♗b4 Black would have had a hard time saving his position. **23.♗a5** 1-0.

243   28.♖xe6+! 1-0 Capitelli-Masters, Dublin 2012; 28...♔xe6 29.♗c4+ ♔e7 30.♗xg8+−.

244   27.♖xe2! ♕xe2 28.♖e1! 28.cxd5 was played in the game Ding Liren-Rapport, Biel 2013. **28...♕xd2 29.♖xe8+ ♔f7 30.♖e1+−**

245   21...♖xd5! 22.♕xd5 ♖d8 and Black won, Vijayalakshmi-Phadke, Chennai 2013.

246   28.♖b7! 1-0 Cormican-O'Grady, Limerick ch-IRL 2013; 28...♖xf2+ 29.♔e3+− (29.♔xf2? ♕xb7); 28...♕xb7 29.♕h7+ ♔d6 30.♕xb7+−.

247   34.♖e1! 1-0 Inarkiev-Yakovich, Vladivostok 2012; 34...♕xe1 35.♕e8+ ♔f5 36.♕xe1+−.

248   42.♖e8! ♕xe8 43.♕e2+ ♔d5 44.♕xe8 d3 45.♕xf7+ ♔d4 46.♕xb3 1-0 G.Jones-Zhou Jianchao, Atlantic City 2016.

249   66.♖c7! 66.♕c1+ was played in the game Nepomniachtchi-Salem, St Petersburg Wch rapid 2018. **66...♕xc7 67.♕c1+ ♔b3 68.♕xc7+−**

250   39.♖b8! 1-0 P.H.Nielsen-Galyas, Germany Bundesliga 2012/13; 39...♕xb8 40.♕h8+ ♔f7 41.♕xb8+−.

251   32.♕xg7+! ♔xg7 33.♖8h7+! 33.♖1h7+? ♔g6 and now, if White captures the queen, the h8-rook is hanging. This means he has to go for a perpetual: 34.♖h6+ (34.♖xd7? ♖xh8−+) 34...♔f7 35.♖6h7+=. **33...♔g8 34.♖xd7** and White won in Simantsev-Maes, Police 2013.

252   87.♕h5+! 87.♕f5+ was played in the game Karjakin-Gelfand, Moscow blitz 2008. **87...♕xh5 88.e8♕+ ♔f6 89.♕xh5+−**

253   105.♕d5+! ♕xd5 106.g8♕+ ♔f6 107.♕xd5+− Van Malder-Hilwerda, Borne jr 2018 (adjusted).

254   28...♗xc3! 29.♕xc3 ♖a3 30.♕b4 ♖xf3 31.♗xc4 ♕b6 0-1 Brunner-Kamsky, Eilat tt 2012.

255   19.d6! ♗xd6 20.♕d2 Or 20.♕d3+−. **20...♗c5 21.♕xd7** and White won, Rooze-Buchäckert, Triesen 2013.

256   48...♘xe2 49.♔xe2 d1♕+! Luring the king to d1 by using a double check as a preparatory move. 0-1 Navara-Bacrot, France tt 2012; 50.♔xd1 ♖b1+ 51.♔c2 ♖xh1−+.

257   53.a7! ♖c2+ 54.♗e2 ♖a2 55.a8♕+! Luring the rook to a8 and simultaneously unpinning the bishop. **55...♖xa8 56.♗f3+ ♔d3 57.♗xa8** and White won, Ramirez-Kaidanov, St Louis ch-USA 2012.

258   27.♖xe5! 27.♖xb8 was played in Warmerdam-S.Elgersma, Rotterdam ch-NED jr 2015. After 27...♖xb8 28.♖xe5! White is clearly better, but he still has to work for a bit to bring home the full point. Reversing the move order (starting with 27.♖xe5) would have been much easier for White. **27...♘xe5** 27...♖xe5 28.♖xb8+−; 27...♖xb5 28.♖xe8+ ♔d7 29.axb5 ♖xe8 30.bxc6+−. **28.♖xb8 ♖xb8 29.♗xe5+ ♔c6 30.♗xb8+−**

259 19.♗h6! ♕xh6 20.♕f7+ ♔d8 21.♕xf8+ ♔xf8 22.♖xf8+ ♔d7 23.♖xa8+− Swapnil-Goorden, Vlissingen 2013 (adjusted).

260 41...♕d5+! 42.♔g1 ♖f1+! 43.♔xf1 ♕h1+ 44.♔f2 ♕xh2+ 45.♔e3 ♕xb2−+ Giri-Carlsen, Shamkir 2018 (analysis).

261 10.♗xe4! 1-0 Grischuk-Duda, Chess.com blitz m 2018; 10...♗xe4 (10...♕xe4 11.♖e1+−) 11.♘c3 ♕e6 12.♘xe4 ♕xe4 13.♖e1+−.

262 29.♖xg6! 1-0 Kvon-Romanov, Al-Ain tt 2012; 29...fxg6 30.♖xe4 ♕f6 31.♖xe7+−.

263 8.c3 ♗c5 8...♗a5 9.♗a3±. **9.d4** ♗b6 10.♗a3± B.Veltkamp-Lai, Rotterdam ch-NED U20 2015.

264 24.♗e3! 24.gxh7 was played in the game Rasmussen-Miedema, Helsingor 2017. **24...♗xe3 25.♖xh7+ ♔xg6 26.♖xd7 ♗xd7 27.♘xe3+−**

265 48.♖xb7! 48.♖d8 was played in the game Ragger-Cornette, Germany Bundesliga 2017/18. **48...♖xb7 49.♖c8+ ♔d5 50.♖xc2+−**

266 31.♗xb6+! axb6 32.♖a8+ ♔d7 33.♖xg8 hxg5 34.♖xg7 and since Black will also lose a second pawn, he resigned: 34...♖e2 (34...♖e5 35.♖xf7+; 34...f6 35.♖xe7+ is a winning pawn ending for White) 35.a4 ♖b2 36.♖xf7+ ♔e6 37.♖f3+− (Vitiugov-Wojtaszek, Shenzhen 2018).

267 27...♗a4! 0-1 Lobanov-Reinderman, Dieren 2018; 28.♕xa4 ♕d2+ 29.♔f1 ♕xd1+ 30.♕xd1 ♖xd1+ 31.♔e2 ♖xh1.

268 46...♖a1+! 47.♔e2 47.♔g2 ♖g1#. **47...♖e1+** 0-1 Cools-Hovhanisian, Brasschaat 2012.

269 72.♕e8+ 72.♗xa4 was played in the game Pruijssers-Werle, Haarlem 2017. **72...♔f6 73.♕h8++−**

270 32.♖4f5+! ♔d6 32...♔e6 33.♖5f6+ ♔e5 34.f4#. **33.♖5f6+!** 1-0 F.Erwich-J.van Foreest, Netherlands tt 2012/13; 33...♔c5 (33...♔e5 34.f4#) 34.♖c7+ ♔b5 35.♖b7+ ♔a5 36.♖xb2+−.

271 41...♖g3+! 42.♔xh4 42.♔h2 ♗xb4−+. **42...♖g1+! 43.♗xe1 ♖h1+** 0-1 Zuiderweg-Hilwerda, Groningen 2018.

272 28.♗xg6! and White won (28...hxg6 29.♖fxd4+−), Nimzowitsch-Spielmann, Hamburg 1910.

273 48.e5+! 48.f4 was played in the game Wiersma-M.Senders, Netherlands tt 2014/15. **48...♔f5 49.♖f7+ ♔xe5 50.♖e7+ ♔f5 51.♖xe1+−**

274 22.♕h8+! ♔e7 23.♖xf7+! 1-0 Sochacki-Lorscheid, Paris 2012; 23...♔xf7 24.♕xh7+ ♔f6 25.♕xc7+−.

275 51.♖f7+! ♔g8 52.♕h3! and Black is lost, e.g. **52...♔xf7 53.♕h7+ ♔e8 54.♕g8+** (or 54.♕h8+) **54...♔d7 55.♕xb8+−** R.Byrne-Tarjan, Oberlin ch-USA 1975 (adjusted).

276 30...♖xc3+! 31.♔xc3 ♗b4+! 32.♔xb4 ♕a5+ 33.♔c4 ♕a6+ and as White loses his queen, he resigned, Honfi-Tal, Sukhumi 1972.

277 15.♗xd4! ♕xd4 15...♗xd4 16.♕h6 ♕d6 17.♕h7+ (17.♖xd4 transposes) 17...♔f8 18.♖xd4! ♕xd4 19.♕h8+ ♕xh8 20.♖xh8+ and like in the game, White wins material thanks to a skewer! **16.♕e1** and White won in Nakamura-Caruana, Elancourt 2013. Many queen moves are good: 16.♕f4; 16.♕g5; 16.♕e2; but not 16.♕c2 when Black can move away the queen with gain of tempo: 16...♕e3+−+.

278 11...♘xe3! 11...♗xb3?! was played in the game Hofstra-Pauwels, Borne jr 2015, but White could have limited the damage with 12.♔b1!. The bishop on b3 is trapped. 12.axb3? was played in the game and after 12...♘xe3 13.♕xe3 ♗g5 White resigned. **12.fxe6** 12.♕xe3 ♗g5!−+. **12...fxe6 13.♖e1 ♘xf1−+** followed by 14...♗g5.

279 20...♖xe3! 21.♕xe3 21.d6 ♖xf3 (protecting the rook on a8 with the queen was also fine) 22.dxc7 ♖xf1+−+ was played in the game R.Danov-Grigorov, Skopje 2013. **21...♗d4−+**

280 32.♘xb5! ♖xb5 32...♕c6 33.♘d6++−. **33.♕xa4 ♕a7 34.♕xa7 ♖xb2+ 35.♖xb2 ♖xb2+ 36.♔h3** and White won, E.l'Ami-P.Ypma, Groningen 2014.

281 46...♖f6! 47.♗f5 ♖xf5! 48.♕xf5 ♖f6 49.♕xf6 ♗xf6 50.♔f3 ♗c7 51.♔g4 ♔d6 52.♔h5 ♔e5 0-1 Colin-Van den Doel, Rochefort 2019; 53.♔h6 ♔f4 54.g7 ♗xg7+ 55.♔xg7 ♔g3−+.

282   16.♘h6! 1-0 Gormally-Granda Zuniga, Douglas 2014; 16...gxh6 17.♗h5+−.

283   47...♘h3+! 48.gxh3 48.♔h2 ♘xf2+ 49.♔g3 ♘xg4−+. **48...♖g7** and Black won, Morozevich-Caruana, Thessaloniki 2013.

284   24.♘g5+! ♘xg5 25.♖d5+− Jumabayev-Shankland, Biel 2016 (analysis).

285   1.♕h4+! ♔g8 2.♕g3+ ♔h8 3.♗c3+− (analysis).

286   39.♕c8+! 39.♖c5 was played in the game Mamedyarov-Kuzubov, Tbilisi playoff rapid 2017. **39...♔h7 40.♕a6+−**

287   23.♗xc6! 23.♘xc6 was played in the game E.l'Ami-Nabaty, Golden Sands 2012. **23...♗xc6 24.♕a6+−**

288   31.c5! bxc5 31...♕e7 32.cxb6+−; 31...♕d7 32.♗c6+−. **32.♖xc7+! ♕xc7 33.♖b7 ♕xb7 34.♗xb7+−** and White won, Maletin-Lyaskovsky, Russia tt 2012.

289   52.♗e1! ♖c4 53.♖xd4 ♖xc5 53...♖xd4 54.♗c3. **54.♖d6** 1-0 Nakamura-Nepomniachtchi, Baku blitz 2015.

290   28...♖xe3! 29.♖xe3 ♕e5 30.♔f2 ♕xh2+ 31.♔f1 ♕xd2 and Black won in Choladze-Feduk, Albena 2011.

291   27.♘xe5! 27.♕f5 was played in the game Corstjens-Wouters, Borne jr 2013. **27...♖xe5 28.♕h5! ♘f7** 28...♖xe2? 29.♕xe8+ ♖xe8 30.♖xe8#. **29.♖xe5 ♖xe5 30.♖xe5 ♕xe5** 30...♘xe5? 31.♕e8#. **31.♕xf7+−**

292   20.♗c2! Keeping the e4-pawn protected, while luring the black rook to d8 as the d4♗ is under attack. The game Muse-Breder, Germany Bundesliga 2011/12, continued 20.♗e2 ♖d8 21.♗b2? ♕xe4 (this is why the bishop should be placed on c2 instead of e2!) 22.♗f3 ♗xf2+ 23.♔xf2 ♖xd1 24.♗xe4 ♘xe4+ and Black was better. **20...♖d8** 20...♗c3 21.f4 ♕f6 22.e5+−. **21.♗b2 ♗xf2+ 22.♔xf2** 22.♖xf2? ♖xd1+ (check!) **22...♖xd1 23.♗xe5+−**

293   18.♖xf7! ♗xf7 (18...♖xf7 19.♗xe6+−) and as now Black's light-squared bishop is pinned, White can attack Black's other pinned bishop: **19.♗f6** (19.♗h6 is also good) 1-0 in the game Alekhine-Mikulka, Olomouc sim 1923.

294   7...g5! 8.♗g3 g4 9.♘e5 ♘e4 10.♕xg4 ♗xd2+ and Black is winning, although the game ended in a draw, Ernst-Papin, Berlin Wch blitz 2015.

295   31...♖xg5! 0-1 Paulet-Kabatianski, Netherlands tt 2012/13; 32.hxg5 h4 33.e5 hxg3+−+.

296   39.♗xg6! ♖g8 39...fxg6 40.♕b6 ♕xb6 41.cxb6+−; 39...♖f8 40.♗xh5+−. **40.♗xf7!** 1-0 Ding Liren-Topalov, Wenzhou (m) 2018; 40...♖xf7 41.♕b6+−.

297   16.♘xd7! ♘xd7 17.♘c7! ♖xc7 18.♗xc7 ♖xc7 19.b4 and White won, Mamedyarov-Carlsen, Moscow blitz 2013.

298   12.♖d4! ♗f5 12...♕c7 13.♖xg4 ♘xe5 14.♗f4+− was played in the game Pradeep-Firat, Chennai Wch U20 2011. **13.♕d1/d2+−**

299   11.♘xc6! 11.e5 ♗xg2 (11...dxe5 12.♘xc6 bxc6 – see 11.♘xc6; or 12...♕xd3 13.♘e7+!+−) 12.exf6 ♗xh1 13.♘e6! fxe6 14.f7+ ♖xf7 15.♗xd8 ♗f3 16.♗h4 is also good for White, but the text is much better. **11...bxc6 12.e5! dxe5 13.♕f3! ♕e7 14.♘e4+−** Sekanina-Ramik, Czechia tt 2012/13.

300   38.g4! 38.♖f7 ♖2f4+−+. **38...hxg4 39.♖f7 ♖2f4** 39...♔g6 40.♖xf5 ♖xf5 41.♔xg4+−. **40.♗xf5+ ♔g8 41.♔g5! ♖xc4 42.♔g6** and White won, Adair-Sarakauskas, England 4NCL 2017/18.

301   31.♕f4! 31.♗xf5 ♗xb2=. **31...♕b7** 31...♕xf4 32.gxf4 and ♗xf5 next, removing the defender of the black bishop. **32.♕d2!+−** Meier-Caruana, Baden-Baden 2013 (analysis).

302   30.♘xg7! ♔xg7 The game Karssen-Klein, Bussum 2013, continued 30...♖g6 31.♘f5 and White was much better, though eventually Black won (54). **31.♕xf4±**

303   22.♖xa7! ♕xa7 23.♕xb4 ♖b8 24.♕a3 1-0 Admiraal-Blom, Escaldes 2018.

304   27.♘xb7! ♕xb7 28.♖b1 ♘c4 28...♕c7 29.♖xb2+− was played in the game Kazarian-Van Wessel, Netherlands tt 2016/17. **29.♕xc4** and White wins.

305   30...b5! 31.axb5 31.♘g1 bxc4 32.♕xc4+ ♔d8−+ was played in the game T.Burg-Bischoff, Deizisau 2012. **31...axb5 32.♗xb5 ♗xb5 33.♕xb5 ♕f1+ 34.♘g1 ♕xb5−+**

306 19...♕xf5! 20.exf5 20.♖bd1 was played in the game E.l'Ami-L.Bensdorp, Hengelo jr 1997, after which Black soon won. **20...♗xf3−+**

307 19.♘xd5! ♕xd5 19...♖g6 20.♘xf6+ (or 20.♘xe7 ♖xh6 21.♘xc8+ ♕e6 22.♖xe6+ fxe6 23.♖e1+−) 20...♕xf6 21.♕d2+−. **20.♕xf6+−** Jobava-Van Wely, Dubai Wch rapid 2014.

308 No! 47.♘e8? ♖e7! 47...♖c8 48.♘f6+±. **48.♘d6** 48.♘f6+ ♖xf6−+. **48...♖xd6−+** The pinned e5-pawn is a bad defender! Timman-Smits, Helmond rapid 2012.

309 20...g5! 0-1 Verstraeten-Harika, Vlissingen 2013; 21.♗c7 ♖d7 22.♗e5 ♖xe5−+ A pinned piece is a bad defender!

310 26.♘fe7+! ♔f7 27.♘h8+! ♔xe7 28.♕xc5+ and White won in Ris-Gazis, Agios Kirykos 2011.

311 34.♘f6+! ♕xf6 34...gxf6 35.♕xg6+ ♔h8 36.♖xh6#; 34...♔xf6 35.♕xg6; 34...♔h8 35.♕xg6 fxg6 36.♘xe8 ♖xe8? 37.♖xh6#. **35.♗xf6** and White won, Jumabayev-Vallejo Pons, Moscow 2016.

312 27...♗xf4! 28.♖xf4 28.exf4 ♖xd4 29.♖fc1 (29.♘e4 ♖xe4 30.♗xe4 ♕xc5+−+; 29.♖cc1 ♖xd2+−+) 29...♘d3−+. **28...♘d3!** 29.♕xd3 ♕xc5 and Black won, Hayrapetyan-Mchedlishvili, Dubai 2013.

313 7.♘c4! ♕d8 8.♘xd5 ♕xd5 8...b5 9.♕xb5 ♕xd5 10.♘e5 ♗d7 11.♘xd7 ♕xd7 and White is a pawn up with a clearly better position. 9.♘b6 axb6 10.♕xa8± Timofeev-Paravyan, Russia tt rapid 2018.

314 36...♕e3! Threatening 37...♕xg1#. 36...♕xe2 37.♕xd4 ♗xg2+ 38.♖xg2 ♕xe1+ 39.♖g1 ♕e4+ 40.♕xe4 fxe4 was played in the game Kalle-De Strycker, Antwerpen tt jr 2012, and now after 41.d7 White wins back the rook: 41...♔g8 (41...♖c7?! 42.♖d1!; 41...♖c6?? 42.e7+−) 42.dxc8♕ ♖xc8=. **37.♖f1** 37.♗f2 ♕xf2 38.♕e1 ♗xg2+ 39.♖xg2 ♕xe1+−+. **37...♕xe2 38.♖fg1 ♗xg2+ 39.♖xg2 ♕f1+ 40.♖g1 ♕xg1#**

315 19.♕e4! St. Andrew's Cross, the 'clean' cross-pin! 1-0 Guseinov-Natarajan, Dubai 2008; 19...♘e7 20.♗xe7+−, removing the defender. If instead 19.♕f3 ♘xe5!.

316 20.♖ge1! A Maltese Cross – a vertical and a horizontal pin! Tempting is 20.♖xg7+ ♔f8 21.♖g8+ ♔xg8 22.♕g5+ ♔f8 23.♕d8+, but White has no more than a perpetual: 23...♖e8 24.♕d6+ ♖e7 (24...♔g8? 25.♕f6+−) 25.♕d8+. **20...♖xe1** 20...♖xd2? 21.♖e8#; 20...♕h4 21.♕xe2+− was played in the game Adhiban-Abasov, Wijk aan Zee 2016. **21.♕xf2+−**

317 27...♖f7! An Oblique Cross: a diagonal and a vertical pin! 0-1 Ostos-Jimenez Fraga, Panama City 2013; 28.♕xb8 ♖f1#; 28.♕xf7 ♕xh2#.

318 No! 30.♖d3? 31.♖d1! A Maltese Cross! 1-0 Giri-Shirov, Reykjavik Ech tt 2015; 31...♖xe3 (31...♖xd1 32.♖xc3+−) 32.♖xd8+ ♗f8 33.♕xe3+−.

319 No! 1...♖c2 2.♖c1 White counter-pins by a Maltese Cross! 1-0 Chatard-Amateur, Paris 1906.

320 No! 23...♖xe4 24.♘g3, attacking the cross-pinned bishop! White wins material, Rutten-Bayings, Breda 2018 (adjusted).

321 25.♖xd5! ♕xd5 26.♖d1! An Oblique Cross! **26...♕xb3 27.♖xd8+ ♔f7 28.axb3** and White wins, Bedouin-Vaisser, France tt 2015 (analysis).

322 57.♖c7+! ♖d7 57...♔f6 58.♕h8#; 57...♔h6 58.♕h8#. **58.♕c8!** An Oblique Cross; 1-0 Canal-Schmid, Venice 1953; 58...♖xc7 or 58...♖e7 59.♕xe6+−.

323 39.♕e6+! ♕f7 39...♗f7 40.♕c8++−. **40.♖f3!** An Oblique Cross! **40...♕xe6** 40...♖f5 41.♕c8+ ♕e8 42.♕xe8+ ♗xe8 43.♖xf5+−; 40...♗f5 41.♖xf5! ♖xf5 42.♕c8+ ♕f8 43.♗xf8+−. **41.♖f8#** Sutovsky-A.Onischuk, Poikovsky 2013.

324 19...♗f5+! After 19...♗xb2 20.♗xb2 ♗f5+ 21.♘d3 ♕e2 22.♕a3 ♗xd3+, as played in the game Halosar-Poschauko, Graz 1941, Black is better, but the text wins immediately! 20.♗d3 20.♔a1 ♗xb2+ (luring away the bishop) 21.♗xb2 ♕e1+ 22.♗c1 ♕xc1#. **20...♕e2!** St. Andrew's Cross. **21.♕xa3** 21.♗xf5 ♕xa6−+. **21...♕xd3+ 22.♔a1 ♕b1#**

325   9.♘xc6! bxc6 10.♕xd5! St. Andrew's Cross. **10...♗xe3** 10...cxb5 11.♕xa8+–.
11.♕xc6+ ♔e7 12.♕e8+ ♔f6 13.♕xe3 1-0 Ducarmon-A.van den Berg, Vlissingen 2013. 13.fxe3 was also good, but White has to be careful after 13...♘e7. Now 14.♘c4!+– is an important in-between move as 14.♕xh8? ♕xe3+ 15.♔f1 (15.♗e2?? ♗g4/♗a6–+) 15...♗f4+ leads to a draw.

326   37.♗g7+! ♔g8 38.♔b3 Zugzwang! 1-0 Van Kampen-Kvetny, Basel 2013; 38...f5 39.gxf6+–.

327   14.♗xg7! ♔xg7 15.♘xa2 ♕xa2 **16.♕c3!** An eternal pin! **16...d5** 16...h6 17.♖xd6+–; 16...♕a1+ 17.♔d2 ♕a4 18.g5+–. **17.g5** 17.♖xd5 and g4-g5 next was also good. **17...♔g8 18.gxf6** and White won in Warmerdam-Mustafin, Batumi Ech jr 2014.

328   22.♗xd5! exd5 23.♖xc7 ♖xc7 **24.♘c5!+–** Tying down Black's king and bishop! As the king has to defend his rook and the bishop has to stay on c8 to protect the a6-pawn, Black has only pawn moves (24...♗b7 25.♘xb7+–). He will quickly run out of those, which means Black will find himself in zugzwang soon. 1-0 Zhou Weiqi-Izzat, Canberra 2015.

329   10...d5! 10...0-0 was played in the game Westerweele-Van de Wynckele, Netherlands tt 2013/14. **11.♗b3** 11.exd6 ♗xc3+–+. **11...d4–+**

330   19.♘b6! 1-0 Ftacnik-Cernousek, Banska Stiavnica 2011; 19...axb6 20.♖xd6+–.

331   34.♖xd5! exd5 34...♕xd5 35.♖xf8+ ♔xf8 36.♕h8#. **35.e6** and White won, Rogic-Zecevic, Croatia tt 2012.

332   27...♖h6! 27...♕xh4 was played in the game Halfhide-M.Senders, Netherlands tt 2013/14. **28.♖xd8+ ♔h7** 28...♖xd8? 29.♕xd8+ (check!) 29...♔h7 30.♕h4+–. **29.♘xe4** 29.♕xh6+ ♕xh6 and ...♕h1# is coming; 29.♕xg5 ♖h1# – Anderssen's Mate. **29...♕xd8!** **30.♕xh6+** 30.♕xd8 (a pinned piece is a bad defender!) 30...♖h1#; 30.♘g5+ ♕xg5 31.♕xg5 ♖h1#. **30...gxh6–+**

333   34.♕f4! f5 34...♕e7 35.♘c6 (or 35.♘f3 ♖e6 36.♘g5+–) 35...♗xc6 36.♖xe5+–; 34...♖e7 35.♕xc7 ♖xc7 36.♖xe4+–. **35.♘c6!** 1-0

Rozum-Ipatov, Yerevan Ech 2014; 35...♗xc6 36.♖xe5+–; 35...♖e7 36.♘xe7++–; 35...♕xc6 36.♕xe5+–. If instead 35.♘f3 ♖e7.

334   34...♖xd4! 35.cxd4 ♗b4 36.♖d1 ♗e2! 37.♖e1 e3 37...♗g4 or 37...♗h5–+ is also good. **38.♘f3** 38.♖xe2 exd2–+. **38...♗xf3** **39.♖xe3 ♗e4** and Black won, A.van Beek-Brenninkmeijer, Netherlands tt 2017/18.

335   36...♗xg2+! 36...♖xd3 was played in the game Marinkovic-Abramovic, Belgrade 1991. **37.♖xg2 ♕f3! 38.h3** 38.♗xf3? ♖d1+–+; 38.♕e1 ♖xd3–+. **38...♕f1+ 39.♔h2 ♕xb1**

336   25.♗d3! ♘c5 26.♗xc5 26.♗f1 ♘b3 27.♕d1 was also winning. **26...bxc5 27.♗f1** and White won, Bezemer-J.Markus, Amsterdam 2012.

337   18...♖xa6! 18...♗xf3 was played in the game Carlsen-Akobian, Riyadh Wch blitz 2017. **19.♕xa6 ♗c4–+**

338   8.♗xf7+! 8.♗b3 was played in the game Jazbinsek-Navinsek, Slovakia tt 2005/06. **8...♔xf7 9.♘g5+ ♔g8 10.♘e6+–**

339   17...f4! 18.♗xf4 The game Gomez Sanjuan-Sanchez Saez, Mislata 2016, continued 18.♗xc5 dxc5 19.a5 ♘d6 0-1. **18...♖xf4 19.♕xf4 ♗h6–+**

340   15.c3! ♕xc3 15...♕b5 16.♖a5+–. **16.♖c1 ♕xc1** 16...♕b4 17.♖b1 ♕c3 18.♖b3+–. **17.♕xc1** and White won in Hoang Thi Bao Tram-Makropoulou, Mardin Wch tt W 2011.

341   23.a5! 23...♖f7 was played in the game Kruijsen-Looijer, Rijswijk ch-NED jr W 2012. **24.♕c5 ♖xe7! 25.♕xe7 ♗f6–+.**

342   8.♗xf6! ♗xf6 9.♗d5 and White won in the game Ye Rongguang-Van Wely, Antwerp 1997.

343   23.♖xc6! 23.♘c4 was played in the game C.IJzermans-Beerdsen, Utrecht 2016. **23...bxc6 24.♘c4 ♕a2 25.♘c3+–**

344   9.♘c4! 9.h5 ♘xe5 10.dxe5 ♗e4. **9...♕c7 10.h5**, trapping the bishop. White is winning, although he still lost in the end, Adair-Nakamura, London rapid 2014.

345   12.axb5! axb5 The game Alb.David-Kravtsiv, Livigno 2012, continued 12...♘a7 13.dxe5 dxe5 14.♕xd8 ♖xd8 15.bxa6 ♗e4 16.♗c4 1-0. **13.d5** and White wins.

346 23.♖xb7! ♖xb7 24.♖c8 ♖c7 24...♕e7 25.♘ac6!+−. **25.♖xd8 ♖c1+ 26.♗f1** and White won, Gleizerov-Venkatesh, Visakhapatnam 2011.

347 28...♖h5! 29.♘h4 ♖xh4! 30.gxh4 ♘f4 0-1 Raljic-Vajic, Bosnjaci 2013; 31.♕g3 ♖g8−+.

348 20...e5! 20...gxf3 was played in the game Cordes-Kafer, Heilbronn 2018. **21.dxe6 c5! 22.fxg4** 22.♘f4 cxd4 23.♘xh5 ♗xe3+ 24.♔f1 ♖xe6−+. **22...♕g6 23.gxf5 cxd4 24.fxg6 ♗xe3+ 25.♔h2 ♖xg6 26.♘f4** 26.exd7? ♖h6+ 27.♗h5 ♖xh5#. **26...♗xf4 27.gxf4 dxc3 28.exd7 ♖xg2+ 29.♔h3 ♖xe2−+**

349 50...♗b4! 0-1 Debashis-Vrolijk, Hoogeveen 2016; 51.♔g3 (51.♔e2/e4 ♘c3+−+) 51...♔d6 52.♔f3 ♘c6−+.

350 25...b4! Shutting off the a5-e1 diagonal and thus threatening 26...♕b/c/d5 or ...♕a6. **26.♕f3 ♕a6 27.♕a8+ ♔d7 28.♗xb4 ♗xb4** and Black won in G.Reichardt-Umudova, Netherlands tt 2017/18.

351 28...f5! 29.♘c3 29.♕c1 ♖c8!−+. **29...♖c8 30.♘b5 ♕a6** 0-1 Papin-Jakovenko, Taganrog 2011.

352 29.♘d5! ♖xd5 29...♗xd5 30.c3+−. **30.c3 ♕xd3 31.exd5** Or 31.cxd5+−. **31...♕xc4 32.dxe6 ♕xe6** and White won, Nimzowitsch-Leonhardt, San Sebastian 1911.

353 31...c5! 32.bxc5 ♗e5 and Black won, Le Cong Cuong-Le Thanh Tai, Ho Chi Minh City ch-VIE 2012.

354 16.♘f5! ♗xf5 16...gxf5 17.g3 ♕xe4 18.♖xe4 fxe4 19.♘h4 exd4 20.♕h5+−. **17.g3 ♕xe4 18.♖xe4 ♗xe4 19.♘d2** and White won, Haslinger-Hamblok, Dieren 2015.

355 29...♘f4+! 30.gxf4 ♗f8 0-1 Kabatianski-Solodovnichenko, Germany tt 2011/12.

356 22...♘f4+! 0-1 Plug-Parligras, Tatranske Zruby 2018; 23.gxf4 ♗f8.

357 29.♖f5! fxg5 30.f3 1-0 J.Polgar-Yilmaz, Yerevan Ech 2014.

358 16...♘c4! 17.♗xc4 b6! and Black won, Sanikidze-Rasmussen, Istanbul ol 2012.

359 11.♗d6! 11.a3 ♕e7 12.♘d6+±. **11...♗xd6 12.a3!** and White won in Toman-Christensen, Marianske Lazne 2012.

360 17.a3! ♗c5 17...♗a5 18.b4. **18.b4 ♗e7 19.♖h3+−** J.van Foreest-Lauber, Novi Sad tt 2016 (adjusted).

361 14.♖d4! 1-0 Zelbel-Pruijssers, Germany Bundesliga 2015/16; if 14...♘g6 or 14...♘h5 15.g4+−.

362 37.♖a7! 38.♗c4 b5 and Black won, Izsak-Iv.Saric, Germany Bundesliga 2012/13.

363 21...♖fg8! 22.♕f7 ♘d8 and Black won, Novruzov-Allahverdiyeva, Baku ch-AZE 2019.

364 21...♖a8! 22.♕c5 ♖dc8−+ Mamedov-Carlsen, Shamkir 2018 (analysis).

365 26...e5! 27.♗xa7 ♖a8 28.♗d4 exd4−+ A.Blees-Alekseev, Amsterdam 2016.

366 18.f4! 18.♗f4 ♕b2 19.♕d1 is the same idea as the text, but in a worse version: ♕xa2 20.♕xa1 ♕xa1 21.♖xa1 ♖xb3 and Black has drawing chances. **18...♕b2 19.♕b1!** and White won, Wojtkiewicz-Wahls, Geneva 1995.

367 24...♘e8! 25.♕g8 f5 0-1 E.Hansen-Kleinman, Athens Wch U20 2012; 26.♕g6 ♗f7−+.

368 17.c4! 17.♕xf1 was played in the game Böhm-Bosboom, Bunschoten-Spakenburg rapid 2018. **17...♕d6** 17...♕d8 18.♘exc6+−. **18.♗xf7** (or 18.♘exc6+−)

369 19.♗g5! ♕h5 20.♗d1! ♘xg3 21.♕xg3! 1-0 So-Nakamura, St Louis blitz 2016.

370 28.♘xg4! ♕xg4 29.h3! ♕xf4 29...♕e6 30.f5 gxf5 31.exf5+−. **30.g3!** and White won, Ibragimov-Nyzhnyk, Moscow 2013.

371 16...♘c4! 17.♕b4 a5 18.♕c5 b6 Or 18.♖c8 19.♗xf8 ♖xc5 20.♗xc5 b6−+. **19.♕c7 ♕xc7 20.♗xc7 ♖ac8−+** (20...♖fc8 is also good) 0-1 T.Blees-Leeftink, Haarlem ch-NED jr 2012.

372 1.g4! ♗h7 2.f5 ♖e4 3.♘xe4 dxe4 4.♖ae1 and White won in Marich-Buljovchich, Yugoslavia 1969.

373 15.g4! ♘xd4 15...hxg4 16.hxg4. If the knight retreats to safety, the pawn marches forward, trapping the bishop: 16...♘g7 17.g5+−. **16.♗xd4** 1-0 I.Sokolov-Bogdanov, Helsingor 2017.

374   21...♛c6! 22.♖d1 ♖a8 23.♘d5 ♛xd5! 0-1 C.Gheorghiu-Tomazini, Ech tt jr 2011; 24.♖xd5 ♖xa7−+.

375   25...♗d4+! 26.♔h1 ♗e3 and Black won, Bakri-A.Haast, Batumi ol W 2018.

376   28.♛d1! ♖a2 28...♗d3 29.♖b3 or 29.♖d4+−. **29.d3 a5 30.♖b1** and White is winning, although the game Gronnestad-Levushkina, Berlin tt W 2014, eventually ended in a draw.

377   10...♗c2! 11.♖d2 ♘b6 0-1 Kyas-Blübaum, Playchess.com blitz 2011.

378   16.h3! ♗h5 16...♗e2 17.♖e1 (or first 17.e5+ ♔d7 (17...♔xe5 18.♖e1+−) 18.♖e1+−) 17...♗a6 18.e5++−. **17.f4!** Threatening 18.e5+ with a fork. **17...♔e7 18.g4 ♘xg4** 18...♗g6 19.f5!. **19.hxg4 ♗xg4** and White won, Taylor-Sengupta, Hastings 2017/18.

379   17.b5! ♛c7 18.♖b4 and White won, Ferro-Dvirnyy, Italy tt 2015.

380   30...♘b7! 30...♖gg8 was played in the game Muschik-Lombaers, Utrecht 2012. **31.♛a7 c5−+**

381   18...♘f5! 19.gxf5 ♗g7 and Black won in Rouffignac-Song, Le Touquet 2011.

382   42.♛c2! and 43.♖d1 next; 1-0 Nepomniachtchi-Kryvoruchko, Antalya Ech tt 2013.

383   18.♘xa2! Luring the queen to a2, while at the same time clearing the third rank for the rook! Of course Black is not obliged to recapture the knight, but then he has nothing to hope for with his unsafe king. **18...♛xa2 19.♖a3** 1-0 Van Kampen-Gerlich, Utrecht 2012.

384   14.h4! Taking away the h4-square from the black queen, while at the same time clearing the h2-square for the rook. 1-0 Kozul-Kuljasevic, Rijeka 2011; 14...♗a6 15.♖h2+−.

385   34...♗c5! Taking away the d6- and e7-squares from the rook. ...♔d7 next traps the rook. 0-1 Sekandar-Peng Zhaoqin, Utrecht 2016.

386   60.♗d7! Taking away the c8-square from the rook. 1-0 Giri-Wojtaszek, Doha 2015; 60...♗e2 61.♔b4+−; 60...g4 61.b4 or 61.♔b4+−; 60...e4 61.♔d4 ♖e5 62.♖a6++−.

387   38...♔f8! and 39...♗e8 next. 0-1 Dominguez Perez-Yu Yangyi, Havana 2015.

388   17.a3! Taking away the b4-square from the black queen. **17...b4** 17...♘d4 18.♛xb8+−. **18.♗f1 ♛xf1 19.♖hxf1 bxc3 20.bxc3** 1-0 Shirov-Kleinman, Reykjavik 2017.

389   31.♛c2! and there is nothing Black can do against 32.♖a4 ! 31.♛a2 (with the idea 32.♖b1 ♛c3 33.♖b3) 31...♘xe4+ (31...a4 32.♛xa4 ♛xa4 33.♖xa4 is no fun for Black either, but compared to 31.♛c2! he can play on for a while) 32.fxe4 ♛xe4 33.♛b1+− was played in the game Kunin-Beeke, Amsterdam 2017. However, the text is more convincing.

390   17.♛d7! Taking away the g4- and h3-squares from the black queen. 18.♖g1 next traps the queen. 1-0 Akdag-Leenhouts, Helsingor 2016.

391   29...♖cf8! And 30...♘e8 cannot be prevented: **30.♘e4 ♘e8** 30...dxe4 31.♗xe4 gives White some counterplay, e.g. 31...♘e8?! 32.d5. **31.♘f6+ ♗xf6 32.♛xf8?** 32.exf6 ♘xg7 33.fxg7 ♖fg8 34.gxh8♛ ♖xh8, but here White still has a tough job defending his position. **32...♖xf8 33.♗xf8 ♗e7** and Black won in Von Meijenfeldt-Maatman, Sneek ch-NED U20 2013.

392   26...♗xd3! 27.cxd3 ♘f7 and Black won, E.l'Ami-C.Van Oosterom, Roosendaal 2012.

393   24...♗xf2+! 25.♔xf2 ♖h4 trapping the queen, as the f3-knight is pinned. 0-1 Suhle-Anderssen, Breslau m 1859.

394   7...♗b4+! 7...♘c5 8.♛a3+−. **8.♗d2 ♘c5 9.♛b5 ♗xd2+ 10.♘bxd2 a6 11.♛xc6 dxc6** 0-1 Ciszek-Pielaet, Naleczow 1987.

395   7...♘b8! 7...♘b4 8.♘a3 a6 (or 8...c6) 9.c3 and White escapes with a black eye. **8.♘d4** 8...e5 c6 (or 8...a6 9.♗c4 (9.♗a4 b5) 9...d5) 9.♗c4 d5−+. **8...a6 9.♗a4 b5** and Black won, Gamboa Gonzalez-Romero Barreto, Santo Domingo ch-VEN 2018.

396   7.♗g5! ♛h5 8.c5 h6 9.cxd6+− In the game Colijn-E.de Boer, Utrecht 2016, White played 9.♗e3? and after 9...♛d5! 10.f3? (10.♘f3 gxf3 (10...♗xc5 11.hxg4±) 11.♘c3 ♛h5 12.cxd6±) 10...♗g3+ Black was even better!

397   9.♗xf7+! ♔xf7 10.♘g5+ ♔g8
11.♘e6 ♕a5 12.♘c4 ♕xe1+ 12...♕a6 13.♘c7
♕a4 14.b3+−; 12...♕b5 13.♘c7 ♕c5 (13...♕a4
14.b3+−) 14.♗e3+−. **13.♕xe1** and White won,
Fell-Villanueva, Buenos Aires 2015.

398   18.♖xa7! ♖xa7 19.♗g5 ♕g6 20.♕e3
Targeting! White attacks the rook while
at the same time threatening to trap the
black queen with 21.♘xe5 or 21.♗h4 as the
g5-bishop is now protected by the queen.
20.♗xe7? ♘f4−+ with a double attack;
20.♘xe5? ♕xg5−+; 20.♗h4? ♕xg5−+. **20...
f6 21.♕xa7 fxg5 22.♘xe5** and White won
in Adams-Baramidze, Baden-Baden 2015.
22.♕xc7 was also winning.

399   21...♗f5! 22.♕xf5 22.♕d2 ♗xc2
23.♕xc2 ♖xe3−+. **22...♖xe3 23.♖d3** White
cannot defend the knight, as the queen will
be trapped, e.g. 23.♘d4 g6−+. **23...♖xe2** and
Black won in Rzayev-Safarli, Baku 2010. 23...
g6 was also good.

400   18.♕xb3! 18.dxe6 was played in
the game Kaidanov-Kengis, Moscow 1986.
18...♗xe5 19.d6! ♕c5 20.♘a4! ♕a5 21.f4+−

401   No! 34...♘xe4 35.♘xe4 ♕xe2
36.♘d6! e4 36...♖a8? 37.♘b2, trapping
the queen! **37.♘xe8+** 37.♘b2 exf3 38.♖xe2
♖xe2 39.♕f4 is also winning for White.
37...♗xe8 38.♘e5 and White won in Sieber-
Osmanodja, Dresden W 2018.

402   Yes! **14...♗g4! 15.♗xf6 ♕d7!**
15...♗xf3 16.♗xd8 and White is a piece up.
16.♗f5 ♗xf5 17.♗xg7 17.♖ad1 ♗g4 (17...gxf6?
18.♖xd5+−) 18.♕xd5 (18.♖xd5 ♗xf3 19.♖xd7
♗c6−+) 18...♕xd5 19.♖xd5 gxf6−+; 17.♗b2
♗g4−+. **17...♔xg7** and Black won, Hebden-A.
van de Oudeweetering, Hoogeveen 2003.

403   No! 27.♗xh6? g5! 27...♕xh5?
28.♕xg7#; 27...gxh6 28.♖xh6+ ♔h7
29.♖xh7+−. **28.♕g4 ♘f4 29.♖h4 ♘e2+!** 29...
gxh4 30.♗xf4=. **30.♔f1 gxh4∓** A.Haast-L.van
Foreest, Amsterdam blitz 2016.

404   Yes! **19.♘c6! ♕xc3 20.♗c1! ♖b6**
20...♕a3 21.♘xb8 ♕c5 22.♘xd7+−. **21.♔a1
♕xc2** 21...♗f6 22.e5!. **22.♕xc2** and White
won, Arizmendi Martinez-Milov, Biel 2001.

405   42...♕xe3+! 43.♕xe3 d2 44.♕e4+ g6
0-1 S.Zhigalko-Carlsen, Berlin Wch rapid 2015.

406   47...♕xg5! 0-1 Klein-Wiersma,
Netherlands tt 2016/17; 48.♕xg5 e2−+.

407   24.♕xg7+ 1-0 Van der Hagen-
Albertus, Meppel jr 2017; 24...♕xg7 25.♖xg7+
♔xg7 26.d7+−.

408   27.♕d8! ♕xd8 28.e7+ ♕d5 28...♔h8
29.exd8♕+−. **29.♗xd5+ cxd5 30.e8♕+−**
Spassky-Donner, Leiden 1970 (analysis).

409   No! **1.♖xf2? ♖h2+!** 1...exf2 2.♔xf2
with a theoretical draw was what White
had in mind. **2.♔xh2 exf2,** a double attack
on a piece and the promotion square, 0-1
Palkovi-J.Polgar, Budapest 1989.

410   51.d7! 1-0 Vachier-Lagrave-Karjakin,
Leuven blitz 2018; 51...♔e7 52.f6+! gxf6
53.gxf6+ ♔d8 54.f7 ♔e7 55.f8♕+ (or 55.d8♕+
♔xd8 56.f8♕++−) 55...♔xf8 56.d8♕++−.

411   28.♕xe6+! ♕xe6 29.d7 ♖c8
30.d8♕+! 1-0 Moradiabadi-Bollen, Dieren
2015; 30...♖xd8 31.♖xd8+ ♔f7 32.♖1d7+ ♔f6
33.♖d6 or 33.♖xb7+−.

412   48.♖a3! 48.b7? ♖d1+ 49.♔h2 ♖d2+!
(49...♖b1? 50.♖a3+ e3 51.♖b3=) 50.♔h3
(50.♔g1 ♖b2−+) 50...♖d7−+. **48...♖xa3
49.b7 ♖xa2 50.b8♕ ♖d2 51.♕b5** ½-½
Mammadova-Krumina, Batumi ol W 2018.

413   29.♕xb6 cxb6 30.c7 ♕c8 31.♘d6
♗xd6 32.exd6 ♔f8 33.d7 ♕xd7 34.c8♕++−
Bezemer-H.Jonkman, Amsterdam 2016
(adjusted).

414   17.♗g5! ♕xg5 18.e7+ cxd5 Better is
18...♗e6, but after 19.exf8♕+ ♖xf8 20.♖xb7!
(or 20.♖xe6+ ♘xe6 21.♕xd6+−) 20...♕f6
(20...♘xb7 21.♖xe6+ ♔f7 22.♗xf7+ ♔xf7
23.♘xb7+−; 20...cxd5 21.♕g7+) 21.♗xe6+
♘xe6 22.♕xf6 White is winning. **19.♕h8+**
1-0 Balog-Van Dooren, Germany Bundesliga
B 2017/18; 19...♔f7 (19...♔xh8 20.exf8♕#)
20.♕xf8+ ♔e6 21.e8♕+ ♕e7 22.♕e/fxe7#.

415   32...dxe4! 32...c4 33.♘g4!= was played
in the game Polak-Van Kerkhof, Delft 2017.
33.dxe4 ♗xe4!−+ 34.♖xe4 Or 34.fxe4 h3+
(34...♖xf1 35.♖xf1 h3+−+) 35.♔g1 ♖xf1+ (35...
h2+−+) 36.♖xf1 h2+ 37.♔g2 ♖xf1 38.♔xf1
h1♕+. **34...♖xe4** Or 34...h3+ 35.♔xh3 (35.♔g1
♖xe4 transposes to 34...♖xe4; 35...h2+−+)
35...♖xe4−+. **35.fxe4 h3+ 36.♔g1** 36.♔xh3
♖xf1−+. **36...h2+ 37.♔g2 ♖xf1 38.♔xf1 h1♕+**

416 41...♖h1+! 42.♔xh1 gxf2 43.♖f6 43.♖f3 ♖h4+ 44.♖h3 f1♕+−+. **43...♖h4+ 44.♖h3 ♔f6!** 44...♖xh3+? 45.gxh3 ♔f6 46.♔g2=. **45.♖xh4 f1♕+ 46.♔h2 ♕xb5−+** Yuan-M.Muzychuk, Sochi Wch W 2015 (analysis).

417 30.♘g6! hxg6 30...♖xf4 31.♘xe7+ ♔f7 32.♖xf4+ ♔xe7 33.hxg7+−. **31.♕xf8+!** 1-0 Wang Jue-Bhakti, Manila Ach W 2013; 31...♕xf8 32.♖xf8+ ♔xf8 33.h7+−; 31.h7+? ♔xh7 32.♕xf8 ♕h4+ 33.♔g1 ♕xd4+ and Black is still in the game.

418 33.♖xg7+! 33.dxc7 was played in the game Gelfand-Grischuk, Elancourt 2013. **33...♖xg7 34.♖xg7+ ♔xg7 35.♕xc7+ ♕xc7 36.dxc7 ♘xf3 37.♗d6** Or 37.♔g2 ♖xh2+ 38.♔xf3 ♖c2 39.♗c5!+− (interference!). **37...♖g5 38.♗g3+−**

419 34.♖c7+! 34.a7 ♖a3=. **34...♔d3** 34...♔c5 35.♗a7 ♔b5 36.♖xc5+ ♖xc5 37.♗xc5 ♔xc5 38.a7+−. **35.♖xc3+ ♔xc3** 35...♗xc3 36.a7+−. **36.♗e5!** 1-0 Fischer-Euwe, Leipzig ol 1960; 36...♗xe5 37.a7+−.

420 26.♕d4! 26.♖e1 ♖dd5=. **26...♕g5** 26...♖xd4 27.f8♕+ ♔g6 28.♕f6#; 26...♖f8 27.♖c5+−. **27.♖c5** Again luring away the d8♖. **27...♖xd4 28.f8♕+ ♔g6 29.♕f7+** 1-0 Anand-Caruana, St Louis 2017; 29...♔h6 30.♖f6++−.

421 Yes! 51...♖f4! 52.♗xf4 gxf4 53.♔f2 h2 54.♔g2 hxg1♕+ 55.♔xg1 b4! (55...♔f6? 56.a4=) 0-1 Sanal-Rublevsky, Serbia tt 2017.

422 53...♖c5! 0-1 Karpov-Seirawan, St Louis blitz m 2012; 54.♖c6 (54.♔xc5 c2−+) 54...♖xc6 55.dxc6 c2−+.

423 61...♖h4! 61...♖a3 was played in the game Ernst-Pavlidis, Hoogeveen 2015. **62.♔xh4** 62.♖e7+ ♔g8 63.♔g6 (63.♖xe5 h2 64.♖e1 h1♕−+) 63...♖g4+ and Black's h-pawn will decide the game. **62...h2−+**

424 57.♖a5+! ♔b4 57...♔c6 58.♖d5! ♖xd5 59.exd5++−. **58.♖d5 exd5 59.d8♕ d4 60.c5 d3** 60...♖xc5 61.♕a5++−. **61.c6** 1-0 Malakhov-Fedoseev, Antalya Ech tt 2017.

425 42.♖c4! ♖xc6 43.dxc6 ♕a3 44.c7+− Rustemov-Mchedlishvili, Germany Bundesliga 2012/13 (analysis).

426 46.♕xe8+! ♕xe8 47.♗c6 1-0 Van Wely-Sukandar, Leiden 2016.

427 35...♕xf1+! 36.♔xf1 ♗b2 and Black won in the game Bereolos-Milman, Philadelphia 2001.

428 56...b2! 57.♔c2 ♘d2! 0-1 Gelfand-Carlsen, London ct 2013; 58.♗xb2 (58.♔xd2 b1♕) 58...axb2 59.♔xb2 ♘c4+ 60.♔c3 ♘xe5−+.

429 67...g3! Obstructing the bishop's range, or luring it to a square where this defender can be captured. 0-1 Richter-Acs, Germany Bundesliga 2013/14; 68.♗xg3 (68.fxg3 h2 69.♔e2 ♖a3 (69...h1♕? 70.♖xh1 ♗xh1 71.♔xd3) 70.♖c8+ ♔f7 71.♖c7+ ♔e8 72.♖c8+ ♔d7 73.♖c7+ ♔d8−+) 68...♖xg3 69.fxg3 h2−+.

430 41...♖xe3! 0-1 Hendriks-Sengupta, Leiden 2013; 42.fxe3 ♗d1−+; 42.♖xe3 c1♕−+.

431 54.♖xe4! 1-0 Docx-Rijnaarts, Netherlands tt 2015/16; 54...♖xe4 55.♗b8+−.

432 47.♗f6! ♖xf6 47...♗xf6 48.f8♕++−. **48.♖a6+** 1-0 Adhiban-Minero Pineda, Baku ol 2016; 48...♔e7 (48...♔xd5 49.♖xf6 ♗xf6 50.f8♕+−) 49.♖xf6 ♔f8 (49...♔xf6 50.f8♕++−) 50.♖xf4+−.

433 44.♖xc4+ 1-0 Ganguly-Sethuraman, Makati Ach 2018; 44...bxc4 (44...♔a3 45.♕a5#) 45.♕b6+ ♔c3 (45...♔a3 46.♕a5#; 45...♔a4 46.♕xb2+−) 46.h8♕++−.

434 38.♕xf7+! ♔xf7 39.b7 ♕xd5+ 39...♕b2 40.♖b3+−. **40.♖f3+!** Getting out of the check by giving check! Now Black has no time to pick up the b7-pawn, so White queens. 1-0 Nemet-Hendriks, Dieren 1988.

435 32.♘e6+! fxe6 33.♖xd7+ 1-0 B.Hansen-Schmidt, Denmark tt 2012/13; 33...♔xd7 34.♖xc8 ♔xc8 35.f7+−.

436 39...♗xc5! 40.♗xc5 40.♔g3 ♘f3−+ and ...h3-h2 next.. **40...♘e2+** Or 40...h2 41.♘g3 ♘e2+!−+. **41.♔d3 h2** and Black won in Gajewski-Ragger, France tt 2017.

437 40...f2+! 41.♔f1 ♕xd4 42.♖xd4 ♖h5! 0-1 Yu Yangyi-Nepomniachtchi, Antalya Wch tt 2013; 43.♖d2 g3! – luring away the h-pawn (44.hxg3 ♖h1+ 45.♔e2 f1♕+−+) or, in case of 44.h3 ♖xh3!, luring away the g-pawn! 45.gxh3 g2+ 46.♔xg2 f1♕+−+.

438 44...♖xf2+! 44...gxf5 was played in the game Giri-Carlsen, Stavanger blitz 2015. **45.♔xf2 c2 46.♖c5 ♖xc5 47.bxc5 c1♕** and Black is winning.

439 42.♖xd7+! 1-0 Hommerson-Van Opheusden, Utrecht 2014; 42...♔xd7 43.a7 ♖a2 44.♗xa2+–.

440 15.♕xg8+! ♘xg8 16.h7 0-0-0 17.h8♕ and White won in Abreu Delgado-Marin, Cartagena 2012.

441 33...♗xf2+! 0-1 Cheparinov-G.Jones, Italy tt 2013; 34.♔xf2 c2 35.♖e1 c1♕ 36.♖xc1 ♖xc1–+.

442 32.♗xa6! fxg3 33.hxg3 1-0 Giri-Nepomniachtchi, Wijk aan Zee 2017; 33...♖xc2 34.d7+–; 33...♗xa6 34.d7+–; 33...♗d7 34.♗b5+–.

443 62.♖g8! With a double threat: 63.b8♕ or 63.e5#. **62...♖b6+** 62...♖xb7 63.e5#. **63.♔c7 ♖xb7+ 64.♔xb7 f3 65.♔c6 ♔e5** 65...f2 66.♔d6 f1♕ 67.e5#. **66.♖e8+ ♔f4 67.♔d5 f6** 67...♔xg4 68.♖f8+–; 67...f2 68.♖f8+–. **68.♖f8** 1-0 Carlsen-Hracek, Germany Bundesliga 2006/07.

444 48...♖h1! First clearing the a1-square and after 49.♖xa2 ♖xh2+ 50.♔f3, Black captures the defender: 50...♖xe2–+. 0-1 Gelfand-Radjabov, Palma de Mallorca 2017.

445 51...♖b1+! Chasing the king. **52.♔g2 ♖b2** Trading off the defender. **53.♖xb2** 53.♘xd8 ♖xd2+ 54.♔f3 ♖xd7–+. **53...axb2 54.♘xd8 b1♕–+** Van der Werf-Admiraal, Netherlands tt 2015/16 (analysis).

446 28.♖d1+! Chasing! **28...♔c6 29.♕d7+!** Either luring away the rook or chasing the king. 1-0 Iordachescu-Petrosyan, Yerevan Ech 2014; 29...♔b6 (29...♖xd7 30.exd7+–) 30.♖b1+ (chasing away the king in order to win material) 30...♔a7 31.♕xc7+–.

447 23.f5! Targeting. **23...♗h5 24.f6 ♗g6** 24...gxf6 25.♖xh5+–. **25.♖e8+!** Luring away the king. **25...♔xe8 26.fxg7+–** C.de Wit-F. Erwich, Rotterdam 2015 (analysis).

448 34.♘c6! Targeting! 1-0 Aronian-Giri, Moscow 2016; 34...♖e8 35.♘e7+ ♔f8 (35...♖xe7 36.b8♕+ ♖e8 37.♕xe8#) 36.♘c8+–. Interference!

449 63...e2! 64.♖e6 ♖f3+! Targeting! 64...e1♕? 65.♖xe1 ♖xe1 66.♔g5+–. **65.♔g2 ♖e3** Interference! **66.♖xe3 dxe3–+** Ernst-Kovalenko, Moscow 2015 (adjusted).

450 46...♖b1+! 0-1 V.Stefansson-E.l'Ami, Reykjavik 2018; 47.♔f2 d2–+. Not 46...d2? 47.♔e2.

451 54...f3! 0-1 Tolnai-Adorjan, Budapest ch-HUN 1992; 55.♔d3 (55.♖a6 f2–+ 56.♖a1 ♖g1–+) 55...♖g1!–+ (55...f2? 56.♔e2=).

452 48.f6! ♔g6 48...♖d6 49.f7 ♔g7 50.♖a8+–. **49.f7!** Luring the king to an unfavourable square. **49...♔g7** 49...♔xf7 50.d8♕+. **50.♖a8+–** Kazarian-Markantonaki, Reykjavik Ech tt W 2015 (analysis).

453 59.♖h8! 59.♖h7+ was played in the game Juanes Garcia-Gomez Dieguez, Gijon tt 2011. **59...♖c1** 59...♔xh8 60.e7+–. **60.e7 ♖f1+ 61.♔g4 ♖g1+ 62.♔f3+–**

454 38...♖xe1+! 39.♔xe1 ♖h1+ 40.♔d2 g2 41.a7 g1♕ 42.♔c2 42.a8♕ ♕c1#. **42...♕d1+ 43.♔c3 ♕a1+** 0-1 Suba-Okhotnik, Rijeka Wch sr 2011; 44.♕b2 (44.♔b3 ♖b1+ 45.♔c2 ♕a2+ 46.♔c3 ♖c1#; 44.♔d2 ♕c1#; 44.♔c2 ♖e1–+) 44...♕xa7 or 44...♖c1+ 45.♔b3 ♖b1–+.

455 39...♖gxg2+! 39...e2? 40.♖xe5. **40.♗xg2** 40.♔h1 e2 41.♗xe2 ♖gxe2–+. **40...♖b1+! 41.♗f1 e2–+** Ja.Broekmeulen-Reinderman, Netherlands tt 2014/15 (analysis).

456 54.♖c8! ♖f2+ 55.♔d3 ♖f3+ 56.♔d4 1-0 Nakamura-Svidler, Thessaloniki 2013; 56...♖xf6 57.e7 ♖f4+ 58.♔e3 ♖f1 59.♔e2+–.

457 36.♗d5! ♔f6 37.♗xb7! 1-0 Dobrov-Bar, Groningen 2014; 37...♘xb7 38.a6+–.

458 39...g4! 40.♔d2 40.hxg4 ♗xg2! 41.♘xg2 h3–+. **40...♗xg2 41.♘xg2 gxh3** 0-1 Cruz Lledo-I.Sokolov, Stockholm 2016/17.

459 39.b4! ♘d3 40.b5 axb5 40...♘c5 41.♗xb7! ♘xb7 (41...axb5 42.a6 transposes to the game) 42.bxa6+–. **41.♗xb7 ♘c5 42.a6 ♘xa6 43.♗xa6** and White won, Tal-Murey, Tel Aviv 1990.

460 58.b5! 1-0 Tomashevsky-Radjabov, Palma de Mallorca 2017; 58...axb5 (58...bxa5 59.b6+–) 59.a6 ♖a7 60.♗b7+–.

461 45.h6! f5 45...gxh6 46.g7 ♖c8 47.g8♕ ♖xg8+ 48.♗xg8+–. **46.h7 ♖c8 47.♗g8** 1-0 Bartel-Duijn, Porto Carras tt 2018.

462 **45.a6! bxa6** 45...♔d6 46.a7 wins for White. He creates a second passed pawn with f2-f3 and g3-g4 while Black's rook is tied to the defence of a8 and his king has to defend c5. **46.♖xc5+! ♖xc5 47.b7 ♖c4 48.b8♕+** and White won, Van Eijndhoven-Rutten, Veldhoven tt 2017/18.

463 **52...♗xe3+!** 52...♗xc3? 53.♘xd5 ♔xd5 54.gxh4 gxh4 55.♔g2 is a draw because Black has the 'wrong' bishop; 52...hxg3+ 53.♔xg3 ♗xe3 54.h4=. **53.♔xe3 g4! 54.gxh4** 54.hxg4 h3 55.♔f2 h2−+. **54...gxh3** and Black's h-pawn is unstoppable. 0-1 M.Karthikeyan-Eljanov, Doha 2014.

464 **57.d4!** Line clearance. 57.♔b2 was played in the game Giri-Van den Doel, Amstelveen ch-NED rapid 2017. **57...cxd4 58.♗xf5 gxf5** 58...♗h5 59.♗d3+− and f4-f5 next. **59.g6 hxg6 60.♔b2+−** Or 60.♔b1 d3 61.♔c1+−. But not 60.h7?? d3 61.h8♕ d2 62.♕g7+ ♔b8 63.♕f8+ ♔b7 64.♕e7+ ♔a6−+.

465 **29...♗xd4+!** 29...♔xe6? 30.♗h3+ ♔d6 (30...♔f6 blocks the h8-a1 diagonal, and so ...♗xd4+ is no longer a threat: 31.♗xc8=) 31.♗xc8 and as Black does not control the f5-square, the bishop sacrifice does not work here: 31...♗xd4+? 32.cxd4 c3 33.bxc3 bxc3 34.♗f5+−. 29...bxc3 30.bxc3 ♗xd4+! transposes. **30.♔f1** 30.cxd4 ♔xe6 31.♗h3+ ♔f6! (controlling the f5-square) 32.♗xc8 c3−+. **30...♔xe6** 30...bxc3 31.bxc3 ♔xe6 transposes. **31.♗h3+ ♔d6 32.♗xc8 bxc3 33.bxc3 ♗xc3** and Black won in Cisneros Belenguer-Moskalenko, Banyoles 2000.

466 **36...c3! 37.♖xe4** 37.♗xe4 ♖xe4! 38.♖xe4 ♖xe4 39.♖xe4 cxb2; 37.bxc3 b2 38.♖xb2 ♗xg2−+. **37...♖xe4** 0-1 Ponomariov-Radjabov, Eilat tt 2012; 38.♗xe4 ♖xe4! 39.♖xe4 cxb2−+.

467 **31...bxc2! 32.♖xb5 c4! 33.♖b7+** 33.dxc4 d3−+. **33...♔f6 34.♘c1 ♗xc1 35.♖c7 c3** 35...cxd3 wins as well. **36.bxc3 ♗f4** 0-1 TheLancer-Sevian, Chess.com blitz 2017.

468 **33.d7! ♖xb3+ 34.♖xb3 ♕d8** 34...♕f5+ 35.♖bd3 ♗f6 36.♘xf6+−. **35.e7** 1-0 Kramnik-E.l'Ami, Douglas 2018; 35...♕xe7 36.d8♕+−. The computerish 35.♖e3 is also winning, e.g. 35...♗f8 36.♘e5 ♖c7 37.♘f7.

469 **36...♖e8! 37.♖xb7+** 37.♕xe8 ♕c1+ 38.♕e1 d2+−; 37.♕d1 ♕e2+ 38.♕xe2 dxe2+ 39.♔e1 c2−+; 37.♘xb2 ♖xe1+ 38.♔xe1 cxb2−+. **37...♕xb7 38.♕xe8 ♕b1+** 0-1 Topalov-Caruana, London 2016; 39.♕e1 c2−+.

470 **29...b4! 30.♖b5** After 30.cxb4 the pawn blocks the b-file, which means White can no longer defend with ♖b5: 30...b2−+. **30...a5! 31.cxb4** 31.♖xa5 b2−+. **31...a4 32.♖d5 b2 33.♖d1 a3−+** Nakamura-Karjakin, Stavanger 2018 (analysis).

471 **36.cxb4! gxf5** 36...♖xc6 37.b5 ♖e6 38.b6 gxf5 (38...axb6 39.a7 ♖e8 40.cxb6+−) 39.b7 ♖e1+ 40.♔f2 ♖b1 41.c6+−. **37.b5 ♔f8 38.b6 axb6 39.cxb6 ♖xc6 40.b7** 1-0 T.Willemze-Van Kerkhof, Netherlands tt 2012/13; 40...♖b6 41.a7+−.

472 **53.♖c6! bxc6 54.b6 ♖c8 55.b7 ♖b8 56.♔c5** 56.a7 ♖xb7 57.a8♕ wins as well, but the text is more accurate as Black is forced to play 56...h4, after which the rook's pawn is lost. **56...h4** 56...♔f5 57.♔xc6 and after 58.a7, Black has to give his rook. **57.a7 ♖xb7 58.a8♕ ♖h7** 58...♖g7 59.♕d8++−. **59.♕g8+ ♔h6 60.gxh4** and White won in Karjakin-Morozevich, Tashkent 2012.

473 **33.♗a6! ♗f6** 33...bxa6 34.c6 ♖xb6 35.c7 ♖c6 36.d7+−. **34.♗xb7 ♖xb7 35.c6 ♖xb6 36.♖c1!** ♗xb2 36...♖b8 37.c7 ♖c8 38.d7 ♖xc7 39.♖xc7+−. **37.d7** 1-0 Carlsen-Grischuk, Linares 2009; 37...♗f6 38.c7+−; 37...♗xc1 38.d8♕+ ♔g7 39.♕xb6+−.

474 **42.dxc7! ♖f8 43.c5! ♖e8+ 44.♔d3 bxc5 45.b6 ♖c8 46.b7 ♖xc7 47.b8♕** and White won, R.Reichardt-L.Baselmans, Assen ch-NED jr 2017.

475 **44.♖xe6! ♖xe6 45.♔b1** 1-0 Decoster-Fedorchuk, Maastricht 2015; 45...♖e1+ 46.♔c2 ♖f1 47.g6 ♔d6 48.g7.

476 White resigned here, but he is actually winning: **30.♖d6! cxd6** and since now the connection between the rook on d8 and the pawn on d2 is interrupted, White does not have to fear 31...♖c1+ (30...♖xd6 31.g8♕++−): **31.f7 ♖c1+ 32.♔xd2+−** Torre Repetto-Parker, New York simultaneous 1924.

477 59.e6+! ♔h7 and here White resigned, but he is winning after **60.♕xb2 ♕xb2 61.e7** and White queens, Schrickx-Provoost, Vlissingen 2015.

478 35...♕xc8! The game Negi-Wen Yang, Mashhad Ach 2011, saw 35...♕xe6 36.♖xd8+! and Black resigned, because of ♖f8 37.♖xf8+ ♔xf8 38.♘xe6+ ♔e7 39.♘g5 e2 40.♘f3+−. If 35...e2 36.♘xd7 e1♕+ 37.♖c1+−. **36.♕xc8 e2 37.♕xd8+ ♖f8 38.♕d5+ ♔h8=**

479 40...♖d8! 40...♔h7 41.♕h3+ ♔g8 42.♕xh2. **41.♕xd8+ ♔h7 42.♕d3+ g6−+** Karpatchev-Potapov, St Petersburg ch-RUS 1998 (analysis).

480 40.♕xg8+! 40.a8♕? ♕e2+ (or 40...♕g4+ 41.♔h1 ♖h3#) 41.♔g1 ♖f1#. **40...♔xg8 41.a8♕+ ♕xa8 42.♖xa8+ ♔g7 43.♔xf3+−** S.Kuipers-Shyam, Leiden 2017 (adjusted).

481 48.♗f1! 48.hxg3 h3 was played in the game Fructuoso-Corstjens, Leiden 2014. **48...gxh2** 48...♔c5 49.♗g2+−. **49.a8♕+** Or 49.♔g2+ ♖xg2 50.a8♕++−. **49...♖xa8 50.♗g2+−**

482 39...e3! 40.♗xc6 40.♖xd2 exd2 41.♔c2 ♗xg2−+. **40...e2! 41.♖xd2 41.♖c1 ♖d1−+. 41...e1♕+ 42.♔c2 bxc6** 0-1 Matlakov-M.Muzychuk, Gibraltar 2015.

483 36.g7! 36.♘g4 was played in the game F.Erwich-Bonnmann, Germany tt 2013/14. **36...♗f3** 36...♗h7 37.♖c7 ♖h4 38.♔d1+− and ♘xh7 cannot be prevented. **37.♖d7!+−** Preventing 37...♖d1# and preparing g7-g8♕+.

484 58...♕e3+! 58...♕f3+ was played in the game Hopman-La.Ootes, Wijk aan Zee 2012. **59.♕xe3 dxe3 60.♖g2** 60.♖e4 a3 61.♖xe3 a2−+. **60...♗d2** 60...a3 also wins, e.g. 61.♖a2 (61.♔g4 ♗d2 transposes) 61...♗d2−+ and..e3-e2 next. **61.♔g4 a3 62.♔f3** 62.♖g1 e2−+. **62...a2 63.♖g1 ♗c3−+**

485 42.♖xf7+ ♔h6 43.♖xf5! ♖c1+ **44.♔e2** 1-0 P.Ypma-Beerdsen, Dieren 2015 44...gxf5 45.e6 ♖b1 46.e7 ♖b8 47.♗f7 or 47.♗c6+−.

486 28...axb4! 29.♘xc6 b3 30.♖xc7 ♘d6 0-1 Nisipeanu-Caruana, Dortmund 2015.

487 No! 68.♘b5 ♘xb5 69.♔xe4 ♘d6+! Covering the f5-square. 69...h4? 70.♘f5+ ♔g4 71.♘xh4=. **70.♔e5 h4 71.♔xd6 h3 72.e4** 72.♘f5+ ♔f4!−+. **72...h2 73.e5 h1♕** and Black won in Van Delft-T.Burg, Amsterdam 2014. 68.♘c8, with the same idea, holds the draw, e.g. 68...♔f5+ (68...♘xc8 69.♔xe4 ♘d6+ 70.♔d5 h4 71.♔xd6 h3 72.♘f3 ♔f2 73.♔e5 ♔xe2 74.♘g1+=) 69.♔xe4 ♘xd4 70.♔xd4 h4 71.♘d6 h3 72.♘e4+ ♔g2 73.♔e3 h2 74.♘f2 (just in time!) 74.♔g3 75.♘h1+ ♔g2 76.♘f2.

488 66.♘f8+! 66.♖e5 was played in the game Caruana-Ding Liren, Berlin ct 2018. **66...♔g8 67.h6 ♔xf8 68.h7 ♘xe6+ 69.♔g4 ♘xg5 70.h8♕+ ♔e7 71.♔xg5+−**

489 42...♘c1! 43.gxf3 43.♘c3 ♘e2+−+. **43...♘a2! 44.♔f1** 44.♘d2 c3 45.♘b3 c2−+. **44...c3 45.♘xc3** 45.♔e2 c2 46.♔d2 c1♕+. **45...♘xc3−+** Laznicka-Shirov, Novy Bor m 2012 (analysis).

490 40.♖xg6+! 40.♔f2 was played in the game Caruana-Nakamura, St Louis 2014. **40...♖xg6 41.e6 ♔h7 42.e7 ♖g8 43.♔f6!** On its way to f7 to support the e-pawn, and shouldering the black king. 43...♖g6+ 44.♔f7 ♖g7+ 45.♔e6 ♖g8 46.♔d7 ♖g7 47.♔d8+−

491 42...♗e3+! An important intermediate check, covering the b6-square with gain of tempo! 42...c1♕+? 43.♗xc1 ♗xc1 44.♖xb4=; 42...b3? 43.♖b6+! ♔h7 44.♖c6=. **43.♔h2** 43.♔f1 ♗c4+−+. **43...b3** and ...c1♕ followed by ...♗xc1 and ...b3-b2-b1♕ is next; 0-1 C.Braun-Dambacher, Maastricht 2015.

492 35.♖xf7! ♔xf7 36.♗c4+ ♔e7 37.♗xa2 ♖xc3 38.a6 ♖a3 38...♖c1+ 39.♔f2 ♖d1 40.a7 ♖d8 41.♗d5!+−. **39.♗b3! c4 40.♗c2** 40.a7 was also good. **40...♖a1+ 41.♔f2** 1-0 Thorfinnsson-Jensson, Reykjavik ch-ISL 2016.

493 43...c3! 43...♗d3 was played in the game Colijn-Maris, Dieren 2012; 43...♔d7 44.♗d2 and White is just in time to stop Black's passed pawn. **44.♔xc3** Now the king is blocking the a5-e1 diagonal for his bishop. 44.♗xc3 h3−+; 44.bxc3 b2−+. **44...♔d7!** 44...h3? 45.♗c7. **45.e5 h3 46.e6+ ♔c8** Or 46...♔d6 47.e7 ♗b5 48.♗b4+ ♔d5−+; 46...♔c6? 47.e7 ♔d7 48.♗c7=. **47.e7 ♗b5−+**

494 56.♖c2! Threatening 57.♖h2.
56...♘xe3 56...♖xh5 57.♖h2+–. **57.♖xc6+**
57.♖h2? ♘f1+–+. **57...♔d7 58.♖c5** Thus, the
h5-pawn serves as a block. **58...f5** 58...♖xh5
59.♖xh5 gxh5 60.h7+–; 58...gxh5 59.h7+–.
59.hxg6 ♖xh6 60.♔f4 1-0 Nanu-Postny,
France tt 2012; 60...♘g2+ 61.♔g5 ♖h8 62.g7
♖g8 63.♔f6+–.

495 38...♖e8! 39.♔e1 a4! Clearing the
a5-square for the bishop, thus provoking
40.c6. Now the a7-g1 diagonal has become
accessible to Black's bishop: **40...♗b6!** and
the threat of 41...♗f2+ followed by 42...e1♕+
can only be stopped by **41.♗xe2 ♖xe2+–+**
Shirov-E.Sveshnikov, Riga rapid m 2014
(analysis).

496 35...♗e5! 36.♗h3 ♖f1+ Luring
the rook. **37.♖xf1 ♗h2+!** Attracting the
king. **38.♔xh2 gxf1♕+–+** Carlsen-Vachier-
Lagrave, Biel 2018 (analysis).

497 98.♖g4! ♗f6 98...♔xg4 99.d8♕++–.
99.♖g7! Threatening both 100.♖f7 and
100.♖e7. **99...♔b4** 99...♔e4 100.♖e7+ (or
100.♖g6 ♗h4 (100...♔e5 101.♖xf6+–)
101.♖g4++–). **100.♖f7! ♖e4+ 101.♔f8 ♖f4**
102.♖xf6 ♖xf6+ 103.♔e7 1-0 Li Chao-
Neiksans, France tt 2017.

498 30.♖f7+! Luring away the queen.
30...♕xf7 31.♕c8+ ♕e8 32.d7 ♔f7
33.dxe8♕+ ♖xe8 34.♕b7+! ♖e7 35.c6!
e4 Clearing the e5-square for the bishop.
36.c7 36.fxe4? ♖xb7 37.cxb7 ♗e5–+. **36...**
e3 Threatening mate in two by ...e3-e2-e1♕.
37.♕d5+! ♔f6 37...♔e6 38.♕xe6+ ♔xe6
39.c8♕++–. **38.♕d6+ ♔f7 39.♕xe7+** In the
game Serper-Nikolaidis, St Petersburg 1993,
White first repeated moves with 39.♕d5+
♔f6 40.♕d6+ ♔f7 and then played 41.♕xe7+.
If 39.c8♕? e2+ 40.♔xf2 e1♕#. **39...♔xe7**
40.c8♕+–

499 31...♖d2+! 32.♔e1 32.♔xd2 ♘c4+
33.♔c3 ♘xe5 34.♔d4 ♘c6+ 35.♔d5 ♘d8
and only Black can be better. **32...♖d1+=**
Guramishvili-J.van Foreest, Wijk aan Zee
2017 (analysis).

500 26...♕xg2+! 27.♔xg2 ♖8f2+
28.♔g3 ♖f3+ 29.♔g4 ♖f4+= T.V.Petrosian-
Matanovic, Kiev tt 1959 (analysis).

501 32.♕xg7+ 32.♖g3 f5!–+ was played
in the game Kevlishvili-Nijboer, Netherlands
tt 2014/15. **32...♔xg7 33.♖g3+ ♔h6 34.♖h3+**
♔g6 35.♖g3+=

502 70...♖a8+! 71.bxa8♕ ♕xa8+
72.♔b5 ♕d5+ 73.♔a6 73.♔b4? ♕c5+ 74.♔b3
♕xb6+–+. **73...♕a8+** ½-½ J.Polgar-G.Jones,
London 2012.

503 28.♖xc6+! bxc6 29.♕a8+ ♔c7
30.♕a7+ ♔c8 31.♕a8+ ½-½ Gao Rui-
A.l'Ami, Reykjavik 2015.

504 45.♖xa7! ♗xc5 46.♖b7+ ♔a8
47.♖a7+ ♔b8 ½-½ De Kruyf-Van Baardewijk,
Nijmegen 2013.

505 25...♖f1+! Using the double check to
make a draw instead of winning material or
delivering mate, as we have seen earlier and
will see later in this book! **26.♔g2** 26.♔xf1?
♗h3#. **26...♖f2+ 27.♔g1** 27.♔h1? ♗f3+ 28.♔g1
♖g2+ 29.♔h1 ♖xd2#. **27...♖f1+=** Sreeves-
Gupta, London 2010 (analysis).

506 34...♖b1+! 34...♖g2 was played in
Gelfand-Kramnik, Moscow blitz 2013.
35.♔e2 35.♔d2? ♖xf1 36.♗xf1 ♖xd7. **35...♖b2+**
36.♔e1 ♖b1+ 37.♔f2 ♖b2+ 38.♔g1 38.♗e2 is
not a good idea, as the bishop has to keep the
knight protected: 38...♔xd7. **38...♖g2+ 39.♔h1**
♖f2+ 39...♖xg3+ 40.♔h2. **40.♔g1 ♖g2+=**

507 40.♕h8+! ♔e7 41.♕h4+! 41.♕xg7+?
♔d8–+. **41...♔e8 42.♕h8+=** Khismatullin-
Brodsky, Russia tt 2015 (analysis).

508 55...♕xf3+! 56.gxf3 ♘h2+ 57.♔g1
♘xf3+ 58.♔f1 58.♔h1? ♖h2#. **58...♘h2+** ½-½
Kevlishvili-Van den Doel, Amsterdam m
2015.

509 38.♖e8+! 38.♘d6 was played in the
game F.Erwich-Den Heeten, Leiden ch-NED
jr 2000. **38...♔f7** 38...♔h7 39.♖e7+=. **39.♘d6+**
♔g7 40.♖e7+=

510 50.g8♘+! An underpromotion!
Maybe you would have expected such a
move in the previous chapter, but as its
main goal is to make a draw, I think this
exercise is better included here! **50...♔xh5**
51.♘f6+ ♔h6 52.♘g8+ ♔h7 53.♘f6+ ♔h6
53...♔h8? 54.♖g8#. **54.♘g8+ ♔h5 55.♘f6+**
♔h4 56.♖g4+ ♔h3 57.♖g3+ ♔h4 58.♖g4+=
Nijboer-Sumets, Haarlem 2014 (analysis).

511   57...g3+! 57...♖xf2+ was played in the game S.Zhigalko-Badelka, Minsk ch-BLR 2017. **58.fxg3 g4 59.d7 ♖f2+ 60.♔h1 ♖f1+ 61.♔g2 ♖f2+=**

512   34...♕xf2+! 34...♗g7 was played in the game Vereggen-Böhm, Netherlands tt 2014/15. **35.♔xf2 ♗d4+ 36.♔e2 ♖g2+ 37.♔d1 ♖g1+ 38.♔d2 ♖g2+ 39.♔c1 ♖g1+=**

513   49...♘xh3+! 50.♔h1 50.gxh3? ♕xf2+ 51.♔h1 ♕h2#; 50.♔f1? ♕xf2#. **50...♘xf2+ 51.♔g1 ♘h3+=** Aronian-Caruana, Wijk aan Zee 2014 (analysis).

514   46...♖e1+! The game Aronian-Caruana, Paris blitz 2018, continued 46...♕f8 47.♕h5+ ♔g8 48.♖g6+ 1-0. **47.♔h2 ♖h1+! 48.♔xh1 ♕e1+ 49.♔h2 ♕g3+ 50.♔g1 ♕e1+=**

515   38...♖g1+! 39.♔h2 39.♔xg1 ♕d1+ 40.♔g2 ♕f3+ 41.♔h2 ♕h5+ (or 41...♕xf2+ 42.♔h3 ♕f1+ 43.♔g3 ♕g1+=) 42.♔g1 ♕d1+=. **39...♖h1+! 40.♔g2** 40.♔xh1 ♕d1+ transposes to the above line. **40...♖g1+ ½-½** Smyslov-Tal, Bled/Zagreb/Belgrade ct 1959.

516   38...♖e1+! The game A.Braun-Siebrecht, Vienna 2005, continued 38...♕b5+ 39.♔f3 ♕xb1 40.♖d8#. **39.♔xe1** 39.♔f3? ♕xd2−+; 39.♔d3? ♕xb1+−+. **39...♕xb1+ 40.♖d1** 40.♔e2 ♕e4+ 41.♔d1 ♕b1+=. **40...♕e4+ 41.♔f1 ♕h1+ 42.♔e2 ♕e4+ 43.♔d2 ♕d4+=**

517   28...♕f3+! 29.♔f1 ♕xd3+ 30.♔e1 ♖e3+! 31.fxe3 ♕xe3+ 32.♔d1 ♕d3+ 33.♔e1 ♕e3+ 34.♔d1 ♕d3+ ½-½ Karjakin-Gelfand, Tashkent 2012.

518   37.♖xf8+! ♔xf8 37...♖xf8? 38.♕h7#. **38.♕d6+ ♔g8 39.♕xg6+ ♔f8** and now White can choose how to give a perpetual: **40.♕xh6+** 40.♕f5+ ♔g8 41.♕h7+ (41.♕g6+=). **40...♔g8 41.♕h7+ ♔f8 42.♕h6+=** There is no mate for White as the black queens cover all the mating squares! Vachier-Lagrave-Aronian, Bilbao 2013 (analysis).

519   29...♕f1+! 29...♘g3+? 30.♔h2 ♘f1+ 31.♖xf1 ♕xf1 32.♕e8#. **30.♖xf1** 30.♔h2? ♗g1+ 31.♔h1 ♘g3#/♘f2#. **30...♘g3+ 31.♔h2 ♘xf1+ 32.♔h1 ♘g3+=** Naroditsky-Oratovsky, Benasque 2015 (analysis).

520   26.♕xh7+! 26.♖h3 f5−+. **26...♔xh7 27.♖h3+ ♔g6 28.f5+!** Blocking the black king's escape route. **28...exf5 29.♖g3+ ♔h7 30.♖h3+=** Mira-Romanov, San Salvador 2015 (analysis).

521   36.♘xe6! ♗xe6 Black has to recapture the knight, otherwise White will play 37.♘c7+ followed by a discovered check. **37.♕xc6+ ♗d7** 37...♖d7 38.♕c8+ (or 38.♕a8++−) 38...♖d8 39.♕/♖xd8#. **38.♖xd7! ♖xd7 39.♕c8+ ♖d8 40.♕c6+ ♖d7 41.♕c8+ ½-½** Gunina-M.Muzychuk, Baku ol W 2016.

522   36...♕e3+! 37.♔h1 ♖xf1+ 38.♗xf1 ♕f3+ 39.♕g2 39.♗g2 ♕d1+ 40.♗f1 ♕f3+=. **39...♕h5+ 40.♕h3** 40.♔g1 ♕c5+=. **40...♕f3+ 41.♕g2** (41.♔g1 ♕f2+ (41...♕e3+=) 42.♔h1 ♕f3+=) **½-½** Fedorovsky-Rapport, Germany Bundesliga 2015/16.

523   38.♖xg7+! ♔xg7 39.♕xd4+ ♔f7 40.♕d7+ ½-½ Ptacek-Walica, Frydek-Mistek 2014; 40...♖e7 41.♕d5+ ♔f6 (41...♖e6 42.♕d7+ ♔f6 43.♕d4+ ♔e7 44.♕xa7+=) 42.♕d4+ ♔e5 43.♕d6+ ♔f7 44.♕d7+ ♖e7 45.♕d5+=.

524   25.♘h6+! ♔g7 25...♔h8? 26.♘f7+ ♔g7 27.♕h6+ ♔g8 28.♕h8#. **26.♕e7+ ♔xh6 27.♕h4+ ♔g7 28.♕e7+ ♔h6** 28...♔g8 29.♕xe6+ ♔h8 30.♕h3+ ♔g8 31.♕e6+= ♔g7? 32.♕xd7++−. **29.♕h4+ ♔g7 30.♕e7+ ♔h6 ½-½** Grischuk-Wang Hao, Elancourt 2013.

525   34...♘h2! 34...♘e3 was played in the game Werthebach-F.Erwich, Germany tt 2009/10. **35.♖c8+ ♔h7 36.♖cc7 ♘f3+ 37.♔f1** 37.♔h1? ♖h2#. **37...♖d2!** and White cannot prevent a perpetual with ...♘h2+−f3+−h2+ etc. We saw the same drawing mechanism in Exercise 508, Kevlishvili-Van den Doel. Not 37...♘h2+? 38.♔e1 ♘f3+ 39.♔d1 and the king walks away.

526   25.♖xd5+! cxd5 26.e6+! Blocking the escape route for the black king. **26...fxe6** 26...♔e8? 27.♕c6+ ♔d7 28.♕xd7#. **27.♕b5+ ♔c8** 27...c6? 28.♕b7+ ♔e8 29.♕e7#. **28.♕a6+ ♔d7** 28...♔b8? 29.♗xa7+ ♔a8 30.♗b6+ ♔b8 31.♕a7+ ♔c8 32.♕xc7#. **29.♕b5+=** Vachtfeidl-Taylor, ch-GB cr 2010 (analysis).

527 35...♕g2+! 36.♔f5 ♕c2+! 37.♔g5
♕d2+! 37...♕g2+? 38.♔h6 ♕d2+ 39.♔g5
♕h2+ 40.♕h5 ♕d6+ 41.♔g5++–. **38.♔h5**
♕h2+ 39.♔g5 ♕d2+= Cheparinov-Sutovsky,
Poikovsky 2013.

528 33.♘e4! ½-½ Vachier-Lagrave-
Aronian, Wijk aan Zee 2015; 33...♕xd4
(33...♕xe1 34.♘f6+ ♔h8 (34...♔g7 35.♘xh5+=)
35.♕g5 ♔g7 36.♘xh5+ ♔h7 37.♘f6+=)
34.♘f6+ ♔h8 (34...♔g7 35.♘xh5+ gxh5
36.♕g5+ ♔h7 37.♕xh5+ ♔g7 38.♕g5+=)
35.♕g5 ♕d2 36.♖e3 ♔g7 37.♘xh5+ ♔g8
38.♘f6+= ♔h8? 39.♕h6#.

529 23.f5! Clearing the c1-h6 diagonal,
while protecting the rook. 23.♖h6+ was
played in the game Riazantsev-Edouard,
France tt 2012. **23...♖xd2** 23...♖xf7? 24.♕h6#.
24.♘g5+ ♔h8 25.♖h6+ ♔g8 26.♖g6+=

530 36...♖h2+! 36...♘d3+ was played
in the game Brinkmann-R.Reichardt,
Skopje tt 2015. **37.♘xh2 ♕xh2+ 38.♔f1**
♕h1+ 38...♕h3+ 39.♔e2 ♕g2+ transposes.
39.♔e2 ♕g2+ 40.♔d1 40.♔f2 ♕xe4+ 41.♔e3
(41.♔d2? ♕xd5+–+; 41.♔f1 ♕h1+ 42.♕g1
♕f3+=) 41...♕g2+ 42.♔f2 ♕e4+=. **40...♕g1+**
41.♔c2 ♕g2+ 42.♔b1 ♕g1+ 43.♔b2
♕g2+= White cannot avoid perpetual check:
44.♔b3? c4+ 45.♔a4 ♖xa8+–+

531 44.♕h7+! ♔e6 44...♖g7 45.♕h5+ ♔f8
46.♕h8+= ♖g8? 47.♕f6+ ♕f7 48.♕xd6+ ♔g7
(48...♔e8 49.♕d8#) 49.♕h6#. **45.♕h3+ ♔e5**
46.♕g3+ ♔d4 46...♔e6 47.♕h3+=. **47.♕e3+**
♔e5 48.♕g3+= Cs.Horvath-Schoppen,
Dieren 2016 (analysis).

532 41.♖dg1! Defending against 41...♖f1+
and threatening 42.♗f6+. **41...♖xg1 42.♗f6+**
♖xf6 43.♖xg8+ ♕xg8 44.♕xf6+ ♕g7 ½-½
Steinberg-Svidler, Gibraltar 2017; 45.♕d8+
♕g8 46.♕f6+. A well-known drawing
motif. Imagine the h7-pawn were a black
queen – then Black could still not escape
the perpetual. Every time one of the queens
interposes, they block the escape for the king.
Check it out for yourself!

533 60.h4+! 60.♕e7+ ♔h5!–+ was played
in the game Van Wely-Alb.David, Greece tt
2017; 60.♕g7+ ♔g6–+. **60...♔g6** 60...♔xh4?
61.♕h6#. **61.♕g8+ ♔h6 62.♕f8+ ♔g6**
62...♔h7 63.♕f7+ ♔h8 64.♕f8+=. **63.♕g8+**
♔f6 64.♕f8+ ♔e6 65.♕e8+ ♔d6 66.♕d8+=

534 94.♕d5+! 94.♕e6+ was played in the
game Sarbok-Hirneise, Germany Bundesliga
2013/14. **94...♔f8 95.♕d8+!** If the black king
reaches the e-file, it will run away from the
checks via the queenside. **95...♔f7 96.♕d7+!**
♔g6 And now the most straightforward way
to draw is **97.♕e6+ ♔h7** (97...♔h5? 98.g4+
♔g5 99.h4+ ♔xh4 100.♕h6#) **98.♕f7+ ♔h8**
99.♕f8+ ♔h7 100.♕f7+ ♔h6 101.♕e6+.

535 55.♖xa2! 55.♖xe4 was played in the
game Topalov-Caruana, Thessaloniki 2013;
55.♕h4+ ♕h7 56.♕f6+ ♕g7 57.♕h4+ ♔g8–+.
55...♖xa2 55...♕xa2 56.♕f6+ ♔g8 57.♕g5+
♔f8 58.♕e7+=. **56.♕h4+ ♔g7** 56...♕h7
57.♕d8+! (this is why White lured the rook
to a2!) 57...♔g7 (57...♕g8 58.♕h4+=) 58.♕e7+
♔h8 (58...♔h6? 59.♕g5#) 59.♕d8+=. **57.♕g5+**
♔f7 58.♕e7+ ♔g6 59.♕g5+ ♔h7 60.♕h5+=

536 No! 141...♕f2 142.♕b1+ e1♘! 142...
e1♕ 143.♕d3+ and White gives a perpetual,
e.g. 143...♕ee2 144.♕b1+ ♕fe1 145.♕f5+
♕2f2 146.♕d3+= (see also the comments in
Exercise 532, Steinberg-Svidler). **143.♕b5+**
♕e2 144.♕f5+ ♕f3+ 145.♕xf3+ ♘xf3 No
stalemate: **146.g4 hxg4 147.h5 g3 148.h6 g2#**
Ali-Adams, Baku ol 2016 (analysis).

537 No! 37.♔c2! 37.♔b4 c5+! 38.♔a5
(38.♔xc5? ♕c6+ 39.♔b4 ♕b6+ 40.♔a4 ♕b3+
41.♔a5 b6+ 42.♔xa6 ♕xc4+ 43.♔xb6 ♖b3+
44.♔a5 ♕b5#; 38.dxc5? ♕d2+ 39.♔a4 ♕c2+
40.♔a5; see Exercise 594 in Chapter 9 for the
continuation of this line) 38...♕d8+ 39.♔a4
♕b6=. **37...♖f2+ 38.♔b3!** 38.♔d3 ♖d2+!
39.♔xd2 ♕xd4+ and White cannot escape
perpetual check. If the white king flees to h5,
Black has ...♕f3+ followed by ...♕h3+-f5+ or
vice versa in case of ...♔g6; 38.♔b1 ♖xb2+!=
39.♔xb2 (39.♔a1? ♕xd4+, the b7♖ prevents
♕xb7#!) 39...♕xd4+ with a perpetual, e.g.
40.♔b3 ♕d3+ 41.♔b2 (41.♔b4? a5+ 42.♔xa5
♕xa3+ 43.♔b6 ♕a7#.) 41...♕d2+; 38.♔c1 ♖f1+
does not bring White any further. **38...♖xb2+**
39.♔c3! Chess is not checkers! 39.♔xb2
♕xd4+, see 38.♔b1. **39...♕xg7 40.♖xg7**
♖e2 41.♔d3 ♖a2 42.d5 1-0 Fontaine-Najer,
Germany Bundesliga 2011/12.

538 37...♖c8! 37...♕c7 was played in Adams-Motylev, Germany Bundesliga 2014/15. **38.♕xf7+ ♖c7 39.♕f8 ♖c8 40.♕e7+ ♖c7 41.♕d6 ♖c6** with perpetual pursuit: draw.

539 23...♖d3+! 24.♔a4 ♗d6! 25.♖b3 25.♘b3? ♖c4+−+; 25.♖b4?! a6! 26.♖b3 (26.♘b3 b5+ 27.♔a5 ♗c7+−+) 26...♖d5 27.♖xb6 ♖xb6 28.♗xb6 ♖xd2∓. **25...♖d5 26.♖b5 ♖d3 27.♖b3 ♖d5 28.♖b5 ♖d3** ½-½ Navara-Vachier-Lagrave, Biel 2018.

540 No! After the tempting **65...♖c5?** White has a stalemate trick: **66.♔xh4! ♖xg5** ½-½ Hübner-Adorjan, Bad Lauterberg ct m 1980. Winning was 65...♔xh3!.

541 No! **42.♖xb5?** White has several ways to win, e.g. 42.♔d3 ♖d7+ 43.♔c3 ♖c7+ 44.♖c5 ♖b7 45.♔d4 ♖d7+ 46.♖d5 ♖b7 (46...♖c7 47.♖xb5 ♖b7 and compared to the game, here White can protect his rook: 48.♔c5/♔c4+−) 47.♔c5+−. **42...♖b7! 43.♖xb7** Stalemate! 43.♖d5 ♖xb4 is a theoretically drawn ending, but of course White can still try a little. ½-½ Khalifman-Yuffa, Moscow 2016.

542 No! **50...♘xh3? 51.♖xh3! ♖b3+ 52.♔f4!** 52.♔g2? was what Black had expected: 52...♖xh3 53.♔xh3 ♔e5! 54.♔g2 ♔e4 55.♔f2 ♔f4−+. **52...♖xh3** Stalemate! ½-½ Almagro Llamas-Moskalenko, Spain tt 2013. 52...♖b4+ 53.♔f3 ♔g5 54.♔g2 is a theoretically drawn endgame (the Philidor position). It's beyond the scope of this book to go into this in more detail here.

543 No! **123...♘e3+ 124.♔e1 ♖g1+ 125.♔f2 ♖g2+** and now **126.♔e1!** saves White! (the game Buksa-Guramishvili, Teheran Wch W 2017, continued 126.♔xe3? ♖xa2 0-1). **126...♖xa2** is stalemate. If Black does not take the rook, the ♖+♘ vs ♖ ending is a theoretical draw.

544 **75...♕g7+! 76.♔xe6 ♕g6+! 77.♔xg6** Stalemate! Gopal-Esipenko, Tegernsee 2017 (analysis).

545 **64...♖g7+! 65.fxg7 ♖g6+ 66.♔xg6** ½-½ S.Hansen-Bok, Germany Bundesliga 2016/17.

546 White resigned here, but after **1.♕f6+! ♔g8 2.♕g7+! ♔xg7 3.h6+ ♔f7** it would have been stalemate! Bartolovich-Abkin, St Petersburg 1902.

547 Black resigned here, but he could have held the draw! **42...♕g7+!** Reversing the move order is not a good idea: 42...♖xh3+? 43.♔xh3 ♕h8+ 44.♗h6! ♕xh6+ 45.♔g3 ♕g5+ 46.♔h2 ♕h6+ 47.♔g1 ♕c1+ 48.♖d1 and Black runs out of checks. **43.♖xg7** 43.♔h4? ♕xd7−+. **43...♖xh3+! 44.♔xh3** Stalemate! Klinova-Spence, Gibraltar 2006.

548 **62...♖f4+! 63.♕xf4 ♕g2+! 64.♔xg2** Stalemate! ½-½ Vidit-Gelfand, Poikovsky 2018.

549 **6.h8♕+/♖+/♗+!** 6...♗xh8 7.♔h7 ♗e5 8.g7+! ♗xg7 Stalemate! L.Kaiev, 1932.

550 **1...a1♕!** 1...♔a5? 2.♖h8! a1♕ 3.♖a8+ ♔b4 4.♖xa1+−. **2.♖xb7+ ♔a3 3.♖a7+ ♔b4!** 3...♔b2? 4.♖xa1 ♔xa1 5.♔e4+−. **4.♖xa1** Stalemate! 4.♖a4+ ♕xa4 5.♗xa4 ♔xa4 6.♔e4?! ♔b3 7.♔d3 (7.♔d5? ♔b4−+) 7...♔b4 8.♔d2 ♔xc4 9.♔c2=. Mieses-Post, Mannheim 1914 (analysis).

551 **42.♖xg7+! ♔xg7 43.♖a7+ ♔h8** White has done everything right, but instead of sacrificing to draw, he resigned here! After **44.♖xh7+! ♔xh7** (44...♔g8 45.♕e6+ ♔xh7 transposes) **45.♘g5+! fxg5** (45...♔h6 46.♘f3 and only White can win) **46.♕xg6+! ♔h8 47.♕g7+ ♔xg7** it would have been stalemate! Campora-Zhou Weiqi, Seville 2003.

552 **4.♖b7+!** 4.♖a7+ ♘e7 5.♖xe7+ ♔xe7 6.♖b7+ (6.d6+? ♔xd6 7.♖b6+ ♔c7−+. This is the difference between 4.♖a7+ and 4.♖b7+: on b7 the rook can be captured by the king) 6...♔d6! 7.♖xh7 stalemate! See also Exercise 542 for the same motif. **4...♘e7 5.♖xe7+ ♔xe7 6.d6+!** 6.♖a7+? ♔d6! 7.♖xh7=. **6...♔e6 7.d7+ ♔e7** 7...♔xd7 8.♖a7+−. **8.d8♕+! ♔xd8 9.♖a8+ ♔e7 10.♖a7+−** V.Kovalenko & S.Makhno, 1978.

553 No! **47.♖xe1! ♖xb3+ 48.♔h2!** 48.♔g2? ♖g3+ 49.♔h2 ♖g2+ 50.♔h1 ♖g1+=. **48...♖b2+ 49.♔h1 ♖h2+ 50.♔xh2 ♔f8 51.♕h8#** E.l'Ami-Smeets, Chess.com blitz m 2014 (analysis).

554 No! **55.♔d5! ♖d4+** 55...♖e5+ 56.♔c6 ♖c5+ 57.♔d7 ♖c7+ 58.♔xc7#. **56.♔e6 ♖xd6+** 56...♖e4+ 57.♔d7 ♖e7+ 58.♔c6 ♖c7+ 59.♕xc7#. **57.♔e7** and Black runs out of checks: **57...♖e6+** 57...♖d7+ 58.♖xd7/♕xd7#. **58.♕xe6+−** Krasenkow-Ivanov, Stockholm 2012/13 (analysis).

555 No! 63.♖e5+ ♔d6 64.♖d5+ ♔c6 65.♖d6+ 65.♖c5+ ♖xc5−+. **65...♔c5 66.♖d5+ ♔b4 67.♖b5+ ♔c3 68.♖b3+ ♔d2 69.♖d3+** 69.♖b2+ ♖c2−+. **69...♔c2 70.♖d2+** 70.♖c3+ ♖xc3+−+. **70...♔c1** Now White has no more 'safe' checks: **71.♖c2+ ♔xc2** Or 71.♖d1+ ♔xd1. 0-1 L.van Foreest-Leenhouts, Amsterdam 2017 (analysis).

556 No! **40...♖f2+ 41.♔e1** 41.♔g1? ♖xg2+ and if White now follows the same method as in the game, he can no longer cross the third rank. **41...♖e2+ 42.♔d1 ♖d2+ 43.♔c1 ♖c2+ 44.♔b1 ♖c1+ 45.♔a2 ♖a1+ 46.♔b3 ♖a3+ 47.♔c2 ♖c3+ 48.♔d2 ♖d3+ 49.♔e2 ♖e3+ 50.♔f2 ♖f3+ 51.♔g1 ♖f1+ 52.♔h2 ♖h1+ 53.♔g3 ♖h3+ 54.♔f4 ♖f3+ 55.♔e5 ♖f5+ 56.♔d6 ♖f6+ 57.♔c5 ♖c6+ 58.♔b5** 1-0 E.l'Ami-Van Wely, Wolvega 2010; 58...♖c5+ 59.dxc5!+−; 58...♖b6+ 59.♖xb6!+−.

557 **70.♕a6+!** 70.♕a2+ was played in the game T.Burg-Narciso Dublan, La Massana 2013. **70...♔c3** 70...♔c5 71.♕a5+ ♔c4 (71...♔c6? 72.♕a8+ and thanks to the skewer, White wins the queen!) 72.♕a6+ and Black can choose between a draw via stalemate or a draw by perpetual check: 72...♔c5 (72...♔d4 73.♕d3+!=) 73.♕a5+ ♔d4 74.♕xb4+=. **71.♕d3+! ♔xd3** Or 71...♔xd3, stalemate.

558 **61...♕d2+! 62.♔f1** 62.♔h3 ♕h6+ (or 62...♕e3+=) 63.♔g3 ♕e3+; 62.♔f3 ♕c3+! 63.♕xc3 stalemate! **62...♕e1+ 63.♔g2 ♕d2+ 64.♔f3 ♕c3+! 65.♕xc3** ½-½ Najer-Lomasov, Moscow tt 2018.

559 **49...♕g2+! 50.♔e3 ♘d5+! 51.♔d4** 51.♗xd5 ♕d2+ 52.♔f3 (52.♔xd2 is stalemate) 52...♕f2+ 53.♔e4 ♕d4+ 54.♔f3 ♕f2+=. **51...♕f2+ 52.♔xd5** 52.♔e5 ♕xb2+ 53.♔e6 ♕f6+ 54.♔xd5 ♕d4+ transposes; 52.♔c4? ♘b6+−+; 52.♔d3 ♕f3+. By moving to the second rank the king can't escape from the perpetual either, e.g. 53.♔c2 (or 53.♔d2 ♕f2+ 54.♔c1 ♕e3+=) 53...♕e2+ 54.♔c1 ♕e3+=; 52.♔e4? ♘f6+. **52...♕d4+ 53.♔xd4** Stalemate! 53.♔e6 ♕f6+ 54.♔d5 ♕d4+ 55.♔c6 ♕b6+, combining the stalemate motif with perpetual check. ½-½ Jakovenko-Gelfand, Khanty-Mansiysk 2015.

560 **54...g2!** ½-½ E.Sveshnikov-Piskov, Bled 1990; 55.♘xg2 ♔g1=; 55.♔xg2 ♔g3=.

561 **75.♔c7!** ♗xc7 75...♗h4 76.♔b8 ♗e4 77.a8♕ ♗xa8 78.♔xa8 would have been a better try for Black, but this is also a theoretical draw. **76.♔xc7 ♘d5+ 77.♔b8 ♘b6** 77...♔c6 78.a8♕. **78.♔c7 ♘d5+ 79.♔b8 ♘b6 80.♔c7 ♘d5+ 81.♔b8 ♘b6** ½-½ Van der Poel-Schouten, Netherlands tt 2018/19.

562 **43.♘xg4+! ♗xg4 44.♘xe5! ♘xe5 45.♔f4 ♘d3+ 46.♔xg4 ♔g2** 46...♘xb4 47.e5 c5 48.e6 c4 49.♔f5 (49.e7? ♘d5! 50.e8♕ ♘f6+−+) 49...♘d5 (49...c3 50.e7 c2 51.e8♕ c1♕ 52.♕h5+ ♔g2 53.♕g5+ ♕xg5+ 54.♔xg5=) 50.♔e5 ♘e7 51.♔d4=. **47.♔f5 ♘xb4 48.e5 ♔f3 49.e6 ♘d5 50.♔e5 ♘f4 51.♔d6 ♘xe6 52.♔xe6** ½-½ Van Delft-La.Ootes, Netherlands tt 2013/14.

563 **4.c7+ ♔a8** 4...♔c8 5.♘e7+ ♔d7 6.c8♕+ ♕xc8 7.♘xc8 ♔xc8. **5.c8♕+!** Or 5.c8♖+. **5...♕xc8 6.♘c7+ ♔b8 7.♘a6+ ♔a8 8.♘c7+=** E.Iriarte, 1957.

564 **7.♗e4+! ♔xe4 8.♔b2 ♔d3 9.♔c1 a3** Stalemate; or 9...♔c3 stalemate; or 9...♔c4 10.♔xc2 with a theoretical draw. F.Lazard, 1909.

565 **5.f8♕/♖+! ♕xf8 6.g7+! ♕xg7** 6...♔xg7 7.♗h6+=. **7.♗f6! ♕xf6** Stalemate! F.Aitov, 1967.

566 **106.♖b8+! ♔xd7** 106...♔e7? 107. d8♕+. **107.♖b7+** Now Black can choose between a draw by stalemate, a draw by perpetual check or a draw due to insufficient material. With some sense of humour he opted for the latter: **107...♔c7** ½-½ Le Quang Liem-Peralta, Gibraltar 2019. 107...♔c6 108.♖c7+ ♔xc7 stalemate! (108...♔d5 109.♖xc5+ ♔xc5=); 107...♔c8 108.♖b8+ ♔d7 (108...♔xb8 stalemate!; 108...♔c7 109.♖c8+ ♔xc8 stalemate!; or 109...♔d6 110.♖xc5 ♔xc5=) 109.♖b7+ ♔d6 110.♖b6+ ♔d5. Now there is no stalemate or perpetual check, but 111.♖b5, pinning the queen, leads to a draw.

567 **65...♕g1+! 66.♔h3 ♘df1+ 67.♕g2 ♕h1#** A beautiful mate! A St. Andrew's Cross, although in this case it is of course not relevant that the queen on a8 is hanging after 68.♕xf1, as this is not a legal option. 0-1 Capablanca-Alekhine, Buenos Aires Wch m 1927.

568 43...♖g2+! The game Hou Yifan-Nakamura, Chess.com blitz m 2018, continued 43...♖g3+ 44.♔h4 ♖h2 and here White resigned, but after 45.c8♕, protecting the h3-pawn, White is totally winning!. **44.♔h4 g5+ 45.♔h5 ♖xh3#** Ladder Mate, which is also known as Lawnmower Mate.

569 **39.♖d6+! ♔f7 40.♗xc4+** 1-0 F.Erwich-Litwak, Belgium tt 2011/12; 40...♔e8 41.♖d8#.

570 **27.♘f6+! ♔h8 28.♖xh6+ gxh6 29.♖g8#** The Arabian Mate, Andriasyan-B. Burg, Groningen 2013.

571 **25...♕h1+!** 0-1 Milos-Carlsson, Istanbul ol 2012; 26.♗xh1 ♘h2+ 27.♔e1 ♖g1#. This mating pattern reminds of the brilliant game Ivanchuk-Jussupow, Brussels rapid 1991. We highly recommend you to check that one out for yourself!

572 **21.♘e8+!** Interference! 1-0 Carlsen-Anand, Zurich blitz 2014; 21...♔g8 22.♕h8+ (or 22.♕xe6+ ♔h8 23.♖xf8#) 22...♔xh8 23.♖xf8#.

573 **13...♘xf3+! 14.♔f1 ♗d3+! 15.♕xd3 ♖e1#** 0-1 NN-Severino, Naples 1723.

574 **29.♖f7+!** 1-0 Smeets-M.Haast, Netherlands tt 2012/13; 29...♔g8 30.♖f8+ ♔h7 31.♖h8#.

575 **29.♕g6+! ♖xg6** 29...fxg6 30.hxg6#. **30.hxg6+ ♔g8 31.♖h8#** Anderssen's Mate. Quesada Perez-Rapport, Tsaghkadzor Wch tt 2015 (analysis).

576 **39.♘f7+! ♔g8 40.♕h8+!** 1-0 Matlakov-Nabaty, Batumi Ech 2018; 40...♘xh8 41.♘h6#.

577 **49...♘f1+!** 0-1 Granda Zuniga-Ducarmon, Barcelona 2014; 50.♔h1 ♕h2+! (blocking!) 51.♘xh2 ♘g3#, Suffocation Mate.

578 **1.♕g8+! ♖xg8 2.♘f7+ ♔g7 3.♗h6#** Miedema-Beerdsen, Arnhem 2015 (analysis).

579 **3.♖b8+! ♔xa6 4.♖b6+!** Blocking! 4...♖xb6 5.♘c5#** Gurevich, 1927.

580 **45...♕b4+! 46.♔d5 ♗e4+!** 0-1 Shirov-Sevian, Stockholm 2016; 47.♕xe4 ♕c5#.

581 **42.♘d5+!** Clearing the third rank for the queen: 1-0 Alb.David-Boerkamp,

Vlissingen 2016; 42...♔a4 43.♘b6+! (luring away the queen) 43...♕xb6 (43...♔b4 44.♕a3#) 44.♕a3#; 42...♕xd5 43.♕c3+ (43.♕a3+ ♔c4 44.♕c3#) 43...♔a4 44.♕a3#; 42...cxd5 43.♕a3+ ♔c4 44.♕c3#.

582 **33.♘g6+! ♔g8 34.♕g7+!** Blocking and clearing in one move! **34...♖xg7 35.♘h6#** Plug-Farrand, London 2011.

583 **19.♘xh7+! ♗xh7 20.♕xf6+ gxf6 21.♗h6#** Boden's Mate, Jackova-Korenova, Germany FrauenBundesliga 2005/06 (adjusted).

584 **26.♖f8+! ♖xf8 27.♕h8+! ♔f7** 27...♔xh8 28.exf8♕#. **28.exf8♕+ ♔e6 29.♕f/hf6#** Kramnik-Shirov, Monaco rapid 1997 (analysis).

585 **31.♖d5+!** Clearing the diagonal for the queen. 1-0 Klepke-Schoppen, Borne jr 2013; 31...♔e7 (31...cxd5 32.♕d6#) 32.♖d7+ ♔f6 (32...♔f8 33.♗h7/33.♗e6#) 33.♗e4+ (putting the bishop on other squares along the b1-h7 diagonal, except g6, will also do) ♔e6 34.♕f5#.

586 **38.♕xe6+! ♔c6** 38...♔d8 39.♕e8#. **39.♕e8+!** 1-0 Nakamura-Sasikiran, Istanbul ol 2012; 39...♔b7 40.♕b5+ ♔c8 41.♖e8#.

587 **38.♖xe5+!** The game Gaprindashvili-Veröci, Yugoslavia 1974, continued 38.♕g4+ ♔h6 39.♕g7+ ♔h5 40.♕g4+ ♔h6 41.♕g7+ ½-½. **38...fxe5 39.g4+ ♔h4 40.♕e7+ ♕g5 41.g3#**

588 **72...♕d5+! 73.♔h7 ♕f5+** 0-1 Salgado Lopez-Cuenca Jimenez, Linares ch-ESP 2018; 74.♔g7 ♕g6+ (or 74...♕f7+ 75.♔h6 ♕g6#) 75.♔f8 ♕f7#.

589 **31.♕e5+! ♔g8 32.♕xd5+** 1-0 Ivanchuk-Almasi, Varadero 2016; 32...♔g7 33.♕d7+ ♔g8 34.♕h7#; 32...♔h8 33.♕h5+ ♔g7 34.♕h7#.

590 **52.♘g6+!** 52.♖e2 was played in the game Charbonneau-Oussedik, Pro League rapid 2017. **52...♖xg6** 52...fxg6 53.f7+ ♖e5 54.♕xe5+ ♖g7 55.f8♕+ (55.♕e8+/55.♕b8+ ♖g8 56.♕xg8#) 55...♖g8 56.♕exg7#; 52...hxg6 53.♕h4#. **53.♖xe8+ ♖g8 54.♖xg8+ ♔xg8 55.♕d8#**

591   26.♖xe6+! fxe6 27.♕g6+ ♔f7 28.♕g8+ ♖f8 29.♕xe6+ 1-0 Zimmermann-Guthrie, London 2012. If the queen on d8 had been a rook, we would now have had a checkmate pattern called the Epaulette Mate. With the queen on d8, Black can block the check, although he will still be mated on the next move: 29...♕e7 30.♕xe7#.

592   35...♗c6+! A Novotny interference! Black sacrifices his bishop on a square where it can be taken by two white pieces, but whichever piece makes the capture, it interferes with the other's range. **36.♖xc6** 36.♗xc6 ♕c1+ 37.♔g2 ♖e2#. **36...♕f3+ 37.♔g1 ♕d1+ 38.♔f2 ♖e2#** Van Osch-Werle, Hoogeveen 2016 (adjusted).

593   49.♖h5+! Blocking! After 49.g5+ ♔h5 the black king escapes. **49...gxh5 50.g5+ ♔h7 51.♖e7+ ♔g8 52.♖e8+ ♔h7 53.g6+ ♔h6 54.♖h8#** Vachier-Lagrave-G.Jones, Chess. com blitz 2018.

594   40...♖xa3+! 41.bxa3 ♕c3+ 42.♔b6 42.♔a4 ♕xc4+ 43.♔a5 ♕b5#. **42...♕b2+ 43.♔a5 ♕xa3+ 44.♔b6 ♕b4#** Fontaine-Najer, Germany Bundesliga 2011/12 (analysis).

595   36.♕xh6+ ♔xg4 37.♘e3+ ♔f3 38.♕h3+ ♔e2 39.♕g2+ ♔e1 39...♔xe3 40.♕f2#. **40.♕f2#** Plukkel-Haslinger, Amsterdam 2012.

596   41.♘e7+! ♔h8 42.♕g8+! 42.♘g6+ was played in the game Topalov-Bareev, Monaco rapid 2004. **42...♖xg8** Now the black king's escape route is blocked. **43.♘g6+ ♔h7 44.♘e5+ ♔h8 45.♘f7#** Suffocation Mate.

597   60...♖f4+! 61.♘xf4 61.♔h3 ♕h1#. **61...exf4+ 62.♕xf4** 62.♔g2 ♖b2+ 63.♔h3 ♕h1#; 62.♔h4 ♕h1#. **62...♕g1+ 63.♔h4** 63.♔h3 ♘xf4+ 64.♔h4 g5#. **63...g5+ 64.♕xg5 ♕h2#** Van Wely-Hou Yifan, Wijk aan Zee 2013 (analysis).

598   21...♕xg2+! 0-1 Benko-Hartman, Gausdal 1984; 22.♔xg2 ♗f3+ 23.♔g1 ♘h3#, Suffocation Mate.

599   33.♖h7+! ♔xh7 34.♕h4+ ♔g7 35.♕h6# Spoelman-Ernst, Amsterdam ch-NED 2014 (analysis).

600   18.♕xg7+! 1-0 Bindrich-Nisipeanu, Austria Bundesliga 2016/17; 18...♔xg7 19.♖g4+ ♔h8 20.♖g8#, Arabian Mate (19...♔f8 20.♖g8#).

601   34...♕a2+ 35.♔xa2 35.♔c1 ♕a1#. **35...axb2+ 36.♔b1 ♖a1#** M.Keetman-Ja. Broekmeulen, Maastricht 2014.

602   45.♗f4+! ♔xf4 46.♕h6+ ♔g3 47.♕g5# L.van Foreest-Kevlishvili, St Louis 2018.

603   39.♖h6+! ♔xh6 40.♕h8+ ♔g6 41.♕h5# H.van Dijk-Polak, Delft 2013 (analysis).

604   39.♕xg6+! 1-0 Sadvakasov-Karpov, Astana m 2004; 39...♔xg6 40.♖1e6+ ♔h7 41.♖h6#.

605   36...♖g4+! 36...♖xa4 was played in the game Carlsen-Ganguly, Doha Wch rapid 2016. **37.♔xg4 ♕g2+ 38.♔h5 ♕f3#**

606   33...e5+! 33...♕d6+ was played in Köhler-Klapwijk, Amsterdam 2012, but after 34.e5 (34.♔g5? h6+ 35.♔h4 ♕g3#) 34...g5+? (34...♖d4+! 35.♔f3 ♖xc4 36.exd6 ♖xc1–+) 35.♔e4 ♕g6+ 36.♖f5 it was eventually White who mated Black: 36...♖xh3 37.e6 ♖g3 38.♕d4+ ♔g8 39.♕d8+ ♔g7 40.♕f8#. **34.♔g5** 34.♔xe5 ♕d6#. **34...♕e7+ 35.♖f6 ♕xf6#**

607   35.♕xb6+! 1-0 Van Dael-L. Baselmans, Rotterdam ch-NED jr 2015; 35...♔xb6 36.♘d5+ ♔a7 37.♘c6+ ♔a8 38.♘c7/♘b6#.

608   34.♖h8+! ♔xh8 35.♕h5+ ♔g8 36.♕h7+ ♔f8 37.♕h8# Giri-Shirov, Hoogeveen m 2014 (analysis).

609   36.♖h8+! 36.♕h5?? fxg5–+. **36...♔xh8 37.♕h5+ ♔g8 38.♕f7+** 1-0 Malisov-Birnboim, Jerusalem ch-ISR 1996; 38...♔h8 39.♕f8#.

610   38.♖h7+! 1-0 Mamedyarov-Gelfand, Astana Wch rapid 2012; 38...♔xh7 39.♕h5+ ♔g7 40.♕g6+ ♔h8 41.♕h6#.

611   24.♖h8+! 1-0 Serper-Ippolito, Seattle ch-USA 2003; 24...♔xh8 25.♕h2+ ♕h6 26.♕xh6+ (a pinned piece is a bad defender!) 26...♔g8 27.♕h7#.

612   27.♖h7+! 1-0 Zhai Mo-Ni Shiqun, Xinghua ch-CHN W 2013; 27...♔xh7 28.♕h5+ (a pinned piece is a bad defender!) 28...♔g7 29.♕xg6+ ♔h8 30.♕h7#.

613 33...♖xh2+! 34.♔xh2 ♕d2+ 0-1 Guerrero-J.Polgar, Tromsø ol 2014; 35.♔h1 ♕h6+ 36.♔g2 ♕h3#.

614 29...b5+! 30.♔xb5 ♕c4+ 31.♔a5 ♗d8+ 32.♕b6 ♗xb6# Pillsbury-Lasker, St Petersburg 1896.

615 50.♘h6+! 1-0 Beerdsen-Fier, Amsterdam 2017; 50...♔f7 (50...♔xh6 51.♕g5#; 50...♔g6 51.♕g8+ ♔xh6 52.♕g5#) 51.♕f8+ (or 51.♕d7+) 51...♔g6 52.♕g8+ (or 52.♕f5+) 52...♔xh6 53.♕g5#.

616 30.♗f7+! 30.♕f3 was played in the game Bauer-Navara, France tt 2015. 30...♔d7 30...♔xf7 31.♕xe7+ ♔g8 32.♕e6#. 31.♕xe7+ ♔c8 32.♗e6+ ♕d7 33.♕xd7#

617 35.♕f8+! ♖xf8 36.♗h6+ ♔g7 The bishop blocks the escape route for its own king. 36...♔g8 37.♖c8+ ♕d8 38.♖xd8+ ♖e8 39.♖xe8#. **37.♖c8+ ♕d8 38.♖xd8+ ♖e8 39.♖xe8#** Duchess (Computer)-Kaissa (Computer), Toronto 1977 (analysis).

618 31...♗h3+! 32.♔xh3 32.♔h1 ♕f1+ 33.♘g1 ♕g2/♗g2#. **32...♕f1+ 33.♔g4** 33.♔h4 ♗f6+ 34.♔g4 ♕f5#. **33...♕f5+** 0-1 Skembris-Antic, Anogia 2013; 34.♔h4 ♕h5#.

619 26.♗g7+! ♔xg7 27.♖xh7+ ♔f8 27...♘xh7 28.♕xg6+ ♔h8 29.♕g7#. **28.♖h8+ ♔g7 29.♕xg6+ ♔xh8 30.♕g7#** T.Kentstra-Raulji, Den Haag jr 2017 (analysis).

620 1.♖h8+ ♔xh8 2.♖h4+ ♔g8 3.♖h8+ ♔xh8 4.♕h6+ ♔g8 5.♕g7# Lolli's Mate, Zaitsev-Shamkovich, Voronezh 1959 (analysis).

621 24.♖h8+! ♔xh8 25.♖h4+! (25.♕h5+? ♔g8 26.♖h4 f5−+) 1-0 Vitiugov-Kosyrev, Wroclaw Ech rapid 2014; 25...♔g8 (25...gxh4 26.♕h5+ ♔g8 27.♕h7#) 26.♖h8+! ♔xh8 27.♕h5+ (or 27.♕h3+) 27...♔g8 28.♕h7#.

622 24.♖h8+! ♔xh8 25.♖h1+ ♔g8 26.♖h8+ ♔xh8 27.♕h1+ ♔g8 28.♕h7# Damiano's Mate, Spoelman-Ernst, Amsterdam ch-NED 2014 (analysis).

623 35...♖h1+! 36.♗xh1 ♖xh1+! 37.♔xh1 ♗f3+ 37...♕h5+ 38.♔g1 ♗f3 transposes. **38.♔g1 ♕h5** and after a few checks White will be mated on h1: **39.♖xf7+ ♔h6 40.♖h7+ ♔xh7 41.♖d7+ ♔h6** etc. Dimakiling-Bersamina, Manila 2013 (analysis).

624 29.♖xc7+! ♔xc7 30.♖c1+ ♔d7 31.♕b7+ 1-0 Eggleston-Harstad, Dublin 2012; 31...♔e6 (31...♔e8 32.♖c8#) 32.♖e1+ ♔e4 33.♖xe4#.

625 46.♖xh7+! 1-0 Bosboom-Brink, Haarlem 2015; 46...♔xh7 47.♕xa7+ ♔h6 48.♕g7+ ♔h5 49.♕g4+ (or 49.♕g6+ ♔h4 50.♕g4#) 49...♔h6 50.♕g6#.

626 38...♘xf2+! 39.♔xf2 39.♔h1 ♘g3+ 40.♔h2 ♘xf1+ 41.♔h1 ♕h2+ 42.♘xh2 ♘g3#, Suffocation mate. **39...♕c5+** 0-1 Van Weersel-Speelman, England 4NCL 2012/13; 40.♔e1 ♕c3+ 41.♔f2 ♕e3#.

627 1.♕xh6+! ♔xh6 2.♖h3+ ♔g5 3.♘f3+ ♔xg4 4.♖h4+ ♔f5 5.♘g3# (5.♖f4#) 1-0 Nothnagel-Karlsson, 1972 (place unknown).

628 23...♗xg2+! 24.♔xg2 ♕h3+! 25.♔xh3 ♘g5+ 26.♔g2 ♘h4+ 0-1 Ftacnik-Cvitan, Germany Bundesliga 1997/98; 27.♔h1 g2#.

629 19.♕xh6+! 1-0 Cabarkapa-Muskardin, Bosnjaci 2013; 19...♔xh6 20.♖f3 ♘f5 21.♖h3+ ♘h4 22.♖xh4+ ♔g7 23.♖h7#.

630 32.♗xe5+! ♖xe5 33.♕b2+! 1-0 Indjic-C.Cruz, Baku ol 2016; 33...♔d6 (33...♔e4 34.♕d4#) 34.♕h2+ ♔c5 35.♕c7+ ♗c6 36.♕xc6#.

631 27.♖h8+! 1-0 Fier-Aloma Vidal, Batumi ol 2018; 27...♔xh8 28.♖h1+ ♔g8 29.♖h8+ ♔xh8 30.♕h1+ ♖h6 31.♕xh6+ ♔g8 32.♕h7#.

632 16.♖xh7+! ♔xh7 17.♕h2+ ♔g6 18.♕h5+ ♔f6 19.e5+! Clearing the e4-square for the knight. 19.♖d5 was played in the game Jukic-Deljanin, Montenegro tt 2011. **19...♔xe5** 19...dxe5 20.♘e4#. **20.♖e1+ ♔d4** 20...♔f6 21.♘d5#. **21.♖e4#**

633 25.♖xh7+! ♔g8 25...♔xh7 26.♕h5+ ♔g8 27.♖h3+−. **26.♖h8+** 26.♕h5? g6−+. **26...♔xh8 27.♕h5+ ♔g8 28.♖h3 ♗h4 29.♖xh4** 29.♕xh4+− is just as fast. **29... f6 30.♗xe6+** 1-0 Asis Gargatagli-Grafl, Catalunya tt 2012; 30...♔f7 31.♕h8#.

634 21.♕h8+! ♘g8 22.♕xg7+! 1-0 Moiseenko-Aleksandrov, St Petersburg rapid 2014; 22...♔xg7 23.♖h7+ ♔f8 24.♖f7#.

635 29.♕d4+! ♖g7 The rook blocks the escape route for its own king. 30.♖xh7+! ♔xh7 31.♕h4# F.Erwich-Kouwenhoven, Leiden 2014 (analysis).

636   41.♖xe8+! ♘xe8 42.♕h7+ ♔xh7
43.g8♕# Middelveld-Spronkmans,
Netherlands tt 2011/12.

637   31...axb2+! 32.♔b1 ♕a2+! 0-1
Iv.Saric-Vachier-Lagrave, Wijk aan Zee 2015;
33.♔xa2 (33.♔c2 b1♕+−+) 33...b1♕+ 34.♔a3
♕b3#.

638   30.♖xh6+! gxh6 31.♖xh6+ ♔g7
32.♖h7+! (32.♕h5? ♕d4+ 33.♔g2 ♕e4+ 34.♔g1
♕e1+ 35.♔g2 ♕e2+−+) 1-0 Breckenridge-Yu,
Pan American Inter-collegiate 2012;
32...♔xh7 33.♕h5+ ♔g7 34.♕h6#.

639   36...♘xh3+! 0-1 Alekseev-Mamedov,
Batumi Ech 2018; 37.gxh3 ♗h2+ 38.♔xh2
♕xf2+ 39.♔h1 ♕xf1+ 40.♔h2 ♕g2#.

640   21.♘xf7+! ♗xf7 22.♗c7+! ♔xc7
23.♕e5+ ♔xb6 23...♔d8 24.♕d6+ ♘d7
25.♕xd7#. **24.♕c5+ ♔a5 25.b4#** 1-0 Cohn-
Chiszar, 1944 (place unknown).

641   25...♖h1+! 25...♘f5 was played in the
game Schiffers-Chigorin, St Petersburg m
1897. **26.♘xh1 ♗h2+! 27.♔xh2 ♖h8+ 28.♔g3**
28.♔g1 ♖xh1#. **28...♘f5+ 29.♔f4 ♖h4#**

642   27.♖h7+! 27.♖h8+? ♔xh8 28.♕h5+
♕h6+−. **27...♔h8 28.♗g6+ ♔g8 29.♖h8+!** 1-0
Larino Nieto-Solaesa Navalpotro, Madrid
2012; 29...♔xh8 30.♕h5+ ♔g8 31.♕h7#.

643   30.♘f6+! ♕xf6 31.♖xe8+ ♗xe8
32.♕xh7+ ♔xh7 33.g8♕+ ♔h6 34.♖h3+
♕h4 35.♖xh4# A Ladder Mate, also known
as Lawnmower Mate, Hamiti-R.Reichardt,
Porto Carras tt 2018 (adjusted).

644   41...♖c1+! 42.♖f1 ♗f2+! 43.♔xf2
♖c2+ 0-1 Caruana-Carlsen, Moscow blitz
2013; 44.♔e1 (44.♔g1 ♕xg2#) 44...♕g3+
45.♔d1 ♕d3+ 46.♔e1 ♖e2/♕e2#/♕d2#.

645   1.♖xg7+! ♔f8 1...♔h8 2.♖xh7+ ♔g8
3.♖h8#. **2.♖g8+! ♔xg8 3.♖g1+!** 3.♕g2+?
♔f8 4.♕g7+ (White lacks time to cut off the
black king's escape route with 4.♗f6 due to
♕xd3+! 5.♖xd3 ♖e1+ 6.♖d1 ♖xd1#) 4...♔e7
and the black king walks away. **3...♔f8**
4.♗g7+ ♔g8 5.♗f6+ The bishop has arrived
on the f6-square with gain of tempo. See the
difference with the 3.♕g2+ ♔f8 4.♗f6 line.
5...♔f8 6.♖g8+ ♔xg8 7.♕g2+ ♔f8 8.♕g7#
Analysis 2016.

646   31.♖f8+! ♔g7 31...♔xf8 32.♕f7#.
32.♕g8+ 1-0 J.Polgar-Ivanchuk, Monaco
rapid 1995; 32...♔h6 33.♘f7#.

647   31.♕h8+! 1-0 Agrest-Fredericia,
Aarhus W 2012; 31...♔xh8 32.♘xg6+ ♔g8
33.♖h8#.

648   16...♕xb1+! 17.♔xb1 ♘d2+ 0-1
Muhsen-Petr, Pardubice 2018; 18.♔c1/18.♔a1
♘b3#.

649   35.♕f8+! 1-0 Bok-Riemersma,
Netherlands tt 2014/15; 35...♔xf8 36.♗d6+
♔e8 37.♖f8#.

650   9.♕d8+! ♔xd8 10.♗g5+ ♔c7
11.♗d8# Réti-Tartakower, Vienna 1910.
Since this game this mating pattern is known
as Réti's Mate.

651   14.♕h6+ The quickest way to
give mate! 1-0 Keres-Verbac, Berlin 1939;
14...♔xh6 15.♖h4+ ♔g7 16.♗h6#.

652   22.♗xf7+! ♔xf7 22...♔h8 23.♗g7#.
23.fxg6+ ♔e8 23...♔g8 24.gxh7+ ♔xh7
25.♕g7#. **24.♘g7#** E.Tate-Van der Auweraert,
Rotterdam 2015.

653   23...♕xb2+! 24.♔xb2 ♘d3+ 25.♔a3
25.♔b3 ♖b4+ 26.♔a3 ♗b2#. **25...♖b2+** 0-1
L.Danov-Stoynov, Plovdiv rapid 2013; 26.♔b3
♖b4#.

654   21.♕xd7+! ♔xd7 22.♗f5+ ♔e8
23.♗d7+ ♔f8 23...♔d8 24.fxe7/♗xe7#.
24.♗xe7# Anderssen-Dufresne, Berlin 1852.

655   32.♕xh7+! ♔xh7 33.hxg6+ ♔xg6
33...♔g8 34.♖h8#. **34.♗h5+ ♔h7** 34...♔f5
35.♖f4#. **35.♗f3+ ♕h6** 35...♔g6 36.♗e4#.
36.♗e4+ ♔g8 37.♖xh6 and next 38.♖h8,
Anderssen's Mate, Fischer-Myagmarsuren,
Sousse izt 1967 (analysis).

656   32.♕h1+! ♔g6 33.♕h5+! 1-0
Schoorl-Höglauer, Deizisau 2015; 33...♔xh5
34.♘f6+ ♔g6 35.♗h5#.

657   37.♖g7+ ♔h8 37...♔f8 38.♖f4#.
38.♖xh7+ 1-0 Kalisvaart-Aronsson,
Vlissingen 2018; 38...♔xh7 39.♖h4+ ♔g8
40.♖h8#.

658   19.♕xg7+! ♘xg7 20.♖xg7+ ♔h8
21.♖g8+ ♔xg8 22.♖g1+ ♕g5 23.♖xg5#
Anderssen-Suhle, Breslau m 1859. Later this
became known as Pillsbury's Mate.

659   28...♖xg3! 29.♔xg3 29.♘xg3 ♕xh4#.
29...♗g1! Taking away the escape square (h2) from the white king! White is defenceless against the mating threat 30...♕g5. 0-1 Palac-Inarkiev, Yerevan Ech 2014; 30.♘e3 ♘e2+! (clearing the f4-square for the queen; 30...♕g5+ 31.♘g4) 31.♔xe2 ♕f4+ 32.♔h3 ♘g5# Double checkmate!

660   32.♕xh4+! ♔xh4 33.♖h3+ gxh3
34.♖xh3+ ♔g4 35.♖h8 (or 35.♖h7+−) and the mating threat h2-h3 is unstoppable, Sutovsky-Zumsande, London 2013 (analysis).

661   30...g4+! 30...♕xh2 was played in the game Colijn-Roiz, Hoogeveen 2014.
31.♔xg4 ♕g2! Threatening 32...h5+ followed by 33...♕h3#. **32.h4 h5+ 33.♔xh5 ♕xg3 34.f5 ♕xh4#**

662   19.♕xf6+! ♔xf6 20.♗e5+ ♔g5
21.♗g7! Taking away the escape square h6 from the black king! 1-0 T.V.Petrosian-Pachman, Bled 1961; 21...♘f5 22.h4+ (or 22.f4+ ♔g4 23.♘e5+ ♔h5 24.♗f3#) 22...♘xh4 23.gxh4+ ♔f5 (23...♔h5 24.♗f3#) 24.♗h3/♘e3#.

663   25.♖xh7+! ♔xh7 26.♕h4+ ♔g6
27.g4! Threatening 28.♕h5#. 1-0 Adamova-Korchenkova, Tyumen W 2012; 27...♖h8 (27...f5 28.exf5/gxf5#) 28.♕xh8 g5 (28...f5 29.♕h5+ ♔f6 30.♕xf5/g5#) 29.♗d2+ ♔xg4 30.♗e2#.

664   27.♖h5+! ♔xh5 27...gxh5 28.♕g7+ ♔f5 29.♕xh7+ ♔g5 30.h4+ ♔g4 31.♕g6/f3#.
28.♕xh7+ ♔g5 29.♕h4+ ♔f5 30.f3! ♕xd5 30...g5 31.♕e4/♕h7#. **31.♕g4#** Ftacnik-Cicak, Czechia tt 2012/13 (analysis).

665   25...♕xf2+! 26.♔h1 26.♔xf2 ♗e3#.
26...♗xe2 0-1 Scherpenisse-Blankert, Leiden 2012; 27.♗xe2 ♘g3+−+.

666   32.♖xh7+! 1-0 R.Goossens-Sowray, Vlissingen 2014; 32...♔xh7 33.♖h1+ ♕h5 (33...♔g7 34.♕h8#) 34.♖xh5++−.

667   33...♖h1+! 33...dxe3? 34.♖xd7.
34.♔xh1 34.♔f2 dxe3+−+ (check!). **34...♕h3+** The pinned g2-pawn is a bad defender!
35.♔g1 ♕xg2# Tillmann-F.Erwich, Germany tt 2017/18 (analysis).

668   34.♖h8+! ♔xh8 34...♔f7 35.♕f4+ ♔e7 36.♖xe8+ ♔xe8 37.♗xg7+−. **35.♕h6+**

The pinned g7-pawn is a bad defender!
35...♔g8 36.♕xg7# Caruana-Mamedyarov, St Louis blitz 2018 (analysis).

669   20...♗g4+! 21.♔xg4 21.♔e3 ♗xd1−+.
21...♘e5+! 22.fxe5 h5# 0-1 Glücksberg-Najdorf, Warsaw 1935. Savielly Tartakower called this game 'The Polish Immortal'.

670   34.♗xb6+! ♔xb6 34...cxb6 35.c7+−.
35.♖b8+ ♔a7 36.♕c5+ ♔xb8 37.♕b4+ 1-0 Havasi-Nemeth, Budapest 2016; 37...♔c8 38.♕b7+ ♔d8 39.♕b8#.

671   14...♗xf2+! 15.♔xf2 ♕c5+ 0-1 Todorcevic-Kovacevic, Ljubljana/Portoroz 1989; 16.♔f1 ♘h5 and now White has to 'invest' material not to get mated, e.g. 17.♖e2 (17.♘e2 ♘e3+ 18.♔f1 ♘xg3#; 17.♗h1 ♗xh3+ 18.♗g2 (18.♔e2 ♕e3#) 18...♘xg3#) 17...♘xg3+ 18.♔e1 ♘xe2−+, e.g. 19.♔xe2 ♕e3+ 20.♔f1 ♗a6.

672   10.♗xf7+! ♔xf7 11.♘e6! ♘de5
11...♔xe6 12.♕d5+ ♔f6 13.♕f5# The Swallow's Tail Mate, also known as the Guéridon Mate.
12.♕h5+ 12.♘xd8++−. **12...♔g8** 12...♔xe6 13.♕f5#. **13.♘xd8 ♖xd8 14.♘d5** 1-0 Von Holzhausen-Tarrasch, Frankfurt simul 1912.

673   33.♖h8+! ♔g6 34.♖xh6+! ♔f7
34...♔xh6 35.♕h8+ ♔g6 36.♕h5#. **35.♖xf6+** and White won in S.Williams-Van Delft, Amsterdam 2014.

674   26.♖xh7! 1-0 Matikozian-V. Georgiev, Los Angeles 2013; 26...♔xh7 (26...gxf5 27.♖h8#) 27.♕h3+ ♔g8 28.♕h8# Anderssen's Mate.

675   20.♕g6! 1-0 Bronstein-Geller, Moscow ch-URS 1961; 20...fxg6 21.♖xg7+ ♔h8 22.♘xg6#.

676   16...♘g4! 17.h4 ♕xh4! 0-1 Flohr-Pitschak, Moravska Ostrava 1933. See also Exercise 61 (Chernyshov-Les) in the chapter 'Elimination of the Defence' for the same motif. 18.gxh4 (with 18.♘ef3 ♘xf3+ 19.♘xf3 ♗xf3 White only delays the mate) 18...♖h2#, Blackburne's Mate.

677   18.♕d3! 1-0 Zaragatski-R.Vedder, Netherlands tt 2018/19; 18...hxg5 (18...♖f5 19.♕xf5 ♕g8 20.♗xg8 ♔xg8 21.♕f7+ ♔h8 22.♕e8+ ♗f8 23.♕xf8#) 19.♕h3+ ♗h6 20.♕xh6#.

678 13...♘f3+! 14.gxf3 14.♔h1
♖xh2#. **14...♗xf3** 0-1 Knorre-Chigorin,
St Petersburg 1874; 15.h4 (15.hxg3 ♖h1#)
15...♖xh4 and ...♖h1# cannot be prevented.

679 20.♕g6! hxg5 21.f6! 1-0 A.Haast-
Pavlidou, Reykjavik Ech tt 2015.

680 22.♕g6! fxg6 With 22...♘e2+ 23.♔b1
♘c3+ 24.bxc3 or 22...♘b3+ 23.♔b1 Black only
delays the mate. See the main line; 22...hxg5
23.hxg5+ ♗h6 24.♕xh6/♖xh6#. **23.♘xg6+
♔g8 24.♗c4+**, mating, Shirov-Topalov,
Sarajevo 2000 (analysis).

681 22...♗xg3! 23.♕xd5 23.fxg3 f2+
24.♔h1 ♕f3#; 23.hxg3 ♗g2 24.♕xd5 ♕h1#.
23...♗xh2+! 24.♔xh2 24.♔h1 ♗g2#. **24...♗f5+**
0-1 Rjanova-Kashlinskaya, Russia tt W 2013;
25.♔g1 ♕g4+ 26.♔f1 ♕g2#.

682 20.♘h6+! 20.♘f6+ ♔h8 21.♕h5
h6 22.♘e8 is also winning, e.g. 22...♖xe8
23.♕xh6+ ♔g8 24.♕xg7#, but the text leads
to mate. **20...♔h8** 20...gxh6 21.♕f6, mating.
21.♕f6! ♕g4 21...gxf6 22.♗xf6#. **22.♘xg4
gxf6 23.♗xf6+ ♔g8 24.♘h6#** Ding Liren-
Rapport, Tbilisi 2017 (analysis).

683 16.♕h6! gxh6 16...f5 17.♘g6+ ♔g8
18.♕xg7#; 16...g6 17.♘xg6+ (17.♗xf7+ ♔g8
18.♕g7#) 17...♔g8 18.♕g7#. **17.♘xf7+ ♔g8
18.♘xh6#** Moene-Corstjens, Netherlands tt
2014/15 (adjusted).

684 28...♕f3! 0-1 Andruet-Spassky,
Germany Bundesliga 1987/88; 29.gxf3
♘exf3+ 30.♔h1 ♗h3! and White is
defenceless against 31...♗g2#!

685 29...♖xh3! 30.gxh3 ♕g3+ 31.♔h1
♕xh3+ 32.♔g1 ♖f4! The most convincing
way, since White is defenceless against
33...♕g3+ and 34...♖h4#. Duport-Bellon
Lopez, Gibraltar 2012, continued 32...♕g3+
33.♔h1 ♗xf2 34.♕e3 ♗xe3 35.♖xf8+ ♔g7 0-1.

686 29.♘f6+! ♔h8 29...♔f8 30.♕h5 and
♕f7# is unstoppable; 29...gxf6 30.♕h5 ♖f8
31.♕g6+ ♔h8 32.♕g7#; 32.♕h7#; 32.♖h7#.
30.♕f4!+− 30.♕h5 ♕e3! 31.♕g6 ♕f3+ 32.♔g1
(32.♔e1? ♗xc3+−+) 32...♕e3+ and Black
escapes with a perpetual. **30...♗xc3** 30...
gxf6 31.♕xh6+ ♔g8 32.♕g7#. **31.♕xh6+
gxh6 32.♖h7#** The Arabian Mate, Rozentalis-
Kantsler, Israel tt 2011/12.

687 20.♕g6! hxg5 21.♖h3 ♖fc8 21...♖fd8
22.♖h7 ♔f8 (22...♕e5 23.♕xf7+ ♔xh7
24.♕h5#, Greco's Mate) 23.♕xg7+ ♔e8 and
now White can choose how to mate Black
in 3 moves. One of the options is 24.♕g8+
♔d7 25.♕xf7+ ♔d6 26.♕xc7#. **22.♖e1**
Preventing Black's mating threat (22.♖h7?
♕c1+ 23.♖xc1 ♖xc1#) and controlling the
e-file, so the black king cannot escape. Now
♕g6-h7-h8# is unstoppable. 1-0 Zviagintsev-
Vasquez Schroeder, Khanty-Mansiysk Wch
rapid 2013; 22...♗e4 (22...♕c2 23.♕xf7#;
22...♕e7 23.♕h7+ ♔f8 24.♕h8#) 23.♕xe4 g6
24.♕xg6+ ♔f8 25.♖h8#.

688 13.♘g6+! hxg6 14.h5! 14.♕xg6? ♕a5+
15.c3 ♗xd5−+. **14...♕a5+** 14...fxg5 15.hxg6#,
Greco's Mate. **15.c3** Moving the king also
wins. **15...♕xd5 16.hxg6+ ♔g8 17.♖h8+!**
17.♕h3? ♕e4+, collecting the g6-pawn, after
which the black king can run away. **17...♔xh8
18.♕h3+ ♔g8 19.♕h7#** Damiano's Mate,
Benjamin-Carter, London 1982.

689 26.♗xg6 hxg6 26...♔f8 27.♕h6+
♔g8 28.♗e3 ♖c7 (28...hxg6 29.♕h8+ ♔f7
30.♕g7+ ♔e8 31.♕g8#) 29.♖xh7+ (or
29.♖g3+−) 29...♕xh7 30.♖g3+ ♔f7 31.♕xh7+
♔xf6 32.♖g6+ ♔f5 33.♕h5+ ♔e4 34.♕f3#.
**27.♕xg6+ ♔f8 28.♕h6+ ♔g8 29.♕h8+
♔f7 30.♕g7+ ♔e8 31.♕g8#** 1-0 F.Erwich-
Duijker, Wijk aan Zee rapid 2013.

690 40.♕xh5+! 40.♘f6+ ♗xf6 41.♕xh5+
♔g8 42.♕xg6+ ♗g7 43.♖h5! also wins, only
without the knight! **40...gxh5** 40...♔g8
41.♕xg6+−. **41.♘f6+ ♗xf6** 41...♔h8 42.♖xh5+
♗h6 43.♖xh6+ ♕h7 44.♖xh7#. **42.♖xh5#**
Bologan-Van Haastert, St Vincent tt 2005.

691 1...♕xg3! 2.hxg3 ♗c5! Threatening
3...♖h8#, Greco's Mate. The game Davis-
Avery, 1990 (place unknown) continued
2...♖h8+ 3.♔g1 ♗c5+ 4.♖f2 (4.♗e3 ♗xe3+
5.♖f2 is White's best defence, but Black
is winning anyway, e.g. 5...♖h6 6.♘e2
(6.♔f1 ♘d4, depriving the white king of
the e2-square, thus threatening 7...♖h1#,
and attacking the queen at the same time)
6...♖ah8 7.♔f1 ♖h1+ 8.♘g1 ♘d4 9.♕d1
♗b5−+) 4...♖h1+! 5.♔xh1 ♗xf2 6.g4 ♖h8#,
Greco's Mate. **3.♗e3 ♗xe3 4.♖f2 ♘d4−+**

692 **15.♘xf7!** **♕c8** 15...♔xf7 16.♕xe6+ ♔f8 17.♗g6, mating. **16.♕xe6 ♔f8 17.♘d6** 1-0 Acevedo-Bernal, Bogota 2011.

693 **28...♘f3+! 29.♔h1** 29.gxf3 ♖h5 and now White has to sacrifice material, otherwise Black will play 30...♕xh3 and mate on h2 or h1 next: 30.♕b5 ♕xh3 31.♕xh5 gxh5−+. **29...♖h5** 0-1 Mollekens-F.Erwich, Belgium tt 2008/09; 30.gxf3 (30.♕d3 ♖xh3+ 31.gxh3 ♕xh3#) 30...♕xh3+ 31.♔g1 ♕h2/♕h1#.

694 **21.♖d7!** 21.♕f6 ♗xe5 22.♕xe5=. **21...♖ad8 22.♖xd6! ♖xd6 23.♕f6!** 1-0 Nimzowitsch-E.Nielsen, Copenhagen simul 1930; 23...gxf6 (23...♕xe5 24.♕xe5+−) 24.♖g4+ ♔h8 25.♗xf6#, Morphy's Mate.

695 **11.♕a6!** **♕c5** 11...bxa6 12.♗xa6#, Boden's Mate. **12.♘a4! ♕e3+** 12...♕f2 13.♕xc6+ bxc6 14.♗a6# – again Boden's Mate. **13.♗xe3 bxa6 14.♗xa6+ ♔b8 15.♘e5** 15.♘d4 is also good. **15...♔c7 16.♘xf7** 1-0 Chalupnik-Solozhenkin, Gdynia 1989; 16...♔xf7 17.♗f4+ ♘e5 18.♗xe5+ ♗d6 19.♖xd6 (or 19.♗xg7+−) 19...♖xd6 20.♖d1+−.

696 White resigned after Black's last move ...♕f6-a6, but he is winning! **1.g4+!** **fxg4+ 3.♘xg4+ ♕xb5** 3...g5 4.♕e8+ ♕g6 5.♘f6#. **4.♘f6#** Dekhanov-Yusupov, Soviet Union 1981.

697 **61.♖a8+ ♔e7 62.e5** and 63.♖e8# cannot be averted, Ris-Ingvason, Reykjavik 2013 (adjusted).

698 **52.♘f7+! ♔h7 53.♔f8 ♖h6** 53...♖g6 54.♖h5+ ♖h6 55.♖xh6#. **54.♖g7#** Den Hartog-Weidmann, Hoogeveen 2014.

699 **54.♗d5!** 1-0 Carlsen-Vachier-Lagrave, Shamkir 2015; 54...a1♕ 55.♖f7+ ♔g5 56.♖f5#.

700 **32.f4!** Threatening 33.♗d3#. **32...♗xf4** 32...e5 33.♗d7#. **33.♗xf4** 33.♖xf4+? ♔e5∓. **33...e5** 33...♖d8 34.♗d3#. **34.♗d7#** Analysis 2009.

701 **68...♔f5!** 0-1 Spassky-Bisguier, Gothenburg izt 1955; 69.h8♕ ♖g6+ 70.♔h5 (70.♔h7 ♘g5+) 70...♘f4+ 71.♔h4 ♖g4#.

702 **40...♗g3+! 41.♖xg3 ♖ee1 42.♖xg6+** 0-1 Kurnosov-Topalov, Astana Wch rapid 2012; 42...fxg6 43.♖d8+ (43.f7+ ♔xf7 44.♖d7+ ♔e8−+) 43...♔h7 44.♖d7+ ♔h6 45.g4 ♖a2+, mating.

703 **32.♖h8! g5** 32...♔xh8 33.♕xh6+ ♔g8 34.♖c8+ ♕f8 35.♖xf8#. **33.♖cc8!** 1-0 Bortnyk-Ivanishen, Lutsk rapid 2015; 33...♖a1+ 34.♔h2 f6 (34...gxf4 35.♖cg8#) 35.exf6+ ♕xf6 36.♖cg8+ ♔f7 37.♖f8+ ♔e7 38.♕c7#.

704 **36...♖g7+! 37.♔xd6** 37.♔e8 ♗h5+ 38.♔d8 ♖f8# Ladder Mate/Lawnmower Mate. **37...♖fg5!** and there is nothing White can do about 38...♖d7#. 37...♖h5! comes down to the same. 0-1 B.Fernandez-Kavalek, Tel Aviv ol 1964.

705 **50.♔f6!** 50.♖h8+ was played in the game Eljanov-Nakamura, Baku 2015. **50...♔h6 51.♖h8+ ♖h7 52.♖cg8!** ♖xh8 52...♘b6 53.♖xg6#. **53.♖xh8#**

706 **1.♔f4! ♖e6** 1...fxe4 2.♗h5+ ♔h7 3.♗xf7+ ♕h3 4.♖xh3#. **2.♖h8!** 2...♗h5+? ♔h7 3.♗xf7+ ♖h6−+. **2...fxe4 3.♗h5#** Rossolimo-NN, simul 1944 (place unknown).

707 **33.g5!** 33...♕g2+ was played in the game Rodshtein-Nabaty, Acre ch-ISR 2013. The text move threatens 34...g4#, but after **34.fxg6** the g6-pawn shuts off the e8-h5 diagonal: **34...♕h5+ 35.♗h4 ♕xh4#** An inventive defence was 34.f6 ♗xf6 35.♗e6+, protecting against ...g5-g4# with gain of tempo, but after 35...♔d8 White's light-squared bishop no longer covers the h5-square, so 36...♕h5# is a big threat! And 36.♗g4 (36.♗f7 g4#) blocks the white king's escape route: 36...♕g2#.

708 **44...♘e1! 45.h5** 45.♘f3 f5+ (45...♘xf3 – the pawn ending is winning for Black as well) 46.gxf5 gxf5+ 47.♔xf5 ♘xf3−+. **45...♔e6 46.hxg6 hxg6 47.♘f3 f5+ 48.gxf5+ gxf5#** Ivalinov-J.Polgar, Targovishte 1984.

709 **48...b6+! 49.♔b4 ♖d3! 50.♖h7** 50.c5 ♖xd5−+. **50...a5#** M.Timmermans-Rijnaarts, Amsterdam 2013.

710 **108...♔g2! 109.♕xh6** 109.g5 ♖b4+ 110.♕d4 ♖bxd4#. **109...♖d5!** (109...♖b5? 110.♕c6++−) Cutting off the white king's escape route and preventing 110.♕c6+. Now White can only stop 110...♖h3# by giving his queen (110.♕d2+), so he resigned, Alonso-Flores, Buenos Aires ch-ARG 2015.

711 34.♖g8! ♖xa4 35.♖h5+ gxh5 36.g5#
Goudriaan-Beerdsen, Dieren 2014.

712 30...♘e5+! 30...♗b7 was played in
Gligoric-Commons, Lone Pine 1972. **31.♗xe5**
♖xd1 **32.♗xc7** Probably both players had
stopped calculating here, but after **32...e5!**
there is nothing White can do against ...♖d4#.

713 51...♘f5+! **52.♔xg4 ♕f2!**
Threatening 53...♕g3#. **53.♕xf5+** 53.♕e6+
♔g7 54.♕d7+ ♔h6 and there are no more
checks: 55.♕xf5 ♕g2+ 56.♔h4 gxf5 57.a7
♕g4# (57...♕h2#); 53.♕f3 prevents the mate
on g3, but blocks the f3-square for the king:
53...♕h4#; 53.♕d3 ♕g2+ 54.♕g3 ♕xg3#. **53...
gxf5+ 54.♔xf5 ♕c2+** Black misses mate in
two: 54...♕g2! 55.a7 ♕g6#. **55.♔g4 ♔f6** 0-1
Akshat-Belkhodja, Dieren 2013.

714 35...♖xh3! △ 36.♕xh3 ♕xh3+
37.♔xh3 f3 and 38...♖h8#, Lee-E.l'Ami,
Hoogeveen 2013 (analysis).

715 33.♔b3! Depriving the black king of
the a4-square (and so, threatening 34.♖xd5#)
and clearing the c3-square for the rook.
33...♖h5 33...♖d8 34.♖c3 and ♖c5# next.
34.♖c3 d4 35.♖cc6 (35.♖c7 is also good:
35...♖b8 36.♖a7 d3 37.♖a5#) 1-0 Kojima-
Takahashi, Pattaya 2011; 35...♖b8 36.♖a6 d3
37.♖a5#.

716 53.♔f5! ♖d5+ 53...e1♕ 54.♗g6+
♔h6 55.♖h8#. **54.♗xd5 e1♕** And now the
cleanest road to victory is **55.♗g8+** (the game
E.de Boer-Schoppen, Batumi Ech jr 2014,
continued 55.♗e4 ♕e3 56.f7 ♕g3 57.♖h8+
1-0) **55...♔h6** (55...♔h8 56.♗f7+ ♔h7 57.♗g6+
♔h6 58.♖h8#) **56.♖b7** and Black can only
prevent 57.♖h7# by giving his queen.

717 36...b4! 36...♖a6∓ was played in the
game Nepomniachtchi-Vocaturo, Bergamo
2014. **37.axb4 ♖ca5! 38.bxa5** 38.♕e1 ♖a2+
39.♔c1 ♖a1+ 40.♔d2 ♖xe1–+. **38...♕xa5
39.♕d1** 39.b4 ♕a1+ (39...♕a2+ 40.♔c1 ♕a1#)
40.♔b3 ♕a2#. **39...♕a3+ 40.♔b1 ♕a1#**

718 44.♖c1! Preventing 44...♖b1, after
which White can close the mating net.
44.♔h3? ♘f4+ 45.♔h2 ♖b1–+. **44...♖xa2**
44...♘xc1 45.♔h3 and 46.g4# next; 44...♖b5
45.♖xc2 (or 45.♔g3 ♖g5+ 46.♖xg5+ hxg5
47.♖xc2+–). **45.♔g3!** Threatening 46.♖h1#.

45...♘xc1 46.♔h3 and 47.g4# next. 1-0
So-E.l'Ami, Batumi ol 2018 (analysis).

719 5.♕d1! This exercise could also have
been included in the Chapter 'Defending'
(against stalemate, in this particular
example). 5.♔h2 ♕h1+ (or 5...♕g1+=) 6.♔xh1
stalemate; 5.♔f2 ♕e1+ 6.♔f3 ♕e3+ 7.♔xe3
stalemate. **5...♕xd1+ 6.♔h2** Black cannot
prevent 7.♗g3# and 7.g3# at the same time,
and as the g5-pawn is no longer pinned,
there are no stalemate tricks! And after **6...g4**
(6...♕e1 7.g3+ ♕xg3+ 8.♗xg3#; 6...♕g1+ 7.♔xg1
g4 8.c4+–) there is **7.♗f6#**. Rusinek, 1971.

720 117...♖c2! The game Howell-
Gormally, Coventry ch-GBR 2015, continued
117...♖h2 118.♔g1 ♖g2+ 119.♔f1 ♖h2 120.♔g1
½-½. **118.♘h4+** 118.♔e1 ♖c1+ 119.♔d2 ♗f4+
120.♔d3 ♖c3#. **118...gxh4 119.♖f8+ ♔e3
120.a8♕** 120.♔g1 h3 121.♖f1 (121.a8♕ h2+
122.♔h1 ♖c1+ 123.♔g2 h1♕#) 121...♖a2–+.
120...h3 Threatening 121...♖c1#. **121.♔g1**
121.♕a1 ♗xa1–+; 121.♖f3+ ♔xf3 122.♕f8+
♗f4 and ...♖c1+ next. **121...h2+ 122.♔h1
♖c1+ 123.♔g2 h1♕#**

721 104...♔c4! 104...♔e6 was played in
the game Goryachkina-L.Schut, Belgrade
Ech W 2013. **105.♔e1** 105.♖d4+ ♔c3 106.♖g4
♖h1+ 107.♔g1 (107.♗g1 f2–+) 107...♘xg1
108.♗xg1 d3 109.♔f2 ♔e4 110.♔f1 ♖xg1+
111.♔xg1 ♔e3 112.♔f1 f2 113.♔g2 ♔e2–+;
for 105.♔g1 ♖h1 106.♖d4+ see 105.♖d4+.
105...♔c3! Taking away the d2-square from
the white king. 105...♖h1+? 106.♔d2 and the
king can flee. **106.♖c1+ ♔d3 107.♖d1+ ♔c2**
and 108...♖h1+ cannot be properly averted.
White will be mated in four moves!

722 29.♕h4! Preventing the black king's
escape to the queenside. 29.♗h5++– was
played in the game Grischuk-Caruana, Dubai
Wch blitz 2014, but after the text Black
has no defence against mate, e.g. **29...♕xe5
30.♗h5+ ♔f8 31.♕d8+ ♔g7 32.♕e7+ ♔g8
33.♕f7+ ♔h8 34.♕f8#**

723 34.♕xg6+! hxg6 Otherwise Black is
a rook down. **35.♖h8+ ♔g7 36.♗g5!** Cutting
off the black king's escape route (via f6). Black
cannot stop 37.♖1h7# now; 1-0 Barnaure-
Nevednichy, Targu Mures ch-ROM 2014.

724 39...♕f2+ 40.♔g5 ♖e5+! 41.♗xe5 ♕e3+ 42.♗f4 42.♔f6 ♕xe5#; 42.♔h4 ♕xh6+–+. **42...♕e7#** Gajewski-G.Jones, Iceland tt 2013/14 (analysis).

725 57...♕b2+ 58.♔c5 58.♔d3 ♕d2#. **58...♗e3+ 59.♔d6** 59.♔c6 ♕b6#. **59...♕b8+** 0-1 Vereggen-Mijnheer, Hoogeveen 2016; 60.♔e7 ♗g5#; 60.♔c6 ♕b6#; 60.♕c7 ♗f4+–+.

726 20...♕xh2+! 21.♔xh2 ♖h4+ 22.♔g1 ♖h1# Anderssen's Mate, Van der Borgt-Westerweele, Netherlands tt 2013/14 (analysis).

727 34.♘e6+! 1-0 Bagaturov-Margaritis, Patras 2000; 34...♔h7 35.♕h6+! ♔xh6 36.♖h8#.

728 20.♕g8+! 1-0 Vajda-Li Zuhao Sydney 2014; 20...♔xg8 (20...♖xg8 21.♘f7# is a Smothered Mate) 21.♗xh7+ ♔h8 22.♘g6#.

729 24.♖e8+! 1-0 Devallee-Duchateau, Saint-Lô 2012; 24...♖xe8 (24...♗xe8 25.♕e5+ ♔f8 26.♕e7#) 25.♕h4+ g5 26.♕xg5+ ♖e7 27.♕xe7#.

730 26.♕xg6! hxg6 26...♕c6 27.♘f7#, Smothered Mate, or 27.♕xh7#. **27.♘f7+ ♔h7 28.♘eg5#** Lalic-Vorobiov, Cappelle-la-Grande 2012 (analysis).

731 36.♖g7! 1-0 Vachier-Lagrave-Nepomniachtchi, Wijk aan Zee 2011; 36...♖d1+ 37.♔h2 ♕b8+ 38.g3 ♔xg7 39.♖f7+ ♔h6 40.♖xh7#, Kill Box Mate.

732 12.♕d5! 12.♘d5+? cxd5 13.♕xd5 ♕a5+!–+. **12...♕e7** 12...cxd5 13.♘xd5#; 12...♕e8 13.♕xd6+ ♕e6 14.♕xe6#. **13.♘xh7+ ♖xh7 14.♗g5#** Cebalo-Vasiukov, Sibenik Ech tt sr 2014 (adjusted).

733 42...♖f5! Threatening 43...♖h5#. 42...♖h4+? 43.♕xh4 ♕xh4+ 44.♔g2=. **43.♕e8 ♕h4+!** Chasing the king, making space for the rook, and controlling f2. 0-1 Marshall-Lasker, United States Wch m 1907; 44.♔g2 ♖g5#.

734 34.♗f8+! 34.♘f5+ was played in the game S.Williams-A.l'Ami, Amsterdam 2014. **34...♖xf8** 34...♔xf8 35.♕f6+ ♔e8 36.♕f7+ ♔d8 37.♕d7#; 34...♔h8 35.♕xh6+. **35.♕e7+ ♔h8 36.♕xf8+ ♔h7 37.♕g8#**

735 24...♖c1+! Luring away the rook from the d-file. **25.♖xc1 ♗d3+** 0-1 Basencyan-Ofitserian, Moscow 2015; 26.♖c2 ♕d4! and White cannot prevent 27...♕b2#. The pinned rook is a bad defender!

736 35...♖d1+! 35...fxg3 was played in the game Hug-Kavalek, Haifa ol 1976. **36.♔h2 fxg3+ 37.fxg3 ♕h3+!** The same motif appeared on the board in the final game (play-off; rapid) of the World Championship match 2016 between Carlsen and Karjakin, see Exercise 744. **38.gxh3** 38.♔xh3 ♖h1#. **38...♖7d2+ 39.♖e2 ♖xe2#**

737 19.♘g6+! hxg6 19...♔g8 20.♕xe6+ ♖f7 21.♕xf7#. **20.♕h3+ ♔g8 21.♕xe6+** 1-0 Dgebuadze-Dauw, Bruges 2018; 21...♔h7 (21...♖f7 22.♕xf7+ ♔h7 23.f5 and mate will follow soon) 22.♕h3#, Greco's Mate.

738 35.♖xg5+! Clearing the f5-square. 1-0 R.Vedder-Zelbel, Vlissingen 2014; 35...fxg5 (35...♔xg5 and now White has many ways to deliver mate in 2. One of the options is 36.♕g4+ ♔xh6 37.♖h1# with a Ladder Mate/Lawnmower Mate; 35...♔f7 prevents mate, but loses the queen after 36.♖g7++–) 36.♕f5+ ♔xh6 37.♖h1+ ♔g7 38.♖xh7+ ♔g8 39.♕g6+ ♔f8 40.♖h8#.

739 19.♘e7+! ♔h8 20.♖h1 1-0 Perunovic-Arsovic, Goracici 2015; there is nothing Black can do against 21.♖xh7+ ♔xh7 22.♖h1+ ♕h2 23.♖xh2# with Anastasia's Mate, e.g. 20...g6 21.♕h6+–; 20...h6 21.♖xh6+ gxh6 22.♕xh6#.

740 20.♘fg5! fxg5 21.♘f6+! Blocking and clearing in one move! A similar motif (without the clearing aspect) showed up in Exercises 116 (Gomez-Otero) and 117 (Köhler-Antal) in the chapter 'Elimination of the Defence', but here the blocking leads to a forced mate! **21...♗xf6** The bishop is in the way of its f7-pawn. There is no ...f7-f5. **22.♗e4 ♖e8 23.♗xh7+** 1-0 Gutierrez-Sun Chin, Panama City 2013; 23...♔h8 24.♗g6+ ♔g8 25.♕h7+ ♔f8 26.♕xf7#.

741 37.♕b4+! ♔d5 38.♘f4+ ♔e5 **39.♕d4+ ♔f5 40.f3** A quiet move in the middle of a mating attack. **40...g5 41.g4#** Bacrot-Tisevich, Chess.com blitz 2018.

742 **19.♕g5! ♖xe5** 19...gxf6 20.♖h8+
♔xh8 21.♕h6+ ♔g8 22.exf6 and Lolli's Mate
with 23.♕g7 is next. **20.♖h8+** Attracting
the king or luring away the knight. 1-0
Werle-Wacker, Groningen 2015; 20...♔xh8
(20...♘xh8 21.♕xg7#) 21.♕h6+ (a pinned
piece is a bad defender) 21...♔g8 22.♕xg7#.

743 **29.♕h6!** 29.♘h6+ ♗xh6 0-1 was
the game continuation in Mason-Smerdon,
England 4NCL 2012/13; after 30.♕xh6 Black
gives mate first with 30...♖xf1+ 31.♗xf1 ♗f3+.
29...♗xf1 29...♗xh6 30.♘xh6+ ♔h8 31.♖xf8#,
Ladder Mate/Lawnmower Mate; 29...♖xf7
30.♖e8+ ♗f8 31.♖xf8+ ♖xf8 32.♖xf8#,
Kill Box Mate; 29...♕e3 is the only way to
prevent mate, but after 30.♕xe3 White is
totally winning. **30.♕h8+! ♗xh8 31.♘h6#**
♕h6 followed by ♕h8+ and ♘h6# is not a
trivial mate. Still, the same motif could have
occurred in Schneider-Tal (Luzern ol 1965),
in which the white player also missed this
golden opportunity (30.♕xh6!) and even lost.

744 **49.♖c8+! ♔h7** 49...♗f8 50.♖xf8+!
♔xf8 (50...♔h7 51.♕h6+! ♔xh6 52.♖h8# or
51...gxh6 52.♖5xf7#) 51.♖xf7+ ♔e8 52.♖f8+
♔d7 53.♕f7+ (or 53.♕f5+ ♔c6 54.♖c8+ ♔b7
55.♕d7+ ♔a6 56.♖a8#) 53...♔c6 54.♖c8+ ♔b5
55.♕c4+ ♔a5 56.♖a8#. **50.♕h6+!** 1-0 Carlsen-
Karjakin, New York Wch m playoff rapid
2016; 50...♔xh6 51.♖h8#; 50...gxh6 51.♖xf7#.

745 **21.♖a8+!** 21.♖a7 was played in
Leenhouts-Van Wely, Amsterdam ch-NED
2018. **21...♗xa8** 21...♔xa8 22.♕a4+ ♔b8
transposes. **22.♕a4 ♗b7** Otherwise
♕a4-a7+–c7# or ♕a4-a7+xa8#. **23.♕a7+ ♔c8**
24.♕xb6 Threatening 25.♕c7#. **24...♔b8** Now
White can choose how to mate Black: 24...♗d6
25.♘xd6+ ♔b8 26.♕xb7#; 24...f2+ 25.♖xf2
♘f3+ 26.gxf3+– only delays the mate; see
below. **25.♕xd8+** 25.♕c7+ ♔a8 26.♕xd8+ ♗c8
27.♕xc8#. **25...♗c8 26.♕c7+ ♔a8 27.♕a7#**

746 **23.♕d3+!** 23.♖dh1 ♕d4–+. **23...♗f5**
Blocking the king's escape square. 23...f5
24.♖dh1+–; 23...e4 24.♕xe4+ ♗f5 25.♕e7!
(25.♖dh1? ♗xe4 26.g4 ♗xh1–+) 25...♗e6
(25...♖g8 26.♕f7#) 26.♖h6+ ♔f5 26...♔xh6
27.♖h1+ ♔g6 28.♕h7#) and now White has
several ways to give mate. One option is

27.g4+ ♔xg4 28.♕xe6+ ♔f4 (28...f5 29.♕c4+
f4 30.♖g1+ ♔f3 31.♖h3+ ♔xf2 32.♕f1#)
29.♖xf6+ ♖xf6 30.♕xf6+ ♔e4 31.♖e1+ ♔d5
32.♕e5+ ♔c4 33.♖e4+ ♕d4 34.♖xd4#.
24.♖dh1! ♗xd3 25.g4! Controlling the
f5-square. White has weaved a mating net.
Black resigned, as he is unable to prevent
26.♖1h6#, Ismagambetov-Wen Yang,
Zaozhuang Ach tt 2012.

747 **20...♗xh2+!** 20...♖h8? 21.♕xe7#.
21.♔xh2 ♖h8+ 22.♕h5 ♖xh5+ 23.♔xh5 ♗f6☺
H.Stefansson-Granda Zuniga, Reykjavik
2015 (analysis).

748 **22.♘f5+!** ♔g8 22...gxf5 23.♕g5+ ♔h8
24.♕xf6+ ♔g8 25.♕xf5+–. **23.♘e3+–** and
White won in Reinderman-Ja.Broekmeulen,
Netherlands tt 2017/18.

749 **10...♘d4!** 10...b5 11.♕b3+–
(11.♕xb5? ♗b8). **11.♕xb4 ♗b5+!** The game
Majhi-Warnk, Oberhof 2013, continued
11...♘c2 12.♕c3 ♘xa1 13.♕xg7 ♖f8 14.♗h6
♕e7 15.♕xf8+ ♕xf8 16.♗xf8 ♔xf8 17.♘a3
and White won. **12.♔g1** 12.♔e1? ♘c2+–+.
12...♘e2+ 13.♔f1 ♘d4+=

750 **32...♖e1+! 33.♔xe1 ♖d1+!** Decoying
the king to d1. 0-1 Lentjes-Akshat, Dieren
2013; 34.♔e3 ♖e8+ 35.♔f2 ♕xh5–+; 34.♔c3
♖c8+ 35.♔b4 ♕xh5–+; 34.♔xd1 ♕xh5+,
taking the rook with check, so White has no
time to take the f8♖.

751 **32...♗a2!** 32...♖a5? 33.♗d8! ♖bxb5
34.♗xa5 ♖xa5 35.♖xd4± was played in the
game Van Wely-Iturrizaga, Istanbul ol 2012.
33.♗xa4 ♖xb1=

752 **18.♗xf7+! ♔f8** 18...♔e7 19.♕xh4+
with check, so Black has no time for 19...♖d1#.
19.♗e3! 19.♕xh4? ♖d1#. **19...♕xg4** 19...♗xe3
20.♕xh4 – as the back rank is now protected
by the a1♖, White can safely take the
queen. **20.♗xc5+ ♖d6 21.♗xd6#** Smyslov-
Greenfeld, Beer-Sheva 1990 (analysis).

753 Yes! **20.♖xc6** 20.♖xe8+∓ was played
in Roering-T.Willemze, Netherlands tt
2015/16. **20...♖c2 21.♘b5!** 21.♖xc2? ♖e1#;
21.♖b1 ♘d5 or 21...♘e4–+ attacking the
pinned knight; or 21.♖d1 ♘d5 (or 21...♘e4–+)
22.♖xd5? ♖e1#. **21...♖xc6** ≥ 21...♖xc1+
22.♖xc1=. **22.♘xa7+ ♔d7 23.♘xc6⊗**

754 **37.♕c4!** 37.♖xd5 ♘xe2+ 38.♔f2 ♖xd5 39.♔xe2 is better for White, but the text is winning! **37...♘xh3+ 38.♔h2 ♕xc4 39.♖xd8+ ♔f7 40.bxc4+−** Mkrtchian-Kovalevskaya, Germany Bundesliga W 2014/15 (analysis).

755 **18.♗d2! ♕xa1** 18...♕xd2+ 19.♗xd2 and White remains a piece up. **19.♖e1**, trapping the queen. Flaum-Morris-Suzuki, Philadelphia 2017 (analysis).

756 **21.♘f5!** The game Lai-Sekandar, Rotterdam ch-NED U20 2014, continued 21.♕f2 ♕xd4 22.♘d1 ♖xd1 0-1; 21.♕d2 ♘xf1−+. **21...♖xc2 22.♘xh4=**

757 **39.♖d8+!** 39.♖xc5? ♖xc5 40.♖d8+ (40.♖xa3 ♘xg6−+ was played in the game Van Wely-Narodtsky, London rapid 2014) 40...♔e7! (40...♔g7 41.♗b1=) 41.♖e8+ ♔d7 and White is unable to save his bishop: 42.♖g8 (42.♗h5 ♖c1#) 42...♘xg6 43.♖xg6 ♖c1#. **39...♔g7** 39...♔e7?! 40.♖e8+ and compared to the 39.♖xc5 line, after 40...♔d7 (≥ 40...♔d6 41.♖d1+ ♔d5 42.♖d8+±) 41.♖d1+! (the big difference with rooks on the board) 41...♔c6 42.♗e4+ it is White who is winning. **40.♖xc5 ♖xc5 41.♗b1=**

758 **34.♖d2!** 34.b7? ♖d1+ 35.♔f1 ♖xf1#; 34.♖c2 ♖xb6∓. **34...♖xd2** 34...♖xb6? 35.♖d8+ ♗e8 36.♖xe8#. **35.b7 ♖xg2+ 36.♔xg2 ♗c6+ 37.♔f2 ♗xb7 38.♗xb7 a5 39.♔e3+−** Landa-Ris, Reykjavik 2017 (adjusted).

759 **33.♕c2! ♘xe1** 33...g4 34.♖bd1 ♘xe1 35.♕xf5 ♖xf5 36.♖xd6 ♖ff8 37.♘xc8 ♖xc8 38.♖xe1 and White has the better chances in this ending. **34.♕xf5 ♖xf5 35.♘xd6±** Georgiadis-Mamedyarov, Biel 2018 (analysis).

760 **32.♘ge4!** 32.♕c6 ♖xd2 33.♕e6+ ♔g7 34.♕e7+ ♔h6 35.♕xf8+ ♔g5 and Black has the better chances in the queen endgame; 32.♕b2? ♖xd2 33.♕xd2 ♖f1#. **32...♔g4** 32...♖xf6? 33.♘xf6+ ♔f7 34.♘xd7+−; 32...♖xd2? 33.♕e6+ ♔g7 34.♘xd2+−. **33.♕a1 ♕e2 34.h3** and White won, Gledura-Mista, Hastings 2014/15.

761 **31.♖h1!** 31.♘d6+ ♔d7 32.♖c1 is better for White, but the text is winning! **31...♗xb5** 31...♕xb5 32.♕d6!. The point! Black's king cannot escape via d7 now, so he will be mated: 32...f6 (or he has to

give big material with 32...♕f1+ 33.♖xf1) 33.♕xe6+ ♔d8 (33...♔f8 34.♖xf6+ ♔e8 and here White can choose how to give mate in three moves: 35.♖e1+ (35.♖h8+ ♔d7 36.♖h7+ ♔e8 37.♕e7/♕h8#) 35...♕e2 36.♖xe2+ ♔d7 37.♕e7#) 34.♕d6+ ♔e8 35.♖e1+ ♔f7 36.♖e7+ ♔g8 37.♕e6+ ♔h8 38.♕xf6+ ♔g8 39.♕g7#. **32.♖xc8+** and White won, Nunn-Kristiansen, Katerini Wch sr 50 2014. Or 32.♖h8+ ♔d7 33.♕xc8+ ♔d6 34.♕b8++−.

762 **17.♖xf7!** △ 17...♖xe5 18.♖d1!+− with the deadly threat 19.f4#. Malakhatko-Bacrot, Geneva 2012 (analysis).

763 **44...♖c5! 45.♗e3** 45.♖xc5 ♗xc5−+. **45...♖xc2 46.♕xc2** 46.♗xa7 ♖xe2−+. **46...♕xe3−+** R.Ratsma-De Jong-Muhren, Amsterdam ch-NED W 2015 (analysis).

764 **30...♖xb4+! 31.♔a3 ♖xc2!** 0-1 Anand-Kasparov, New York Wch m 1995; 32.♖xc2 ♖b3+ 33.♔a2 ♖e3+ 34.♔b2 ♖xe1−+.

765 **27...♕e6!** 27...♔h8 28.♕xa4 and now after 28...♘c3 White has 29.♕a6 (or 29.♕c4 △ 29...♕e1+ 30.♕f1). **28.♕xa4 ♘c3** Thanks to Black's 27th move, the a6- and c4-squares are covered by the queen and so White's defence in the 27...♔h8 line is not possible here. **29.♕xe8+** 29.bxc3 ♕e1+ 30.♖xe1 ♖xe1#. **29...♕xe8 30.bxc3 dxc3 31.g3 ♕e7** 0-1 Wemmers-Zanan, Gibraltar 2019.

766 **43.♖e8+! ♖xe8 44.♕xd2 ♕xf3+ 45.♖g2=** But not, as in the actual game, 45.♕g2 ♖e2! (an Oblique Cross!) and White resigned in view of 46.♕xf3 ♖xh2#, Alapin-Alekhine, St Petersburg 1914.

767 **32...♖f4!** Clearing the b1-h7 diagonal. 32...♖f8? 33.fxe4± was played in Tokabayev-Filin, St Petersburg 2011. **33.♕xa8+ ♖f8 34.♕c6 ♕g6+ 35.♔a2 ♕xh5−+.**

768 **33...♕e6!** The game S.Kuipers-Wilschut, Leiden 2018, continued 33...♖f7 34.♕xa5 1-0; 33...♔f8 34.♕xa5 ♕g4+ 35.♔h1 ♖d2 36.♕c5+ ♔f7 37.♕f2+−; 33...♖e6 34.♕xa5 ♕g4+ 35.♔h1 ♖d2 36.♕a8+ ♔f7 37.♕xb7++−. **34.♕xa5** 34.♕xe6+ ♖xe6=. **34...♕g4+ 35.♔h1** 35.♔f2 ♖d2+ 36.♔e3 ♕d7! and White can only prevent 37...♕d3# by giving his queen. **35...♖d2 36.♖f2** 36.♔g1 ♕f3+ 37.♖g2 ♕xg2#. **36...♖xf2 37.♕d5+ ♕e6−+**

769 28...♖a5! 28...♕xg6? 29.♗f4+ ♖d6 30.♕xd4 (or 30.♖e7+−) 30...♔c7 31.♖e7+ ♔xc6 32.♕c4#. **29.♗f4+** 29.♕xd4? hxg6−+. **29...♔a8 30.♗xh5 ♖xa4 31.♗xf7=** Lopez-Bejarano U, Bogota 2011 (analysis).

770 White resigned after 22.♗xg7 f3+, but **22.♖xf4!** would have saved him, as **22...♗xb2?** fails to **23.♖g4+** and now it is White who wins material by executing a discovered attack, Vrolijk-M.de Jong, Dieren 2016.

771 **17.♘c3!** 17.♕xb5 ♗a6 18.♕a4 ♘b6 19.♗xf7+ (19.♕a2 ♗xe2−+) 19...♔xf7∓/−+ was played in the game Houben-Ja.Broekmeulen, Netherlands tt 2012/13. **17...c4 18.♘xb5! cxd3 19.♘xc7=**

772 No! **47.♗xd7? ♗xd7 48.♘b6 ♖d8!** and Black keeps a material advantage. 48...♖a5 was played in the game Ris-Gonda, Germany Bundesliga 2013/14. **49.♖xd6** 49.♘xd7+ ♖xd7. **49...♗h3+!**

773 No! **25.♖f7** 25.♘xd6 ♗xf1−+ was played in the game Majhi-Vuilleumier, Lisbon 2014. **25...♗xc4 26.♖xg7 ♗c5!** In case Black makes a bolthole for the king to prevent ♖g any with a quick mate, White regains the piece with interest: 26...h5 27.♖xc7+! ♔g8 28.♖xc4+−. As the bishop is under attack (and pinned, so the bishop can't move away to keep the threat alive!) White does not have a sound discovered check, e.g. **27.♖g4+** (27.♗xc5 ♔xg7−+) **27...♗xd4+−+.**

774 **8.♘xe5! ♗xf2+!** 8...♗xd1? 9.♘xc6+ ♔f8 10.♘xd8 ♖xd8 11.♖xd1 and Black is a piece and a pawn down. **9.♔xf2** 9.♔f1 ♗xd1 10.♘xc6+ ♗xe1 11.♘xd8 ♖xd8 12.♔xe1 ♗xc2 and Black is an exchange and a pawn up. **9...♕h4+ 10.g3** 10.♔f1 ♗xd1 11.♘f3+ (11.♘xc6+ ♔f8!−+ (11...♔d7? 12.♘e5+!)) 11...♕xe1+ and again Black is an exchange up. **10...♕xh2+ 11.♔f1 ♗h3#** In the game J.Zwirs-L.Beukema, Borne jr 2012, White went for the better 8.h3 and after 8...♗h5, this time he could have taken the e5-pawn, leaving Black with a terrible position. The point is that after 9.♘xe5 (9.g4 ♗g6 10.♘xe5 0-0, with some compensation for the pawn, was played in the game) 9...♗xf2+ 10.♔xf2

♕h4+ White can play 11.g3 as Black has no 11...♕xh2+ ! After 11...♕xh3 12.♘f3+ Black does not have enough compensation for his lost bishop.

775 **22.♕g3!** 22.♕e3? ♗xe2∓ was played in the game Bruggink-Salomons, Waalwijk ch-NED jr 2013. **22...♗xe2 23.♕xg6+ ♔h8 24.♕h6+ ♔g8 25.♕g6+=**

776 **24...♕xd3!** 24...♖xd1+? 25.♖xd1 ♕xa4 26.♖xd8+. **25.♗xd3** 25.♖xd3 ♖xd1+−+. **25...♖xd1+ 26.♖xd1 ♗g4!** 0-1 Zubarev-Vachier-Lagrave, Le Port Marly rapid 2012; 27.♖d2 ♗f5−+.

777 **23...♖e8! 24.♖xe4 ♗h2+ 25.♔xh2 ♖xe4 26.a5 ♖e2 27.f3 ♖xb2 28.♗xf7+ ♔xf7 29.♔g3** 0-1 Ernst-L.van Foreest, Groningen 2018.

778 **20...♘f6! △ 21.♕xc6? ♖b6!**, trapping the queen, Kravtsiv-Kazakovskiy, Stockholm 2016/17 (analysis).

779 **29...♔g8!** 29...♕f4 30.h3 and White won the queen and the game in T.L.Petrosian-Naroditsky, Golden Sands 2012; 29...♕h6 30.♕xd4+ ♔g8? 31.♕h8#; 29...♕g7 30.♗xd4+−. **30.♖xf6** 30.♗xd4 ♕d6−+; 30.♗a3 ♗g4! 31.♖xf6 ♖xf6 32.♕g1 (32.♗xf6 ♖e1+ 33.♕f1 ♖xf1#) 32...♗e2−+ and ...♖f1 is coming. **30...♖xf6 31.♕g1** 31.♕xf6 ♖e1+ 32.♕f1 ♖xf1#. **31...♖ef8** with 32...♖f1 next, winning back the queen.

780 **38...♖g1+! 39.♖xg1** 39.♔c2 ♕xh1−+. **39...♕h7+ 40.♖g6 ♕xg6+ 41.♕e4 ♕xe4#** Bok-Ju Wenjun, Wijk aan Zee 2016 (analysis).

781 **30...♖h8! △ 31.♕xh4+** 31.♖d2 ♔g8−+ was played in the game Timman-Reinderman, Wijk aan Zee 2012. **31...♔g8−+**

782 **21.0-0!** 21...♗e5? 22.♖xe5 (22.♕h5, attacking the pinned bishop and pinning the f7-pawn in order to prevent a defence with ...f7-f6, is also good for White) 22...♕xe5 23.♖e1+−. **22.♗b7 ♖ab8 23.♖xe6 fxe6** and now it's Black who is pinning the queen! Bakhmatov-Malevinsky, 1976 (place unknown).

783 White resigned here, but he could have won the game with **1.♗xf7+! ♔xf7 2.♖f1+ ♔g8 3.♖f8+** (luring away the rook) **3...♖xf8 4.♕g7#** NN-Sonnenschein, Berlin 1937.

784   39...♕f7! (Black's queen is pinned, but so is White's rook!) 39...♖xd7? 40.♖xd7 ♕xd7 41.♕xf8#; 39...♕e6? 40.♖xh7/g7#. **40.♖1d5** 40.♖xf7 ♖xd1+ 41.♔g2 ♖xf7–+. **40...♕g8! 41.♖xc7 ♖f7!** With a knight up, he is winning! Martorelli-Antunes, Reggio Emilia 1985.

785   46.♕f2! 46.♕e3? g5 0-1 was played in the game Jobava-Jakovenko, Russia tt 2015. **46...g5** 46...♖f8 47.g5=. **47.hxg5 hxg5 48.♕b2+** (or 48.♕h2+) and the black king cannot escape the checks: **48...♔h7 49.♕h2+ ♔g8** 49...♔g7 50.♕b2+ ♔g6 51.♕f6+ ♔h7 52.♕xg5; 49...♔g6? 50.♕h5+ ♔g7 51.♕xg5++–. **50.♕a2+ ♔g7 51.♕b2+=.**

786   28...♗d5! 28...♖xc6? 29.♖xd8+ ♔h7 30.♗xe4++–. **29.♖xd8+ ♖xd8 30.♘xd8 ♔f8** and Black will win back the trapped knight, with an equal ending, Kaplan-Ribeiro, Skopje ol 1972.

787   35.♗b4! Moving away the bishop while closing off the b-file, so that Black has no intermediate check on b1. 35.♖e3 was played in the game S.Zhigalko-Carlsen, St Petersburg Wch blitz 2018; 35.♖xf6 is a good alternative, but after 35...♖bxe7 White has to work hard to bring home the full point; 35.♗c5? ♖b1+! (that is why White has to play 35.♗b4) 36.♔h2 ♖xe6. **35...♖xe6** 35...♗e6 36.♕xe8++–; 35...♖xb4 36.♖xe8+ ♗xe8 37.♕xb4+–. **36.♕a8+ ♔h7 37.♕xb7**

788   Yes! **22...♖xc3** (22...♘c5 was played in Kleijn-H.Vedder, Netherlands tt 2014/15) wins a pawn as after **23.♖e3** Black has a discovered attack with **23...♘xf4! 24.♖xc3 ♘e2+–+.**

789   No! **31...♕xg5?** 31...♖f8! wins, e.g. 32.hxg6 ♕a1+! 33.♔g2 ♖xf2+ 34.♔h3 (34.♕xf2 ♖xf2+ 35.♔xf2 ♕f6+ or 35...♕d4+ with a double attack) 34...♕h1+ 35.♔g4 ♖8f4+ 36.♕xf4 ♕d1+ 37.♔g3 ♕g1+ 38.♔h3 ♕f1+ 39.♔g3 ♕g2+ 40.♔h4 ♖xf4+ 41.♔h5 ♕h3#. **32.♕xg5 gxh5 33.♖a8** White counters the pin with a Maltese Cross! 1-0 Acs-Kortchnoi, Ohrid Ech 2001.

790   30...♖xe4! **31.♖xf7+** 31.fxe4 gxf5∓; 31.♕xe4 ♗xf5∓; 31.♘xe4 ♕xf5=; 31.fxg4 ♖xe1 32.♖xf7+ ♖xf7 33.♖xe1=. **31...♗xf7 32.fxe4 ♖f6=** J.Polgar-Yilmaz, Yerevan Ech 2014 (analysis).

791   29...♖c1! 29...♕xg1+ 30.♔xg1 ♗xf4 31.♕d3 ♗g8+ (31...♗g7? 32.♘h5++–) 32.♘xg8 (32.♔f2 ♖g6 33.♕f5 ♖c4=) 32...♔xg8 33.♕f5 ♖c1+=. **30.♖xc1 ♗xf4** Now both the white rook and knight are en prise. **31.♘h5 ♕g5 32.♕b4 ♗d6 33.♕c3+ ♗e5 34.f4** 34.♕c5 ♖g8–+. **34...♗xc3 35.fxg5 b4** 0-1 Bologan-Jakovenko, Poikovsky 2014.

792   24...b2! **25.♔g2 ♖g1! 26.♗f8** 26.♔xg1 ♖a1–+; 26.♖xg1 ♖a1–+. **26...g5** and Black won in an instructive way: **27.♗g7 ♔e7 28.♗e5 f6 29.♗c7 h5 30.♗b6 h4 31.gxh4 gxh4 32.e4 h3+ 33.♔xh3 ♗xf2 34.exd5 exd5** 0-1 Vuilleumier-Vocaturo, Bastia 2016.

793   No! 30.♗e3 defends against 30...♕xf2+ followed by 31...♕xg2#, and traps the queen. However, Black has **30...dxe3! 31.♖xe1 exf2+ 32.♔h1 fxe1♕**–+. Therefore, White resigned in the starting position in Nasuta-Wagner, Maribor Wch jr 2012.

794   Yes! **26.♕xe5! ♗d6??** 26...♗xb4 27.♕xe8 ♕xe8 28.axb4±. **27.♕xf6** 1-0 Zherebukh-Firman, Germany Bundesliga 2011/12; 27...gxf6? 28.♗xf6+ ♔g8 29.♖g4++–.

795   Yes, he can! **13.♖xe7! ♖e8 14.♗xh7+!** 1-0 Landa-Baljé, Vlissingen 2016; 14...♔xh7 15.♕xf7+–; 14...♖xh7 15.♕xe8++–.

796   24.♕xh6! ♖xe5 25.d6! If 25.fxe5 ♗g5 traps the queen, although White seems to have enough compensation after 26.♕xh5 gxh5 27.d6. **25...♖e2** 25...♗f8 26.♗xf7+! ♔xf7 27.♕h7++–. **26.dxe7 ♕xe7 27.f5**+– Iv.Saric-Carlsen, Tromsø ol 2014.

797   13...♘e5! Black does not have to fear **14.♗b4** as he has the beautiful defence **14...♕f3! 15.gxf3?** 15.0-0 ♕xe4 and Black is a pawn up. **15...♘xf3+** 0-1 Amarasena-Kavinda, Teheran Ach jr 2008; 16.♔f1 ♗h3#.

798   28...♗g4! **29.gxf3** 29.♖xa3 fxg2+ 30.♔c2 g1♕–+ was played in the game Popilski-Gabuzyan, Washington 2018; 29.♔e1 ♖xe4 30.♖xe4 f2+ (or 30...♗g3+–+) 31.♔xf2 ♕g3+ 32.♔g1 ♕h2+ 33.♔f2 ♕h4+ 34.♔g1 ♗h2+ 35.♔h1 ♗g3+ 36.♔g1 ♕h2#; 29.♔c2 ♕xa2+–+. **29...♗xf3+ 30.♗e2 ♕xe3 31.♕xe3 ♗xe4** with double-edged play.

799   39...♖h4! 40.♔xh4 g5+ 41.♔xg5 ♔g7 0-1 Lasker-Loman, USA simul 1903.

800 57.♖e5+!+– 1-0 Nunn-Hebden, Katerini Wch sr 50 2014; 57...♖xe5 58.f4+ ♔e4 (58...♔xf4 59.♔f2+–) 59.♔f2 ♔d3 60.♔e1+–.

801 Yes! 36.fxe5! ♖c2 37.♖f2! (37.♖xc2?? dxc2–+) 1-0 Giri-Cornette, France tt 2015; 37...d2 38.♘e3+–.

802 35.♗f6+! 35.♔f2? ♖xd1 36.♔e2 ♖e1+–+. 35...♔xf6? ≥ 35...♔f8 36.♔f2 (or 36.♔f1) 36...♖xd1 37.♔e2 ♖g1 38.♔xd2 ♖xg4 39.♘d5±. 36.♘d5+ ♔e6 37.♘e3+– Bok-Palliser, Eilat tt 2012 (analysis).

803 39.axb5! a4 40.♘c5! a3 40...bxc5 41.b6 a3 42.b7 a2 43.b8♕++– (check!). 41.♘b3 and White won in Nakamura-Kramnik, Antalya Wch tt 2013.

804 No! 51...♖e4? 51...♔e6=. 52.♖xf7+ ♔e8 53.♔xe4 1-0 Karjakin-Kramnik, Moscow blitz 2013; 53...e2 54.♖e7+ ♔f8 55.♔d4+–. 53.♖e7+ ♖xe7 54.fxe7 ♔xe7 55.♔xe3 also wins, e.g. 55...♔d7 56.♔e4 ♔e6 57.a4 ♔d7 58.♔e5 ♔e7 59.a5 and Black is in zugzwang.

805 Yes! 49...♖xf5+! 50.♖xf5 ♖xf5+ 51.♔e3 ♖xf2 52.e7 ♖f6! 0-1 Mamedyarov-Kryvoruchko, Berlin Wch rapid 2015; 53.e8♕ ♖e6+–+.

806 35...♖e1+! 36.♕xe1 ♕d5 37.♔f1 37.♖e2 ♕h1+ 38.♔f2 ♕f3+ 39.♔g1 ♕h1+=. 37...♗b5+ 38.♔g1 38.♖e2 ♕h1+ 39.♔f2 ♕xh2+ 40.♔e3 (40.♔f3 ♕h5+ 41.g4 ♗e2+ 42.♕xe2 ♕xf7+=) 40...♕h6+ 41.♔f3 ♗e2+ 42.♕xe2 ♕f6+=. 38...♗c6 39.♔f1 ♗b5+ 40.♔g1 ½-½ M.de Jong-Wagner, Hoogeveen 2013.

807 52...♘d3! The game Anand-Nakamura, St Louis rapid 2016, continued 52...♘c4 53.b7 ♘xe5 54.fxe5+ ♔f5 55.b8♕ and White won. 53.♔xd3 53.♘xd3 ♖b5–+; 53.b7 ♘b4+ 54.♔d2 ♘a6–+. 53...♖xh3+ 54.♔c2 ♖g3 or 54...♖h2+ 55.♔c3 ♖h3+ 56.♔c4 ♖h1= and ...♖b1 next. 55.♘d7+ ♔f5 56.b7 ♖g8 57.b8♕ ♖xb8 58.♘xb8 ♔xf4=.

808 42...♗xc6! 42...♔g7 was played in the game Mandizha-Krush, USA tt ICC 2013, and Black soon lost after 43.hxg5. 43.dxc6 ♖a2! 44.c7 ♖a3+ 45.♔d2 45.♔d4 ♖a4+ 46.♔d5 (46.♔e5 ♖c4=) 46...♖a8=. 45...♖a2+ 46.♔c1 ♖a5!= with 47...♖c5+ next. The general idea is: as soon as the king steps onto the c-file, there is ...♖a5; otherwise, the checks continue unless White wants to let Black's rook occupy the c-file; or, in case White crosses the middle of the board by ♔d5, the a8-h1 diagonal is blocked and Black can defend by ...♖a8.

An important point is that Black can always liquidate into a theoretically drawn ending, e.g. 47.c8♕ ♖c5+ 48.♕xc5 bxc5 49.♗f3 gxh4 50.gxh4 ♔g7 and Black can shuffle with his king between h8, g8 en g7. He can even give his h-pawn, as White has the 'wrong-coloured bishop'.

809 46.♕xf3! (46.d8♕? ♖c1+ 47.♕xc1 dxc1♕+ 48.♕d1 ♖xd1#) and Black resigned, because after 46...♖c1+ 47.♕d1! ♖xd1+ 48.♔e2 ♖b1 49.d8♕ d1♕+ 50.♕xd1 ♖xd1 51.♔xd1 White wins the pawn ending, 1-0 Ermenkov-Sax, Warsaw jr 1969.

810 41...♗f8! 41...♔h7 was played in the game Hekhuis-Westerweele, Oost-Souburg 2014, but this allowed White to escape with a draw thanks to a 'rampant queen': 42.♕g8+ ♔g6 43.♕xg7+! ♔f5 44.♕e5+ ♔g4 (44...♔g6 45.♕g7+ ♔f5 46.♕e5+ and White combines the two drawing themes of perpetual check and stalemate in one line) 45.♕xh5+! ♔xh5 (45...♔g3 46.♕h3+ ♔xh3=). 42.♕xf8+ ♔h7 and as White's rook pawn can move now, White has no stalemate tricks.

811 1.♗b5+! 1.♔a2 ♖b2+! 2.♔xb2 stalemate!; 1.♔a1 ♖e8 2.♗d3 ♔xa3. 1...♖xb5+ 1...♔xb5 2.♘xb8+–. 2.♔a2 ♖d5 2...♖b7 3.♘c5+–; 2...♖b3 3.♘c5+. 3.♘b6++– Afek, 2015.

812 20...♕f2! 21.♖f1 ♘c5! 21...♕g2 22.♖hg1 ♕h2 23.♖h1=. 22.♕c3 22.dxc5 ♕xc5–+. 22...♘e4 23.♖xf2 ♘xc3 and Black is winning, Klein-Navara, Wijk aan Zee 2015 (analysis).

813 34.♔d4! 34.♔xe4? was played in the game Caruana-Nisipeanu, Bucharest 2012, and after 34...♕e1+ 35.♔f4 (35.♔d4 ♕xf2+ 36.♔e4 ♕e1+ 37.♔d3 ♕f1+ 38.♔d4 ♕f2+=) 35...♕c1 36.♔e4 ♕e1+ the players agreed a draw. 34...♕d1+ 35.♔c5 ♕xa4 36.♔b6! wins for White.

814 **84.♔h4!** 84.♔h2 ♕f2+. **84...♕f2+** 84...♕f4+ 85.♔g4 ♕h2+ 86.♔g5 ♕h6+ 87.♔f5+−. **85.♔h5** 85.♔g5 ♕f4+ 86.♔h5 ♕h2+ transposes. **85...♕h2+ 86.♔h3!** 86.♔g4 ♕f4+ doesn't bring White any further. **86...♕xh3+ 87.♔g5 ♕g3+ 88.♔f6 ♕f3+ 89.♔e7 ♕xb3 90.♕h5+ ♔g7 91.♕g4+** 1-0 Möhring-Kaikamdzozov, Zamardi 1978; 91...♔h7 92.♔f6+−.

815 **1.♕g8!** 1.♕e8 ♕g7!=; 1.♕f8 ♕a3!=. **1...♕a2 2.♕e8 ♕a4 3.♕e5+ ♔a8 4.♕h8 ♕f4 5.♔d7+** Or 5.♔e7+. **5...♕b8 6.♕a1+ ♕a7 7.♕xa7#** Joseph, 1922.

816 **28...♕e1!** (but not 28...♕d1 29.♖h4 ♕h5 30.♖xh5 gxh5 31.♘e3! ♗e6 32.♗xd5 ♗xd5 (32...♗a5 33.♗e4+−; 32...♗xd5 33.♘xd5 ♗xd5 and here the white king will walk to c5, after which he can put his d-pawn in motion. Black can only move his bishop as his other pieces are paralysed) 33.♘f5 with 34.♘e7+ next, and it is White who is winning. Compare this with Exercise 824 (De Wilde-Delabaca) to see the differences) 0-1 Anand-Carlsen, Chennai Wch m 2013; 29.♖h4 ♕xh4−+.

817 **40.♖c4!** 40.♕a4? ♖b1+ 41.♔xb1 ♕b2# was played in the game Hulak-Adorjan, Jakarta 1983; 40.♕xb2 ♖xb2+ 41.♔d2 ♕c3+ 42.♔c1 ♕b2+=. **40...♖xa2 41.♖xc3 ♗xc3 42.♗c4** and White is just a piece up.

818 **33...♗g5! 34.♖e1** 34.♕h5 ♔e7 35.♕h7+ ♔d8 36.♘xg5 ♕xe3 37.♘xe6+ ♖xe6 38.♖g8+ ♖e8 39.♖xe8+ ♔xe8 40.♕g6+ ♔d7 41.♕d6+ ♔c8 42.♕e6+ and White gives perpetual check; 34.♕xg5 ♕xf3+−+; 34.fxg5 ♕xe3−+. **34...♕c2 35.♕xg5 ♖e7** with double-edged play, Topalov-Kramnik, Elista Wch m 2006 (analysis).

819 **41...♕d5+!** 41...g6? 42.♕xf7#. **42.♔h2 ♖d7** and the position is equal: **43.♕h8+ ♔e7 44.♖xd7+ ♔xd7 45.♕xg7 ♕d2** Lobron-He. Gretarsson, Leeuwarden 1995.

820 **28...♕g5+!** 28...♕e7 29.♕xg6+ ♔d7 (29...♔d8 30.♕g8+ ♔d7 31.♖f7=) 30.♖f7= was played in the game A.Blees-Beeke, Amsterdam 2016. **29.♔b1 ♖f4−+.**

821 **13...♕a5+!** Defending by means of targeting! Due to the check, White has no time to mate Black. With gain of tempo, the black queen can go to f5 on the next move, covering the h7-square and preventing checkmate. 0-1 Charbonneau-Hussein, Dresden ol 2008; 14.♔d1 ♕f5!−+. Not 13...♗xg5? 14.hxg5, and Black does not have a good defence against 15.♕h7/8#, e.g. 14...f6 (14...♕a5+ 15.b4! (15.♔d1 f6 is still winning for White, but it is not necessary to allow this) 15...♕xb4+ 16.♗d2+−) 15.g6!+−; 13...♖e8 14.♕h7+ ♔f8 15.♗d6+ ♔e7 (blocking its own king's escape route) 16.♕h8#.

822 **38...♖xg1+!** 38...♖f6 39.♖xg7+! ♖xg7 40.♕xf6+−; 38...♖e5 39.♕g6+ ♔h8 40.d7 ♕a5 41.f4+−. **39.♔xg1 ♖e1+ 40.♔h2 ♗xf7−+** Van Weersel-Khotenashvili, Warsaw Ech tt W 2013 (adjusted).

823 **32...♖d1+! 33.♔xd1 ♕xc2+ 34.♕xc2 ♗xc2+ 35.♔xc2 ♔xh8** and Black won, Brochet-Le Quang Liem, France tt 2012.

824 **22...♕xe3+!** 22...♕xa1+ 23.♔g2 and Black will get mated, e.g. 23...♖d8 24.♕xh7+ ♔f8 25.♕h8#. **23.♔h1 ♕f3+!** Targeting! **24.♔g1 ♕h5** With a rook, knight and bishop, Black has more than enough material for the queen. Compared to a similar defence (...♕d1-h5) in the analysis of Exercise 816 (Anand-Carlsen), Black has much more breathing space here, De Wilde-Delabaca, Amsterdam 2013.

825 **27...♗g5!** 27...♕d8 28.♗f5+ ♔h4 (28...♔g8 29.♕h7#) 29.♖b4! (or 29.♖d4! g5 30.♗xc8+−) 29...g5 30.♗xc8 ♕xc8 31.♖xh4+ gxh4 32.♕xh4+ ♔g7 33.♕g5+ ♔h8 34.♖d4+−. **28.♗f5+ ♗h6−+** Sipila-T.Burg, Deizisau 2013 (analysis).

826 Black threatens 36...♕h3+ 37.♔xh3 ♖h1# or 36...♖h1+ 37.♔xh1 ♕h3+ 38.♔g1 ♕g2#, so White played **36.♖b1! ♕d7** (protecting the rook and clearing the g4-square for the knight) **37.♖g5!** and now it is over (37.♖xd1? ♘g4+ 38.♔h3 (38.♔g1 ♕xd1#) 38...♘xf2+ 39.♔h2 ♕h3+ 40.♔g1 ♕g2#): **37...♘e4 38.♖xd1 ♕xd1 39.♕f4!** 1-0 Nakamura-Topalov, Moscow ct 2016; 39...♕f1 40.♕xf3+−.

827   17...♕f6! 17...♖f8 18.♖g8!; 17...♕xg5 18.♕f7+ ♔d8 19.♕c7+ ♔e8 20.♕f7+=. **18.♕xf6** 18.♖xh7 ♖xh7 19.♘xh7 (19.♕xf6 ♖xh2+ 20.♔g1 ♗xf6−+) 19...♕xf3 (19...♕h8 is also good, but White can complicate things after 20.d4) 20.gxf3 ♖b8 21.b3 ♖b7 22.♘g5 ♗f4 23.h4 ♗c1 24.a4 ♖xb3−+. White can hardly move a piece, while Black will steadily increase his position and pick up the pawns on c3 and d3 (...♗a6 is in the air). **18...♗xf6 19.♖xh7 0-0! 20.♘a3 ♗xg5** and Black won, Karjakin-Carlsen, Bilbao rapid 2007.

828   32.♔c1 32.♔a2 ♖a8+ 33.♕a4 ♖xa4#, Anastasia's Mate. **32...♘b3+ 33.♔b1 ♕c1+ 34.♔a2!** Chess is not checkers! In the game Golmayo Zupide-Loyd, Paris 1867, White took the queen and got mated: 34.♖xc1 ♘d2+ 35.♔a2 ♖a8+ 36.♕a4 ♖xa4#, Anastasia's Mate. **34...♕xc2 35.♕c6!** 35.♕a6 ♘c5!−+; 35.♕a4 ♘xa1∓; 35.♕xb3 ♖a8+ 36.♕a3 ♕c4+ 37.♔b1 ♕e4+−+. **35...♘xa1** 35...♕xc6 36.♘e7+ ♔h7 37.♘xc6 ♘xa1 38.♔xa1±. **36.♔xa1** and White has the better chances.

829   41.♘e7+! ♔h8 41...♔f8? 42.♖d8#; 41...♔h7 42.♖h5+! transposes. **42.♖h5+! gxh5 43.♖g8+ ♔h7 44.♖g7+ ♔h8** 44...♔h6? 45.♘f5/♘g8#. **45.♖g8+=** Kurnosov-Topalov, Astana Wch rapid 2012 (analysis).

830   34.♖xe1 ♖xe1 35.♖d8+ ♔f7 36.♖d7+ ♔e6 36...♔e8 37.♖d8+ ♔xd8 38.♕d2+=. **37.♖d6+! ♔e7** 37...♔xd6 38.♕d2+ ♕d5 39.♕xe1 ♕xb3 40.♕xa5=. **38.♖d7+=** Camilia-Van Weersel, Istanbul ol 2012 (analysis).

831   No! 25...♘g3+ 26.hxg3 ♖f4 Greco's Mate is in the air (...♖/♕h4+), but White can defend against this mating threat by sacrificing his queen: **27.♕xe5+! dxe5 28.e7** with double-edged play, N.Zwirs-T.Dijkhuis, Dieren 2013.

832   34...♘c4! Threatening mate on b2, but also defending the d6-pawn (see the difference with 34...♘d1). The game N.Zwirs-Wedda, Hoogeveen 2018, continued 34...♘d1 35.♗xf7+! ♔f8 (35...♔xf7 36.♖e7+ ♔g8 37.♖g7+ ♔f8 38.♖h8#) 36.♗xd6+ and Black resigned due to 36...♔xf7 37.♖e7+ ♔g8 38.♖g7# or 37...♔f8 38.♖h8#. **35.♗xf7+** 35.♖eh1 ♕b2#; 35.♗xc4 ♕c3+ 36.♔b1 ♕xe1+−+; 35.♗c1 ♕c3+−+. **35...♔f8!** Capturing is not mandatory! **36.♖h8+** 36.♗xd6+ ♘xd6−+. **36...♔xf7 37.♖e7+ ♔g6** and the black king walks away.

833   No! After **23.♕xh7+?** Black resigned in the game Cs.Horvath-Kroeze, Leeuwarden 1993, but he is winning! 23...♔xh7 24.♗d3+ and now Black has a surprising defence: 24...♗e4! (24...♔h8 25.♖h4 with unstoppable mate is what both players had calculated) 25.♖xe4 (25.♗xe4+ blocks the d4-rook, so ♖h4 on the next move is no longer possible: 25...♔h8 26.♗xa8 ♕c2! △ 27.♖h4 ♕b1+ 28.♔e2 ♕xg1−+) 25...♔g8! 26.♖h4+ (26.♖c4+ wins back the queen, but this is not enough – White is too much material behind: 26...♔h8 27.♖xc8 ♖axc8) 26...♖g6−+.

834   38...♖xf2+! 39.♔g1 39.♔xf2 ♘g4+ 40.♔g2 ♘xf6−+. **39...♖h2! 40.♖xh2 ♘f3+ 41.♔g2 ♘xh2−+** Giri-Svidler, Baku 2015 (analysis).

835   28...♕d1+! 28...♕xf6? 29.♕h7#; 28...hxg5? 29.♕h7#. **29.♕xd1** 29.♔xd1 ♘b2+−+. **29...hxg5 30.♕d3 ♔g7** and Black will not get mated, Boleslavsky-Pachman, Saltsjöbaden izt 1948 (analysis).

836   **1...♕b1+! 2.♘e1 ♖c4! 3.♖e3** 3.dxc4 ♕xe4−+; 3.♖xc4 ♕xe1#. **3...♖g4!−+** Geller-Gufeld, Moscow blitz 1961.

837   22...♗f3! Prevents 23.♗d1+ with a quick mate. Now White has nothing better than a perpetual: **23.♕h7+** 23.gxf3?? ♖g8−+. **23...♔g5 24.♕g7+** 24.gxf3 ♕f6! 25.♔h1 (25.h4+ ♔f4 and Black's king is safe here!) 25...♕h8 26.♖g1+ ♔f6−+; 24.h4+ ♔f6−+; 24.g3 (threatening 25.♕h4#) 24...♖h8 25.♕g7+ ♔h5 26.♕xf7+ ♔g4 (26...♔g5? 27.♕g6#) 27.♕g6+ ♕g5−+ (27...♔h3 28.f6 ♘xf6 29.♗f5+ ♔g4 and here also, Black survives – and wins). **24...♔h5 25.♕h7+ ♔g5 26.♕g7+ ♔h5** ½-½ Karjakin-Svidler, Moscow 2011.

838   21...♕xc3! 21...♖xg7 22.♖xg7+ ♔h6 23.♖g8 ♔h7 24.♖8g7+ with a draw was played in the game Shirov-Kramnik, Groningen 1993. **22.♖xc3** 22.bxc3 ♗a3+ 23.♔b1 ♖d1#. **22...♖xg7−+**

839 **94...a6!** The game Miedema-Van Dael, Dieren 2018, continued 94...♖h8? (also, 94...a5?) 95.♕c8+ ♔xc8 stalemate! **95.bxa6 ♕c2+!−+**

840 **38...♕xf6!** 38...♖f8? 39.♖xh6+ ♗xh6 40.♕xh6#; 38...♗xf6? 39.♕xh6#. **39.♕g3** 39.♖xf6 ♗xf6+ with a discovered check! **39...♕xg6 40.♕xg6 ♗f6** 0-1 Postma-La. Ootes, Netherlands tt 2016/17.

841 **71.a8♘!** 71.a8♕ ♕b2+ 72.♔a6 ♕a3+ 73.♔b5 ♕b3+ with a perpetual. **71...♕b2+ 72.♘b6++−** Akopian-Karjakin, Nalchik 2009 (analysis).

842 **35.♗f2!** 35.♗f1 ♖a8−+; 35.♗d1 ♖xe1+−+. **35...♗xf2 36.♖xb2=** Borm-N. Zwirs, Netherlands tt 2013/14 (adjusted).

843 **18.g4!** Saves the knight. In the game Delekta-Geller, Cappelle-la-Grande 1992, White resigned after 18.♘g3? ♕xg3 as 19.hxg3 g5 leads to Greco's Mate! **18...gxf5? 19.gxf5 ♖h6? 20.♖g1±**

844 **20.♖xe8+! ♖xe8 21.♕xf6! ♖e1+ 22.♗f1 ♗h3 23.♗h6!** 1-0 Paszewski-Zakrzewski, Rewal 2011; 23...♖xa1 24.♕f8#.

845 **27.fxe7! ♗d4+** and here White resigned, but after **28.♘e3!** (28.♖f2 e1♕#; 28.♔h1 exf1♕#) **28...♗xe3+ 29.♔h1** he would have been winning, as his rook is now defended by the queen thanks to the clearance of the diagonal with 28.♘e3!. Jonasson-Angantysson, Reykjavik 1986.

846 No! **21.♖xa5 ♖xa5** 21...♖d8 was played in the game. **22.♖c8+ ♗f8 23.♗h6 ♖a1+ 24.♗f1 ♔h8! 25.♖xf8+ ♘g8−+** R.Reichardt-De Groot, Bunschoten-Spakenburg 2015.

847 **34.♘d5+!** 34.♖xf2? ♖e1+; 34.♖g1 ♖e1 and now White can still play 35.♘d5+, but here this move only equalizes: 35...♔d7 (35...cxd5? 36.♕c3++−) 36.♘f6+ ♔c7=. **34...♔d7** 34...cxd5 35.♕c3+ (covering the e1-square) ♔d7 36.♖xf2. **35.♕c8+** 35.♕f6 wins as well, but the text is better since Black will be a full rook down in an endgame in which he only has a few pawns left! 1-0 Nabaty-Khairullin, Rijeka Ech 2010; 35...♔xc8 (35...♔d6 36.♕d8+ ♖d7 (36...♔c5 37.♕xe7+, check!) 37.♕f8+ ♔xd5 38.♖xf2+−. 36.♘xe7+ ♔d7 37.♖xf2+−.

848 Black resigned here, but he is winning after **51.♔xh7** (51...♔f8? 52.e7#) **52.f8♕+ ♔g6 53.♖g7+** (53.♕g7+ ♔f5 54.♕h7+ ♕g6−+) **53...♔h6!** and White does not have a sound discovered check as his queen is attacked twice, Romi-Staldi, Trieste ch-ITA 1954.

849 **36.♕xd1!** 36.♘e2? ♖f1+! (a typical magnet sacrifice) was played in the game So-Giri, Wijk aan Zee 2010. White resigned because of 37.♔xf1 (obliged, as the bishop was pinned) 37...♕f2#; 36.♕xf4 ♕xf4 37.♖xd1 ♕e3+ 38.♔h1 ♕xc3 39.axb5 (39.♗c1 bxa4) 39...♕xa3=. **36...♖f2 37.♕f1 ♖xf1+ 38.♖xf1** and now Black has no time to take on c3 due to White's mating threat: **38...h5 39.♗b2+−**

850 **22.exf6!** 1-0 E.de Groote-S.Kuipers, Netherlands tt 2013/14; 22...♕xf4 (22...gxf6 23.♕xc7+−) 23.fxg7+ ♔e8 24.gxh8♕++−.

851 **35.♗d6!** ♖e7 35...♕xh7 36.♖xf8#; 35...♕xf1+ 36.♖xf1 ♗xd6 and now White has many ways to win the game, e.g. 37.♕h8+ ♔e7 38.♕xc8. **36.♖xf7 ♖xf7 37.♕xg6 ♗xd6 38.♖f1** 1-0 Puranik-Rapport, Zalakaros 2017.

852 **34...♖c8! 35.♕xc8** ♕e5+ f6!−+; 35...♕xa7 ♖xc1#. **35...♘xc8** and Black won in Barua-Michalik, Groningen 2012.

853 **13...g6! 14.♕xg6** 14.♕h3 e5 (chasing away the defender of the bishop) 15.♕g3 ♖xh7−+. **14...♕h4** Now the h7♗ is pinned! **15.♖e1** 15.♗g8? ♕xh2#. **15...♕xh7−+** 0-1 Munoz Monroy-Osorio, Medellin 2013.

854 **9...♘xe4 10.♗xd8** 10.dxe4 ♕g5−+. **10...♗xf2+ 11.♔e2 ♘d4#** Legal's Mate, Claus-Zegers (place and date unknown).

855 **7.♗c4! ♖d4+** 7...♖xg7? 8.♗xd5 ♔xd5 9.a8♕++−; 7...♗c6 8.g8♕ ♖xg8 9.♗xg8=; 7...♖xc4 8.a8♕; 7...♖xc4 8.a8♕ (or 8.g8♕ ♗xg8 9.♗xg8=) 8...♗xa8 9.g8♕=. **8.♗d3!=** 8...♖a4 (8...♖g4 9.♗c4!) 9.♗e4! ♖d4+ (9...♖xe4 10.a8♕ (or 10.g8♕ ♗xg8 11.a8♕=) 10...♖xa8 11.g8♕=) 10.♗d3= S.Hornecker & M.Minski, 2010.

856 **18...♗b1!** Obstructing the back rank with a discovered attack, thus threatening both mate and to capture the rook. 0-1 Hautot-Ringoir, Lommel ch-BEL 2012; 19.♖xb1 (19.♖xe8 ♕d1+ 20.♖e1 ♕xe1#) 19...♖xe2−+.

857 **29.♘xf5!** 1-0 Sipila-C.Braun, Maastricht 2013; 29...gxf5 (29...♗xf5 (a pinned piece is a bad defender!) 30.♕xb6+–; 29...♕c5 30.♕g7#) 30.♖g3+ ♔h7 31.♕g7/♖g7#.

858 **28.♖c8! ♕xc8** 28...♕h4 29.♖xf8+ ♗xf8 30.♕xa5+–. **29.♘e7+ ♔h8 30.♘xc8** and White won, Bräuer-Hahn, Oberhof ch-GER jr 2012.

859 **37.♗h3!** Skewering the queen and rook (37.♕xg4 was played in the game Lanchava-A.Haast, Amstelveen ch-NED rapid W 2018). After the intermediate capture **37...♕xg3+ 38.hxg3** there are still two black pieces under attack: **38...♖f7 39.gxh4+–**

860 **24...b4! 25.♗xb4** 25.♗b2 ♖c2–+. **25...♗xb4 26.♕e3** 26.♕xb4 ♕xd3–+. **26...♖c3** and Black won, N.Guliyev-Aloma Vidal, Navalmoral 2011.

861 **24.♗xd5+!** Both removing an important defender and decoying the queen. 1-0 Goryachkina-Nasybullina, Vladivostok W 2014; 24...♕xd5 (24...♘xd5 25.♕xc4) 25.♘e7+ ♔h7 26.♘xd5+–.

862 **46...♖xg2! 47.♔xg2** 47.♕xd1 ♖xf2+ 48.♔g1 ♖d2–+. **47...♕xe1** and Black won, Leenhouts-Brink, Amsterdam 2017.

863 **27...♖xc1!** 0-1 Delgado Vlaic-Rzayev, Albena 2012; 28.♖xc1 ♘h3+–+; 28.♕xc1 ♘e2+–+.

864 **27...♖xc2!** 0-1 Vrolijk-I.Sokolov, Amsterdam 2018; 28.♕xc2 (28.♘xc2 ♘e2+ 29.♔g2 ♘xc3–+) 28...♕xd4+ 29.♔h1 ♘d3–+.

865 **32.♘xd6 ♖xe3** 32...exd6 33.♖xe5+–, a pinned piece is a bad defender! **33.♘f5+ ♔c6 34.♘xe3** and White won, Hendriks-Lindgren, Hoogeveen 2012.

866 **10.♘xe5! ♘xe5** 10...♗xd1? 11.♘xc6+ (discovered check!) 11...♗e7 12.♘xd8 and White is a piece up. **11.♕xg4±** The pinned knight is a bad defender, Volkers-Warmelink, Groningen 2004.

867 **33...f3+ 34.♔e3 ♗xd3 35.♖xd3 f2!** 0-1 Morozevich-Vidit, Malmö 2018; 36.♖xd8 f1♕–+; 36.♔xf2 ♖xd3–+.

868 **19.♗xd7+!** 19.♗e5? dxe5 20.♗xd7+ ♔e7, capturing is not mandatory! **19...♔xd7 20.♗e5 ♕g6** 20...dxe5? 21.dxe5+ with a discovered check. **21.♗xh8 ♖xh8** and White won, Prohaszka-Pacher, Cappelle-la-Grande 2011.

869 **23...f6! 24.♗g3** 24.♗xf6 ♖f4+ with a double attack, or 24...♖f8∓, pinning the bishop. **24...g4#** Boulahfa-Paulet, Roosendaal 2012.

870 **26.♗xf7+!** ♔xf7 26...♔h8 27.♕g7#; 26...♔f8 27.♕g7+ ♔e7 28.♘f5#. **27.♕g7+ ♔e8 28.♕xc7** and White won in Jaracz-Tiviakov, Germany Bundesliga 2013/14.

871 **23.♗f4!** 1-0 Admiraal-Rosmüller, Vlissingen 2018; 23...♕b6 (23...♘d6 24.c5+–, attacking the pinned piece) and now in the next two moves White lures two pieces to unfavourable squares in order to execute a double attack: 24.♕xb6 ♘xb6 25.♖xd8! (25.♗c7 ♖xd1) 25...♖xd8 26.♗c7+–.

872 **34...♖exe4! 35.dxe4** 35.fxe4 (a pinned piece is a bad defender!) 35...♕xe3–+. **35...♕h4+!** 0-1 Halldorsson-Salama, Iceland tt 2012/13; 36.♔f2 (36.♔f1 ♖d1#) 36...♖d1+ (deflecting the king!) 37.♔xd1 ♕xf2–+.

873 **27...♘c5! 28.0-0** 28.♕xe5 ♘xd3+ 29.♔d2 ♘xe5–+; 28.♖c3 ♕xd6–+. **28...♘xd3** and Black won, Najer-Vachier-Lagrave, Dortmund 2016.

874 **35.♗xg7! ♔xg7 36.♖xb4! cxb4** 36...axb4 (a pinned piece is a bad defender!) 37.♖xa7+–. **37.♕d4+ ♕f6 38.♕xa7** and White won in Korobov-Durarbayli, Rhodes tt 2013.

875 **18...♘a4! 19.♕xb7** 19.♕d8 ♘xc3+ 20.♔d3 ♖fxd8+ 21.♔xc3 ♗f6+–+ skewer!; 19.♕b3 ♘xc3+ 20.♕xc3 ♗f6–+ skewer! As the knight defends the queen, it can't move: 19.♘xa4 ♕xd5–+. **19...♘xc3+** and Black won, Zatonskih-Wemmers, Belgium tt 2013/14.

876 **21.♘h5!** 1-0 Nikolac-Kragelj, Pula 1998; 21...♖xh5 (21...♖xd1 22.♘xf6+, check No. 1; 22...♔f8 (22...♔g7 23.♘xe8++–, check No. 2) 23.♖xd1) 22.♖xd7+–.

877 **40...♕c4!** 0-1 Pel-Van Dooren, Netherlands tt 2016/17; 41.♕xc4 (41.♖f8+ ♔xf8 42.b5+ ♔f7–+) 41...♘xc4 42.♖c7 ♘xa3–+.

Deflecting the queen is not a good idea here: 40...♖xa3? 41.♕xa3 ♗xf7 42.♕a7+ and White wins back the piece by a double attack.

878 **30.♗xd5!** 1-0 Senkyr-Navratil, Czechia tt 2011/12; 30...♕xd5 (30...♘xd5 31.♕xg7#) 31.♘e7++–.

879   29...♗d4+! 0-1 Wei Yi-So, Chess.com blitz m 2018; 30.♕xd4 (30.♘xd4 ♕g2#) 30...♘xf3+ 31.♔f2 ♘xd4–+.

880   22...h5! 23.♗xh5 23.♕xh5 ♖h6 and the queen is trapped. **23...e5 24.♕g2 exd4** and Black won in Scheider-Kotainy, Osterburg 2012.

881   9...e5! 10.0-0 10.♗g3 e4–+; 10.♗xe5 ♘xd3+ 11.♕xd3 ♕xe5–+. **10...exf4** and Black won, Li Chao-Matlakov, St Petersburg tt rapid 2012.

882   30...♘f4! 30...♖xc4 was played in the game Carlier-F.Erwich, Rotterdam rapid 2012. **31.♘xf4** 31.♗xf4 ♖xe2–+; 31.♕f1 ♖xd2–+; 31.♕f3 ♖xc4–+; 31.♖xc2 ♘xe2+–+. **31...♕xc4 32.♕xc4 ♖xc4–+**

883   26.g4! 26.♗d3? ♕xh5=. **26...♘g3** 26...♗h7 27.♗d3 ♘f6 28.♗xh7++–; 26...fxg3 27.♖xf5. **27.gxf5 ♘xf1 28.♔xf1** and White won in Giri-Ding Liren, Wijk aan Zee 2015.

884   13.♖e8! Double deflection! **13...♕xe8** 13...♖xe8 14.♕xd5+! ♕xd5 15.♗xd5+ ♖e6 16.♗xe6#. **14.♗xd5+ ♖xd5 15.♕xd5+ ♕f7 16.♕xa5+–** R.Vedder-Spaans, Netherlands tt 2014/15 (analysis).

885   20.♖f8+! Deflecting the rook or attracting the king to f8. 1-0 Knight-Wolters, Groningen 2012; 20...♔xf8 (20...♖xf8 21.♕xe5+–) 21.♘xd7+ ♔g8 22.♘xe5+–.

886   25...f4! 0-1 Kohlweyer-Van den Doel, Delft 2013; 26.♗xf4 ♗xc3 27.♕xc3 (27. bxc3 ♖xb1–+) 27...♕xf4.

887   22.♖xe7+! ♔xe7 22...♘xe7 23.♕xd4+–. **23.♘f5+ ♔e8 24.♘xd4+–** Hilwerda-Kokje, Leiderdorp jr 2018 (analysis).

888   49.♗h7+! ♖xh7 49...♔h8 50.♗f5+ ♔g8 51.♗xe6++–. **50.♖g4+ ♖g7** 50...♘g7 51.♕xe7+–; 50...♕g7 51.♕xe6++–. **51.♕xe7** 1-0 Fedorchuk-Indjic, Bratto 2011.

889   42.♖e5+! Obstructing the b8-h2 diagonal or decoying the queen. 1-0 Mladenov-Seger, Germany Bundesliga 2013/14; 42...♕xe5 (42...♔xe5 43.f4++–) 43.♕f4+ ♔h5 44.♕h4#.

890   21...♖e1+! Obstructing the back rank or decoying the queen. 0-1 Hatzl-Bachmann, Graz 2014; 22.♕xe1 (22.♗xe1 ♕f1#) 22...♕xf3+ 23.♔g2 ♘xe1+–+.

891   19...♖xc3! 20.♕xa6 20.♕xc3 ♗b4–+. **20...♖d3+!** Interference by a double check! 0-1 Vroombout-Köhler, Amsterdam 2015; 21.♔xd3 ♕xa6+–+.

892   48.♘f4! 1-0 Dreev-Edouard, France tt 2011; 48...♕e7 (48...exf4 49.♕xg7#; 48...♕xg6 49.♘xg6+ ♔h7 50.♖xd6+–) 49.♖xd6 exf4 50.♕xh6+ ♔g8 51.♖g6+–.

893   25...♗xe3! 26.♘xe3 26.♕xe3 ♖xh4–+. **26...♖xh4! 27.f4** 27.♕xh4 ♘xf3+–+. **27...♘g6** and Black won in Bojkovic-Sebag, Gaziantep Ech W 2012.

894   31...♕d1! Attacking the rook and the g4-square. In this case Black does not attack a mating or promotion square – he just wants to give a perpetual on g4. 31...♗h3 32.♕a6 (or 32.♕b5+–). **32.♕c5** 32.♖e2 interrupts the connection between the queen and bishop on the a6-f1 diagonal: 32...♗h3+–; 32.♕c6 ♗d5! preventing the white queen to go to g2 and thus making 33...♕g4+ a big threat (32...♕g4+? 33.♕g2+–). However, after 33.♕c8, Black has another unpleasant surprise: 33...♕f3! with mate. **32...♕g4+ 33.♗g2** 33.♔h1 ♕f3+–. **33...♕d1+** with a perpetual, Mchedlishvili-Aliyev, Al-Ain 2014 (adjusted).

895   56.♖fd8! Preventing the in-between check 56...♖d5+, while at the same time clearing the f8-square for the pawn. Moreover, Black's rook is still hanging! 1-0 Mista-E.Hansen, Germany Bundesliga 2013/14; 56...♖xa8 (56...♔xf7 57.♖xa5+–) 57.f8♕++–; 56.♖xa5 ♔xf8=; 56.♖fc8 ♖d5! 57.♔e2 ♔xf7=; 56.♖g8+ ♔xf7 57.♖xa5 ♔xg8=.

896   37.c5! ♖dd7 37...bxc5 38.♖bxb7+–; 37...♖xc5 38.♖xb7++–. **38.♖xb7!** Luring the rook! **38...♖xb7 39.c6 ♖b8 40.cxd7** and White won, Isgandarov-Guliyev, Baku ch-AZE 2019.

897   35...♖xf1+! 36.♔xf1 ♕c6 Attacking the rook and the mating square h1. **37.♖e4 f5!**, attacking the pinned piece. 0-1 Jumabayev-Kashlinskaya, Douglas 2018.

898   No! 20.♕f5? cross-pins the pawn, but after **20...♖e8!** (moving away the rook and defending the pawn) the bishop and queen are forked! **21.♗c4 b5!∓** Instead, White is much better after 20.♗c4, F.Gheorghiu-Shapiro, New York 1989 (analysis).

899   36.♖xf5! ♕xf5 37.♖xh4+ ♕h7 38.♕h3! 1-0 Kokje-Kaufeld, Belgium tt 2017/18.

900   26.♖xc8! 1-0 Akesson-Vaarala, Västeras 2011; 26...♖xc8 (26...♕xc8 27.♕xd6+−) 27.♘f5+− ♖dc6 28.♕xh6+ ♔g8 29.♕g7#.

901   52.h6+! 52.♕f4 was played in the game Spoelman-Tregubov, Germany Bundesliga 2012/13. **52...♕xh6** 52...♔g6 53.♖g8+ (or 53.♕e4+ ♔xh6 54.♕h1+ (54.♕xd5+−) 54...♔g6 (54...♔g7 55.♕h8+ ♔g6 56.♖g8+ ♕g7 57.♖xg7#) 55.♖g8++−) 53...♔h7 54.♖g7+ ♕xg7 (54...♔h8 55.♕e8#) 55.hxg7+−. **53.♖g8+** Deflection No. 1. **53...♔h7 54.♖h8+** Deflection No. 2. **54...♔xh8 55.♕xh6++−**

902   19.♕d5+! ♕d6 19...♗d7 20.♘e6++−, possible thanks to the square clearance on the previous move; 19...♗d6 and here White has several ways to get a winning advantage, e.g. 20.♘e4 ♗f7 (20...♔e7 21.♘xd6 ♕xd6 22.♗xc5+−) 21.♘xg6+−. **20.♗xc5!** 1-0 Wen Yang-Artemiev, Moscow 2016; 20...♕xd5 21.♗b6#.

903   41.♖f2! In the game Nieuwenhuis-Reinderman, Netherlands tt 2015/16, followed 41.♔h3 ♕h6+ 42.♔g2 ♕d2+ 43.♔h3 ♕h6+ and the players agreed a draw. **41...♕c1** 41...♕h6 42.♖xe5+− (a pinned piece is a bad defender!). **42.♕c6+!** Luring away the defender of the back rank. **42...♖xc6 43.♖f8+ ♖c8 44.♖xc8#**

904   40...g5! 41.♘g6 41.♘g2 ♖a1+ 42.♘e1 ♖xe1+−+. **41...♗d6!** (41...♖xg6? 42.♖d8+ ♔b7 43.♖xf8) 0-1 Kramnik-Aronian, Zurich m 2012; 42.♖g7 ♗xh2+ 43.♔h1 ♖f1#.

905   22.a3! 22.♘c3 was played in Houben-Popilski, Dieren 2012. **22...♘c6 23.♖xc6!** 23.♘xc6? ♗xc6 24.♖xc6 ♖xb3. **23...♗xc6** 23...♖xb3 24.♖xg6!+−, a desperado! **24.♘xc6** and White remains a piece up.

906   31...a2+! 31...♘xd7 was played in the game Soors-Van der Werf, Leiden 2015; 31...♘d5? 32.♖xa3. **32.♗xa2** 32.♔xa2 b1♕+ 33.♔a3 ♕b4+ (33...♕b2+ 34.♔a4 ♕b4#) 34.♔a2 ♕b2#. **32...♘d5** A discovered attack. Black threatens both 33...♖f1, mating, and 33...♘xe3. Moreover, the knight keeps an eye on the c3-square: 33.♕e1 (33.♗xd5 ♖f1+

34.♔a2 ♖a1#; 33.♕d3 ♖f1+ (or 33...♘c3+ 34.♕xc3 ♖f1+ 35.♕e1 ♖xe1#) 34.♖xf1 ♘c3#; 33.♘xb8 ♗xe3−+) 33...♘c3+ 34.♕xc3 ♖f1+ 35.♕e1 ♖xe1#.

907   37...♖xg2+! 38.♔xg2 ♕g4+ 0-1 Xiong-Robson, St Louis ch-USA 2018; 39.♔f1 (the knight is pinned: 39.♔g3 ♕xe6−+) 39...♕f3+ 40.♔g1 ♖h1#, Kill Box Mate.

908   21.♘c6! Interference! 21.♗c4 was played in the game Martin-Schlosser, Germany Bundesliga 2013/14. **21...♗xc6 22.♕xe6+ ♔h8 23.♖f7!** Threatening 24.♖xh7+ ♔xh7 25.♕g6+ ♔h8 26.♕h7# as well as 24.♕e5+ followed by ♕g7#. 23.♕e5+ also wins, e.g. 23...♔g8 24.♗c4+ ♗d5 25.♗xd5+ ♖xd5 26.♕xd5+ ♔h8 27.♕e5+ ♔g8 28.♕xe7. **23...♗d5 24.♕e5+ ♗f6 25.♖xf6 ♖e8** 25...♔g8 26.♖xb6+−. **26.♖f8#**

909   16.♕xh5! Luring away the g-pawn in order to execute a double attack two moves later. **16...h6** 16...gxh5 17.♗xh7+ ♔h8 18.♘exf7+ ♖xf7 19.♘xf7+ ♔xh7 20.♘xd8+−. **17.♘exf7! ♖xf7** 17...gxh5 18.♗h7#. **18.♘xf7** 1-0 Collins-Short, England 4NCL 2015/16.

910   24...b5! 25.♕xb5 25.♕b3 ♗e6!−+, attacking the pinned piece for a third time, suffices to collect the knight! (25...bxc4? 26.♗xc4+−). **25...♗a6,** winning the piece by a skewer: 0-1 (30), Yohan-Patil, Lucknow ch-IND jr 2013.

911   15.d5! 1-0 Omar-Alb.David, Gibraltar 2013; 15...exd5 16.b5, trapping the bishop; 15...♗xd5 16.♗f5 (luring away Defender No. 1 of the bishop) 16...exf5 17.♗xb6 (capturing Defender No. 2 of the bishop) 17...axb6 18.♕xd5+−; 15...♘xd5 (here the knight blocks its own bishop on c6) 16.b5 ♘fe3 (16...♘xc3 17.♗xc3 ♗d5 18.♗xf5, luring away the defender of the bishop: 18...exf5 19.♘xd5 or 19.♕xd5+−) 17.bxc6 bxc6 18.♗xe3 ♘xe3 19.♕a4 ♘xf1 20.♖xf1 (or 20.♗e4+−) 20...♗e7 21.♗e4+−.

912   26.♕h4! 26.♕g7 was played in the game C.van den Berg-Eliskases, Beverwijk 1959. **26...♖g8 27.♖xf6! ♕xf6** 27...♕c5 28.♖c6+ (discovered check) 28...♔f8 29.♖xc5+−. **28.d6+!** Luring away the defender of the queen. **28...♔xd6 29.♕xf6++−**

913   33.b6+! ♔d6 33...♞xb6 34.♖e7+−, pinning the queen; 33...♔xb6 34.♕xd7+−. **34.♕f8+** 1-0 Schoppen-B.van den Berg, Vlissingen 2018; 34...♞e7 35.♖d4+−, skewer!

914   28...♖h4! 29.♗xh4 29.♕xh4 ♕xg2#; 29.♖h1 ♕xh1 30.♗xh4 ♕xa1−+; 29.♕g3 ♖hxf4+ (29...♖fxf4+ is also good) 30.♗xf4+ ♖xf4+−+. **29...♖xf4+ 30.♕xf4+ ♕xf4+ 31.♔e2 ♕xh4−+** Stany-Ikonnikov, Dieren 2014 (analysis).

915   27.♕xf8+! Decoying the king. **27...♔xf8 28.♞g5+** Discovered check. **28...♕f5 29.♞xe6+!** Removing the defender of the pinned queen. White played 29.♞xh7+ and although he was better here, the game Niemelä-Hamalainen, Finland tt 2011/12, ended in a draw. **29...♔e7 30.♖xf5+−**

916   No! 34...♗b4? 35.♞b6! Interference! **35...♗xa3** 35...♕xb6 36.♕a8+ (36.cxb6 ♗xa3 37.b7 is also winning) 36...♔e7 37.cxb6+−; 35...♗e8 36.♕xb4+−. **36.♞xd7+ ♔e7 37.♞xb8+−** Schiennmann-F.Erwich, Germany tt 2014/15 (analysis).

917   14.♗a6! ♞xe5 14...h6 15.♗xh6 ♞xe5 16.♗xb7+−; 14...♗xa6? 15.♞xc6 ♕d7 16.♞e7+ ♕xe7 17.♗xf6+−. **15.dxe5** 1-0 Ree-Je.Piket, Netherlands tt playoff 2000/01; 15...♗xa6 (15...♞d5 16.♗xe7 ♕xe7 17.♕xe7 ♞xe7 18.♗xb7+−) 16.exf6 ♗d6 17.♕h6+−.

918   13.♞d7! ♞g6 13...♖xd7 14.♗xh7+ ♔h8 (14...♞xh7 15.♕xd7) 15.♗f5++−; 13...♞xd7 14.♕xh7#. **14.♞xf8±** Kortchnoi-Timman, Almelo rapid m 2006.

919   39...e3! Clearing the b1-h7 diagonal. **40.♖h8+** 40.fxe3 ♗f5+ 41.♔c3 ♗xh7−+. **40...♔g7** The game Pridorozhni-Safarli, Khanty-Mansiysk Wch blitz 2013, continued 40...♔e7 41.♖h7+ (41.♖xd8 e2!−+) 41...♔f6 42.♖h6+ (42.♞e4+ ♔g6 43.♖e7 e2 44.♖xe6+ ♔g7 45.♖e7+ ♔f8−+) 42...♔g7 43.♖xe6 ♖xd2+ 44.♔c3 exf2 0-1. **41.♖xd8 e2 42.♞f3 gxf3 43.♔d2 fxg2−+**

920   26...f4! Luring the bishop to f4. **27.♗xf4 ♗h4! 28.♗xe5** 28.♕xh4 ♞xf3+ 29.♔f2 ♞xh4−+; 28.♕g2 ♖xf4−+. **28...♗xg3 29.hxg3 ♖xf3** and Black won, Lederman-Kurmann, Gibraltar 2013.

921   39.♕f8! Threatening 40.♕g7#. 39.♕xe8 was played in the game Afek-Klein, Haarlem 2015. After 39...♞h6 40.♕d8! White is still winning, but after the text Black has nothing to hope for. **39...♖g5 40.♖h1+** 40.♖xg5? ♕e1+ 41.♔b2 ♕xe2+ and White will lose his rook, for example: 42.♔b1 ♕d1+ 43.♔b2 ♕d2+−+. Now Black has to interrupt the connection between the rook and the knight: **40...♔g6 41.♕xg8+ ♔f6 42.♕xe8+−**

922   41...♖c1+! Deflecting the rook or attracting the king. 41...♕c7 was played in the game Morozevich-Inarkiev, Moscow 2014. **42.♔xc1** 42.♖xc1 ♕xd4−+. **42...♕c7+** Or 42...♕c8+. **43.♔b1 ♕c2+ 44.♔a1 ♕a2#**

923   35...♗xd5! Luring the bishop to a vulnerable square. **36.♗xd5 ♞d3! 37.♗xf7** 37.♖e2 ♞f4−+, double attack; 37.♖a1 e2−+, promoting. **37...♖e7 38.♖e2 ♞f4 39.♗c4 ♞xe2+ 40.♗xe2 ♖f7** 0-1 Gordon-Fridman, Gibraltar 2013.

924   33.♖f6! Threatening 34.♕h8#, as the a1-h8 diagonal has been interrupted. 33.♕xg6 was played in the game Damen-Den Hartog, Assen ch-NED U20 2017. **33...♔e8** 33...♖d7 34.♕h8+ (chasing the king to e7, while setting up a battery to execute a discovered attack on the next move) 34...♔e7 35.♖xf7+ ♔xf7 36.♕xc3+−. **34.♕h8+** Chasing the king to d7, while setting up a battery to execute a discovered attack on the next move. **34...♔d7 35.♖xd6+ cxd6 36.♕xc3+−**

925   10.e5! ♗xg2 11.exf6 ♗h3 11...♗d5 12.c4 ♗b7 13.♞xe6! fxe6 14.♕xe6+ ♗e7 15.fxg7+−. **12.♕h5! ♗f5** 12...♕xf6 13.♕xh3+− was played in the game Carlsen-Caruana, Bilbao playoff blitz 2012. **13.♞xf5 exf5 14.♖e1+ ♞e5 15.fxg7 ♖xg7 16.f4+−**

926   41.♖h8+! ♔xh8 42.♕xf8+ ♔h7 43.♖f3! Rook lift! **43...♕h6+ 44.♖h3** 1-0 Den Hartog-Dambacher, Netherlands tt 2014/15.

927   27.g5! Obstructing the d8-h4 diagonal. 27.♕e2 was played in the game M.Erwich-Soukup, Germany tt 2014/15. After **27...hxg5 28.fxg5 ♗xg5** the h2-b8 diagonal has been opened (28...♗e5 29.♗xh4+−): **29.♗xg6** Clearing the d-file. **29...♞xg6 30.♗xd6+−**

928 26...♖e1! Interference or luring away the rook: **27.♗xe1** Now the connection between the queen and rook is interrupted: 27.♖xe1 ♘f2+ 28.♔g2 ♘xd1–+; 27.♘xe1 ♘b2–+. **27...♘b2** Discovered attack! **28.♗c3** 28.♘xb2 ♕xf1#. **28...♘xd1 29.♖xd1 ♕e2** 0-1 I.Jones-Dueball, Nice ol 1974.

929 40.♕h7+! 1-0 A.Vovk-E.Hansen, Hoogeveen 2014; 40...♔h6 41.g4+! fxg4 (41...♔g5 42.♕e7+ (or 42.♕g8+ ♕g6 43.♕d8+ ♔h6 44.♕h4+ ♕h5 45.♕xh5#; 42.♗f4+, deflecting the king and winning a queen, is not bad either) 42...♔g6 43.♕f6+ ♔h7 44.♕f7+ ♔g7 45.♕xg7#) 42.♕xe4.

930 18...♗g4! 19.♕xg4 19.♕g3 ♖xe4–+. **19...♕xd3 20.♖fe1** 20.♘c5 ♕xd2–+. **20...f5** 0-1 Bosch-Dreev, Arnhem Ech U20 1989.

931 33.♗xh6! Creating a breach in the wall! 1-0 Shengelia-Sakelsek, Graz 2011; 33...gxh6 (33...♖g8 34.♖c8! g6 (34...gxh6 35.♕xg8#) 35.♕f4 f5 36.♗g7+! (attracting the king) 36...♔xg7 37.♖c7+ ♔f8 38.♘xf5 (line clearance) △ 38...gxf5/exf5 39.♕b4+ ♔e8 40.♕e7#) 34.♘f5! ♖g8 (34...exf5 35.♖xh6#) 35.♖c8!+– (luring away the rook) 35...♖xc8 36.♕g7#.

932 39.♕e7! 1-0 Le Quang Liem-Shankland, Danzhou 2018; 39...a5 (39...♖xe7 40.fxe7+–; 39...♕xe7 40.fxe7+–) 40.♖xf8+! ♖xf8 41.♕g7#.

933 44.♗g6+! ♔xg6 44...♘xg6 45.♕e6+ ♔f8 46.♕c8+ ♔f7 47.♕xb7++–. **45.♕e4+ ♔f7** 45...♔f6 46.♕f5#; 45...♔h6 46.♖h1+ ♘h5 47.♖xh5#. **46.♕xb7++–** H.van Dijk-Polak, Delft 2013 (analysis).

934 25...♘f4! Targeting – the knight is on its way to e2. **26.♖d2 ♖xd4** Decoying the rook. **27.♖xd4 ♘e2+** 0-1 Timman-Bosch, Netherlands tt playoff 2000/01; 28.♖xe2 (28.♔f1 ♘xd4–+) 28...♖xb1+, mating.

935 27.♖xg5! 1-0 Rabatin-Plat, Frydek-Mistek 2013; 27...♖xg5 28.♖xh7+ ♔d6 (28...♔d8 29.♖h8+ (skewer!) 29...♔d7 30.♖xa8+–) 29.♘e4+ (double attack!) 29...♔xd5 30.♘xg5+–.

936 32...♘e3! Threatening 33...♕h2#. **33.♗xe3 ♖xe3 34.♔f2** 34.♕xe3 ♕h1+ 35.♔f2 ♖h2#; 34.♕a8+ ♔g7 35.♕g2 ♖xg3–+.

934... 34...♖xf3+ and Black won in Belous-Bologan, Wroclaw Ech rapid 2014.

937 36.♖c8+! 36.♖xf7 was played in the game Kiik-Tal, Tallinn 1985. See Exercise 968 for the follow-up. **36...♖e8 37.♖xe8+ ♕xe8 38.♖e1 ♕b8** The queen is overloaded. It has to protect both the back rank and the bishop (38...♔f8 39.♕c5++–, double attack; 38...h6 39.♕d5+–, attacking the pinned bishop, while keeping the f7-pawn pinned (preventing 39...f6)): **39.♖xe5! ♕xe5 40.♕c8+ ♕e8 41.♕xe8#**

938 23...♕b7+! 23...♘xf1 24.♖xf1 with compensation. **24.♖f3** 24.♔g1? ♕g2#. **24...♘xc4 25.dxc4 ♖xc3!** 0-1 Koster-Landa, Netherlands tt 2005/06; 26.♕xc3 (26.bxc3 ♕xb1+–+) 26...e4!–+.

939 No! 14...♘xe5? 14...♘e7 was played in the game Popov-Nybäck, Budva Ech 2009. **15.♖xe5!** 15.♘xe5 ♗xb5 16.a4 ♗c4! △ 17.a5 ♗xb3 18.♕xb3 ♗xd4; or 15.dxe5 ♗xb5 16.a4 ♗c4 17.a5 ♗xb3 18.♕xb3 ♘c5 and the bishop escapes. **15...♗xb5 16.a4!** Targeting! **16...♗e8 17.a5** and the bishop is trapped.

940 28...♗g2+! 29.♔xg2 After 29.♗xg2 the bishop obstructs the second rank: 29...♕h2#. **29...♕h3+ 30.♔g1 ♗xe3+ 31.♕xe3 ♖xe3** and Black won, Gordon-Ris, England 4NCL 2018/19.

941 46.♕e4! 1-0 Caruana-Jakovenko, Poikovsky 2011; 46...h5 (46...♕d1 47.♖h1 (47.f4?? ♕xg4+–+) 47...♕xa4 48.f4+–) 47.f4 ♖xg4 (47...hxg4+ 48.♔h4+–) 48.♕e8+ ♔h7 49.♕xh5++–.

942 26.♖c1! ♕b5 26...♕b6 27.♖c5+–; 26...♕f5 27.♖c5+–. **27.♖c5 ♘c4 28.♕c1** (or 28.♕e2 ♕b2 29.♕xc4+–) 1-0 Jakovenko-Sutovsky, Poikovsky 2014.

943 13.c5! ♕xc5 13...♘a5 14.♘b3+–; 13...♖xc5 14.♘a4+–. **14.♘b3 ♕b4** 14...♕b6 15.♘a4+–. **15.axb4 ♕xb4** and White won in Topalov-Karpov, Monaco rapid 1998.

944 26.♕g4+! 1-0 Tiviakov-M.Senders, Groningen 2014; 26...♔xf6 27.♕h4+ (skewer!) ♔g7 28.♕xe7+–; or after 26...♔h7, White sets up a battery first: 27.♕h4! ♔g7 28.♖g6+! (discovered attack!) 28...♔xg6 29.♕xe7 with a winning advantage.

945 **20.♕h4!** 20.♕g5? ♕a1+ 21.♔d2 ♕a5! and Black can still fight, e.g. 22.♗xa5? ♘xe4+ 23.♔e3 ♘xg5–+. **20...♖c8** 20...♔g7 21.♕g5+! ♔h8 22.♗xf6++–. **21.♗xf6+ ♗xf6 22.♕xf6+ ♔g8 23.♗c4!** ♕a1+ 23...♖xc4 24.♖g1+ ♔f8 25.♕xd6+ ♔e8 26.♖g8#. **24.♔d2 ♕a5+ 25.c3** 1-0 Adams-Morrison, England 4NCL 2011/12.

946 No! **13.♘xe5?** 13.h3 was played in the game Carlsen-Caruana, St Louis 2014. **13...♘xe5!** 13...♘xg3 14.♗xf7+ ♔d8 15.♘g6 ♘xf1 (15...♕xf7 16.♘xh8±) 16.♘xe7 ♔xe7 17.♕xf1 ♔xf7 is unclear. **14.♕xh5** The in-between move 14.♗xe5 does not help, as after 14...♕xe5 the knight on h5 is protected by the queen. **14...♗g4 15.♕h4 g5** and the queen is trapped.

947 **22.♕d5! 0-0 23.♘xf7! ♕h5** 23...♘e7 24.♘h6+ (double check!) 24...♔h8 25.♕xa8! (desperado) 25...♖xa8 26.♘xg4+–; 23...♖xf7 24.♕xa8++–. **24.♘d8+!** Interference! **24...♔h8 25.♕xa8** 1-0 Bartel-Ducarmon, Jerusalem Ech 2015.

948 **56.♗xf5+!** By luring away the bishop White can set up a double attack later! **56...♗xf5** 56...♔h5 57.♕f7+ ♔h4 (57...♔h6 58.♕xh7#) 58.♗g3#. **57.♕e8+!** 1-0 Lahaye-Jedlicka, Groningen 2018; 57...♔f6 (57...♔h6 58.♗f8+ and now Black has to interpose his queen not to get mated: 58...♕g7 59.♗xg7++–; 57...♔g7 58.♗e5+, double attack!) 58.♕h8+! (skewer!) 58...♔f7 59.♕xd4+–.

949 **27...♘e3! 28.♖xe3** 28.♗xd6 ♘f1+ 29.♔g1 ♘xg3+ 30.♔h2 ♖h1#. **28...♖dd1 29.♕xd1 ♖xd1** and Black won, Van Wely-Borisek, Reykjavik Ech tt 2015.

950 **23.♗xh7+! ♔xh7** 23...♔h8 24.♖g4 f6 25.♕h5+– and ♗g6+ and ♕h7+ next. **24.♖g4!** 1-0 Kovalev-S.Kuipers, Wijk aan Zee 2019; 24...f6 (24...g6 25.♖h4+ ♔g8 26.♖h8/♕h8#; 24...♔g8 25.♕h5#) 25.♖h4+ ♔g8 (25...♔g6 26.♕h5#) 26.♕xe6+, luring forward the f8♖, the defender of the c8♖: 26...♖f7 27.♕xc8++–.

951 **26.g4!** 26.♖e1 was played in Carlstedt-Maze, Gibraltar 2017. **26...♗xg4** 26...♕xg4+ 27.♔h2 and the bishop is trapped. **27.♖h2 ♕f5 28.♖f1+–** and ♕h6 is on the agenda.

952 **26...h5! 27.♕f5** 27.♕h4 g5 28.♘exg5 fxg5 29.♘xg5 ♖a5 30.♘f3 ♕xh4 31.♘xh4 ♖b5–+. **27...♖a5! 28.♘c5 ♗b6 29.♖c1 ♗xc5** Luring the rook to c5. 0-1 H.Jonkman-Timman, Helmond rapid 2012. Now, after chasing the king to h2, Black will win back the rook with interest: 30.♖xc5 ♕d1+ 31.♔h2 ♕d6+–. 29.♖xc5 30.♖xc5 ♕d1+ 31.♔h2 ♕d6+ is also good.

953 **30.♘g6+!** hxg6 30...fxg6 31.♖xd6 (or 31.♖xd6+–) 31...♕xd6 32.♕xd6 ♖xd6 33.♖e8#; 30...♖xg6 31.♖xd8+ ♕f8 32.♖xf8#. **31.♕h4+ ♔h5** 31...♔g8 32.♕xd8+ ♖xd8 33.♖xd8+ ♔h7 34.♖h3+ ♕h5 35.♖xh5+ gxh5 36.♖xa8+–. **32.♕xd8+ ♖xd8 33.♖xd8+ ♔h7 34.♖ee8** 1-0 Mamedyarov-Timofeev, Moscow 2004; 34...g5 35.♖h8+ ♔g6 36.♖xh5+–; 34.♖h3, pinning the queen, wins as well.

954 **24.♖f4!** ♕g6 24...♖xf4 25.♘e7++–; 24...♕xd3 25.♘e7+ ♔h8 (25...♘xe7 26.♕xd3+–) 26.♘g6+ ♕xg6 27.♖xf8#. **25.♕xd5!** ♕xg5 25...exd5 26.♘e7+ ♔h8 27.♘xg6+–; 25...hxg5 26.♘e7+ ♔h7 27.♕xa8. **26.♕f3!** 1-0 Swinkels-P.Claesen, Belgium tt 2016/17; 26...♕g6 27.♘e7++–.

955 **62.♖c7!** 62...♗e1 was played in the game Bartel-Naiditsch, Dortmund 2012. **63.♗e8** 63.♗e6 ♖c6–+; 63.♗b5 ♖f7–+. **63...♖c8 64.♗b5 ♖f8–+**

956 No! **25...♘xg3?** 25...h6 was played in the game Vallejo Pons-Svane, Germany Bundesliga 2013/14. **26.♗e5!** Targeting! **26...♗d6** 26...♘f5 27.♗c7+–. **27.♗d4!** Unpinning the f-pawn! **27...♕a5 28.fxg3+–**

957 **33.♕c3! ♔f8** 33...♖xc3 34.♖xe8#; 33...♕b8 34.♖xe8+ ♖xe8 35.♕xg7#. **34.♕xc8 ♔xe7 35.♗a3+!** ♔f6 35...♘d6 36.e5+–. **36.♕xe8** and White won, Shoker-Enkhtuul, Al-Ain 2012.

958 **44.♖xa6! bxa6 45.b7 ♕d8** 45...♕c7 46.♘e8++–. **46.♕xh6+! ♔xh6 47.♘xf7+** 1-0 Zviagintsev-Schwarz, Novi Sad tt 2016.

959 **38.g5+! ♔xg5 39.♖g1+ ♔h5** 39...♔f6 40.♖g6#. **40.♘g6!** Double attack on the rook and a mating square. **40...♘g8 41.♘f4+** 1-0 Ivanchuk-Giri, Leon blitz m 2013; 41...♔h6 42.♖g6+ ♔h7 43.♖xd6+–; 41.♘e7 wins as well, but the text is even better.

960 10.♗xf7+! Removing a defender and/ or attracting the king. **10...♔xf7** 10...♖xf7 11.♘e6! (a pinned piece is a bad defender!) dxe6 12.♕xd8+–. **11.♘e6! dxe6** 11...♔xe6 12.♕d5+ ♔f5 and now White has several ways to give mate. One of the options is 13.g4+ ♔xg4 14.♖g1+ ♔h4 15.♕e4+ ♔h3 16.♕g4+ ♔xh2 17.♕g3/♕g2#. **12.♕xd8** and White won, Fischer-Reshevsky, New York ch-USA 1958.

961 43.♖c8! ♖d8 43...♖xc8 44.f6 ♕xf6 45.♕xc8+ ♔h7 46.♕xa8+–. **44.f6** Clearing the h3-c8 diagonal! **44...♕xf6 45.♕d7 ♖xc8** 45...♕g6+ 46.♔f1 (or 46.♔f2 ♕b6+ 47.♔f1+–) 46...♕b1+ 47.♔f2+–. **46.♕xc8+ ♔h7 47.♕xa8** and White won, Van Wely-Beerdsen, Vlissingen 2015.

962 No! 46...♘xb3? 46...e3 was played in Wagner-Aronian, Douglas 2018. **47.♖g8!** 47.♕xb3? ♖b8–+. **47...♕xf5** 47...♕xc3 48.♖xf8+ (check!) ♔b7 49.♖xc3+–; 47...♕xg8 48.♕xf6+–. **48.♖xf8+ ♕xf8 49.♕xb3+–**

963 Yes! 34.♗xf6! ♖xb7 35.cxb7 ♕e4+ 35...♔h7 36.♖c8 ♕e4+ 37.♔h2 ♕xb7 38.♖h8#. **36.f3 ♕xb7 37.♖d1!** 1-0 Basso-Korobov, Minsk Ech 2017; 37...♕c8 (37...♔h7 38.♖d8 and ♖h8# cannot be averted) 38.♖d8+ ♕xd8 39.♗xd8+–.

964 14.dxe5? is not a good idea! ≥ 14.gxf3. **14...♗h6!** Black counterattacks by a cross-pin! **15.♖xf3** And now best was 15.♗xb6 ♗xd2 16.gxf3 axb6 17.exf6 bxa4∓. **15...♗xe3+! 16.♕xe3** 16.♖xe3? ♘g4, attacking the pinned rook. **16...♘xe5! 17.♖g3 bxa4.** Black is a pawn up and his pieces are much better placed, Goudriaan-La.Ootes, Amsterdam 2015.

965 23.♗d2! 23.♖ff1 was played in the game Eisenbeiser-Rademakers, Vlissingen 2012, but now Black could have limited the damage by 23...♗xe4! 24.♖xe4 ♖xf1+ 25.♕xf1 ♖f8!. 23.♖ee2 g3 24.hxg3 ♗g4 25.♗f4 ♕e7 (25...♗xe2 26.♕xe2 ♕f6 27.♕xh5) 26.c5! is better for White, but the text wins decisive material. **23...♗xe4** 23...♕e7 24.♗xf5+–; 23...g3 24.♗xf5! gxh2+ 25.♔h1 ♖xf5 26.♗xf5 ♕xf5 27.♖xe8++–. **24.♖xe4** and the queen is trapped in the middle of the board!

966 18...♕a6! 18...♕c7 was played in the game. The text threatens 19...♖c1 with double checkmate or 19...♖e4+ with a discovered

check. Moreover, after **19.♔g1 f6!** the queen is trapped! Hendriks-J.van Onzen, Arnhem 2011.

967 30.♖xe7! ♕xe5 30...♕xe7 31.♕xd4+–. **31.♖xe6!+–** 0-1 Danielian-Cmilyte, Beijing W blitz 2012; 31...♕xe6 (31...♘xe6 32.♖xe5+–; a pinned piece is a bad defender) 32.♕xd4+–.

968 36...♖xc6! 36...♖xf7? 37.♖c8+ ♕xc8 38.♕xc8+ ♖f8 39.♕e6+ and compared to the text, Black loses his bishop; 36...♕d1+? 37.♖f1++–, getting out of check by giving a discovered check! **37.♕xc6** In the game Kiik-Tal, Tallinn 1985, White tried to be smart by inserting 37.♖xg7+? (taking a pawn with double check), but after 37...♔xg7 38.♕xc6 ♖c7! it was Black who was the smartest. The queen is pinned, and e.g. 39.♕e6 ♖c1# is mate! Therefore, White resigned after 38...♖c7!. **37...♔xf7=.**

969 40.♖xe7! ♕xe7 41.♕xh6+ ♔g8 41...♕h7 42.♕xf8++–. **42.♕xg5+** Luring the black queen away from the blocking square. **42...♕xg5 43.e7+** 1-0 Petersen-Timman, Helsingor 2018; 43...♔g7 44.exf8♕+ ♔xf8 45.fxg5+–.

970 29...♖e1! 30.♖xe1 ♖xe1 31.♕b8+ ♔h7 32.♕xg3 ♖xf1+! 0-1 Bukavshin-Drozdowski, Albena Ech jr 2011; 33.♔xf1 (33.♔h2 ♕xf2–+) 33...♕d1#.

971 24.♘h7+! ♖xh7 Now the rook blocks the escape route for the black king: **25.♕f3+! ♔g6 26.♕g4+ ♔f6 27.♕f4+** and if Black tries to escape to the queenside by **27...♔e7**, White has a double attack: **28.♕e4+ ♔d7 29.♕xh7=** Westerweele-Hmam, El Haouaria 2012 (adjusted).

972 21.♕f3! ♕xg1+ 22.♔d2 22.♔e2? ♗xg4 23.♖xg1 ♗xf3+ 24.♔xf3 g6–+. **22...♕h2** 22...♕xf2+ 23.♕xf2 ♗xf2 24.♖h1+ ♗h4 25.♖xh4#, Anastasia's Mate; 22...♕xa1 23.♕h3#. **23.♖h1 ♕h6+ 24.g5!** 1-0 Shevchenko-Nesterov, Jermuk jr 2017.

973 No! 31.♘xd5?! ≥ 31.♖a2! (threatening 32.♘c1) and White is better. **31...♕xb3 32.♘xf6+ gxf6! 33.♖xb3 e5 34.e4** 34.♖d3 was played in the game Greenfeld-Raznikov, Dieren 2012; 34.dxe5? fxe5 35.♗g5 f6 36.♗h6 ♔h7–+. **34...exf4 35.♘xf4** with compensation.

974   22...♘a2+! 22...♖xd1+ was played in the game Stojanovic-B.Muhren, Tromsø ol 2014. **23.♔c2 ♘ab4+** Or 23...♘cb4+. **24.axb4 ♘xb4+ 25.♔c1** 25.♔c3? ♖xd1 26.♔xb4 ♖f8! (attacking the pinned bishop) 27.♗f4 g5!−+ (again attacking a pinned bishop; but not 27...e5? 28.g3! exf4 29.♗h3+ ♔c7 30.♖xd1+−). **25...♘a2+=**

975   **38.♖h8+! ♔g6 39.♖xh6+!** 1-0 Bronstein-Kortchnoi, Leningrad-Moscow 1962; 39...♔xh6 (39...gxh6 40.♕g8+ (chasing the king in order to execute a skewer on the next move) 40...♔f6 41.♕f8+ ♔g6 42.♕xf3+−) 40.♕h8+ ♔g6 41.♕h5+ (again chasing the king, while setting up a battery to execute a discovered attack on the next move) 41...♔f6 42.g5++−.

976   **48...♕f1+! 49.♕c1 ♗c2+!** 0-1 Areshchenko-Vidit, Martuni 2014; 50.♔xc2 (50.♔a2 ♕xc1−+) 50...♖c8+ 51.♔b3 ♖xc1, winning. This tactic certainly has some similarities with Carlsen's 42...♗f2+ in Exercise 644 (Caruana-Carlsen, Mate Chapter).

977   **13...♘xe4! 14.♗xd8** 14.♘xe4 ♕xh4+ was a better try, although White's position remains terrible. **14...♘xf3+! 15.♔f1** 15.gxf3 ♗f2+ 16.♔f1 ♗h3#. **15...♘ed2+** 15...♘fd2+ 16.♕xd2 transposes (16.♔e1 ♗f2#). **16.♕xd2 ♘xd2+ 17.♔e1 ♘xb1** and Black won in Mohandesi-Barsov, Leuven 2002.

978   **9.e5! g5 10.exf6 gxh4 11.♕xe6+! fxe6** 11...♔e7 12.♕xe7+/fxe7+−. **12.♗g6#** M.Piket-Lont, 1993 (place unknown).

979   **30.♗c2! ♕xc2 31.♘d3 ♔g8** 31...♖xd3 32.♖xd3+−. **32.♕xh7+** Chasing the king to f7, while setting up a battery. **32...♔f7 33.♘e5+ ♔e6 34.♕xc2** and White won, Ding Liren-Inarkiev, Baku 2015.

980   **16...♗h3+!** 16...♖ad8 was played in the game Gvetadze-Melia, Tbilisi ch-GEO W 2009, but after 17.♔g1! White would have had chances to survive. **17.♗g2 ♕xe1+! 18.♔xe1 ♗xg2 19.♖g1 ♖fe8+** Or 19...♖ae8+ 20.♔d2 ♖d8−+. **20.♔d2 ♖ad8−+** Or 20...♖ed8−+.

981   **38.♖c8+! ♔f7** 38...♘xc8 39.♕f8#; 38...♖xc8 39.♕xa5+−. **39.♖c7+ ♔g8** 39...♔e8 40.♘g7+ ♔f8 41.♕xd6++−. **40.♖g7+** 40.♕xa5 ♖xa5 41.♖g7+ transposes. **40...♔h8 41.♕xa5 ♖xa5 42.♖d7!** with a double attack on the knight and the (almost mating) square d8, Van Harten-T.Dijkhuis, Eindhoven rapid 2011 (analysis).

982   **46...♘d5+!** 46...d3 47.♔c3 ♘d5+ 48.♔d2 a3 49.♖c8 a2 50.♖a8 ♘b4−+ was played in the game L.van Foreest-Werle, Netherlands tt 2016/17, but the text is more convincing. **47.♔xa4** 47.♔c4 d3 (luring the king) 48.♔xd3 (48.♔xd5 d2−+) 48...♘b4+−+. **47...d3 48.♖c4** 48.♔b3 d2 (luring the king) 49.♔c2 ♘b4+−+; 48.♖c1 d2 49.♖d1/♖g1 ♘c3+−+. **48...d2 49.♖e4+ ♔f8!** 49...♔d6 50.♖d4 and as the knight is pinned, Black will lose the d2-pawn. **50.♖d4 d1♕+** Or 50...♘c3+−+. **51.♖xd1 ♘c3+ 52.♔b4 ♘xd1−+**

983   **78...♖d5!** 78...♔g7?! was played in the game E.l'Ami-I.Sokolov, Amsterdam ch-NED 2012. **79.♗h6+ ♔e7 80.hxg4 hxg4 81.♗xg4** 81.♗g5+ ♔e8 and White will lose one of his bishops. **81...♖d6+!**

984   **17.♗b5!** 17.♗h7+ ♔xh7 18.♕c2+! (18.♖xd8 ♗xh2+ 19.♔xh2 (19.♔f1? ♖xe2 20.♔xe2 ♗g4+−+) 19...♖xe2=) 18...g6 19.♖xd8 ♖xd8 is better for White, but the move played in the game is winning! **17...♗xh2+ 18.♔f1!** 18.♔xh2? ♕h4+−+; 18.♔h1 ♗d7!= 19.♖xd7? ♕h4−+. **18...♕e7 19.♗xe8 ♕xe2+ 20.♔xe2 ♗g4+ 21.f3 ♖xe8+** 1-0 Naiditsch-Jobava, Budva Ech 2009; 22.♔f2 ♗e6 23.g3 ♗c4 24.♖d2 and the locked-up bishop on h2 will be lost.

985   **1...♕h7+!** A double attack on the king and the rook. It seems White can defend against both threats, but after **2.♖h3** (pinning the queen) it appears the rook is vulnerable here as it is protected by a pawn that is in the line of Black's bishop: 2.♔g1 ♖xd3−+. **2...♖d1+ 3.♔h2 ♖h1+!** Luring the back king to an unfavourable square; see also Exercises 667 (Tillmann-Erwich) and 668 (Caruana-Mamedyarov) in the Mate chapter for the same motif. **4.♔xh1** 4.♔g3 ♕h4+! 5.♖xh4+ gxh4#. **4...♕xh3+** The pinned g2-pawn is a bad defender! **5.♔g1 ♕xg2#** Losekoot, 2015.

986 Yes! **24.♖xc5!** (24.♗f3 was played in Uhlmann-Hennings, Weimar ch-DDR 1968) wins a pawn as after **24...♕xc5 25.♗xf7+ ♔h8 26.♕xc5** (26.♖xd8? ♕xe3+ 27.♔f1 ♖xd8−+) **26...♖xd1+ 27.♔f2 ♖xf7** White has **28.♕h5!** with a double attack! **28...♖d2+ 29.♔e1+−**

987 **36.♗e8!** 36.♗c2 was played in Giri-Pruijssers, Amsterdam ch-NED 2015. **36...♕c7** 36...♕xe8 37.♖xg7+−; 36...d1♕ 37.♖xg7 ♕xe8 (37...♕c2 38.♖g8#) 38.♕xh7#; 36...♖xg5 37.♕f8+ ♔g8 38.♕xg8#. **37.♕f6 ♔g8** 37...d1♕ 38.♕f8+ ♔g8 39.♕/♖xg8#. **38.♖h5!** Preventing 38...d1♕ and threatening 39.♖xg7+ ♖xg7 40.♕xe6+ ♔h8 41.♕e8+ ♔g8 42.♖xg8#. Now: 38...♕d7 39.♖xg7+ ♖xg7 40.♖xg7+ ♕xg7 41.♕xe6+ ♔h8 42.♕xc6+−; 38...♘d8 39.♖xg7+ ♖xg7 40.♖xg7+ ♕xg7 41.♕xd8++−.

988 **39.♗xg6! ♔xg6 40.♘f5! ♕b4** 40...♔xf5 41.♕d3+ ♔g4 42.♕f3# (42.f3#). **41.♕h6+ ♔f7** 41...♔xf5 42.♕h7+ ♔g4 43.f3#. **42.♕xh5+ ♔g8 43.♕g6+** 1-0 H.Vedder-Beeke, Maastricht 2012; 43...♔h8 44.♖xc7+−. Or first 43.♖xc7 ♘xc7 44.♕g6+ ♔h8 45.♕g7#.

989 **30...♖xe3!** Decoying the king. **31.♔xe3** 31.♖c2 ♖d3−+. **31...♘c4+ 32.♔d4 ♘xb2** Did you stop calculating here? Too soon, the line is not finished yet: **33.♔c3** Trapping the knight, but Black has a counterattack! **33...b6!** 0-1 Ducarmon-Warmerdam, Netherlands tt 2018/19; 34.♘xa6 ♘a4+! (an important in-between check!) 35.♔b4 ♖xa6−+, taking the enemy's knight while protecting his own.

990 **20...♕e8! 21.f3** 21.♗f3 e4−+; 21.♕c4 ♗e6 22.♕b4 (22.♕a4 b5 23.♕b4 a5−+) 22...a5 23.♕a4 b5−+; 21.♕b4 a5 loses in the same way. **21...♘d7! 22.♕c2 f5**, trapping the bishop, although White still managed to win in Swinkels-Hoeksema, Netherlands tt 2014/15.

991 **24.♖c1!** After 24.♖d2? Black could have saved himself with 24...♕e4!! (24...♘e4 was played in the game, transposing to 24.♖c1) 25.♖xe4 ♘xe4 and here anything can happen, e.g. 26.♕h5 (26.♕g4 ♘xd2 27.f6 g6 28.♕g5 ♘e4! 29.♕xe5 (29.♕h6? ♘xf6) 29...♖ae8∓) 26...♘xd2 27.f6 gxf6 28.♕h6 ♖a6 29.♕xd2 is unclear; 24.f6 ♕g6!. **24...♘e4** 24...♕xb2 25.f6! g6 26.♕h6, mating. **25.♖xc2**

♘xg5 26.h4, trapping the knight! Vachier-Lagrave-Kravtsiv, Riyadh blitz 2017.

992 **20.♘e8!** 20.♘e6? ♕xe6 21.♕xb8 ♕c6!, taking away the c7-square from the white queen. Also, 22...♗b7 is a threat since after that both the queen and g2 (mate!) are under attack. After 22.♕xa7 Black still plays 22...♗b7 with gain of tempo! White has to prevent mate, after which Black will trap White's queen with 23...♖a8. 20.f3 was played in Carlsen-Vokhidov, St Petersburg Wch rapid 2018. **20...♖a8** 20...♖xe8 21.♕xb8+−. **21.♘xg7 ♔xg7 22.♗xh6+** Deflecting the king. **22...♔xh6 23.♕xf8++−**

993 **14...♖xf3! 15.♗xf3 ♕f8 16.♔e2** If 16.♗e2 ♗b4! pins the queen. **16...b4!** Attacking the white queen and preparing ...♗a6+. **17.♕c4** 17.♕c2 ♗a6+ 18.♔e1 ♗xf3−+. **17...♗xf3+! 18.♔xf3 ♘e5+ 19.♔g3 ♘xc4** and Black won in Akobian-Adhiban, Khanty-Mansiysk Wch tt 2017.

994 **21...♗xa3! 22.♕xa3 ♘b5! 23.♖xc6** 23.♕b2 ♘d6 24.♘c5 (24.♖b4 a5 25.♖a4 ♖xc1+ 26.♕xc1 ♗xa4−+) 24...♘xb7 25.♕xb7 ♕c8−+; 23.♕a4 ♖xc1+ 24.♘xc1 ♕c8 with a double attack (24...♗c6 25.♕xb5 ♕e8 26.♗f1 a6−+); 23.♖xb5 ♖xc1+ 24.♕xc1 ♗xb5−+. **23...♗xc6** 23...♘xa3? 24.♖d6. **24.♖xb5 ♗xb5** and Black won, Kramnik-Caruana, Zurich blitz 2015.

995 **17.h4!** 17.♗b3 was played in Shankland-Gareev, Hawaii rapid 2015. **17...♗d8** 17...♗h6 18.♘e7+, forking the rook and the king; 17...♗xd5 18.♗xd5 (18.exd5 ♗f6 19.d6 is also very promising for White) 18...♗e7 19.♗xb7± (or 19.♗xf7+ ♔xf7? 20.♕b3+! ♔g6 (20...♔f8 21.♖hf1+ ♗f6 22.♖d7) 21.♖d6+ ♗f6 (21...♖xd6 22.♕e6+ ♔h5 23.g4#) 22.h5+ ♔g5 23.♕e3+ ♔g4 24.♕f3+ ♔g5 25.♕f5+ ♔h6 26.♖xf6++−). **18.b4! ♕a4** 18...♗xd5 19.bxa5±. **19.♗b5+−**.

996 **40...♕d3+! 41.♕c2** 41.♔a1 ♕e2 42.♕b1 ♕d2−+ and ...c3-c2 next. **41...♗a2+! 42.♔c1** 42.♔xa2 ♕xc2+−+. **42...♕e3+ 43.♔d1 ♗d5 44.♕c1 ♕d3+ 45.♔e1 ♗f3 46.♔f2 ♕d2+** 0-1 Bivol-Kevlishvili, St Louis 2018; 47.♕xd2 cxd2 48.♖d4 d1♕ 49.♖xd1 ♗xd1−+. 46...♕e2+ or 46...c2 will win as well, but the text is an easy way to collect the point.

997 30...♘f3! 31.♕h6 31.♕g4+ ♖g5–+. **31...♖g5+ 32.♔f1 ♖g6 33.♕h5** 33.♕f4 ♕xh3+! (luring away the rook) 34.♖xh3 (34.♔e2 ♕xh1–+) 34...♖g1+ 35.♔e2 ♖e1#. **33...♖e5** 0-1 Moskalenko-Andreikin, Russia tt 2012.

998 Yes! **49.♗e4!** 49.♕d7 was played in the game Girya-A.l'Ami, Rhodes tt W 2013. **49...♕xb1+ 50.♔h2!** Chess is not checkers! Capturing is not mandatory! 50.♗xb1 d1♕+ 51.♔h2 ♔g8 52.♕c8+ and White can save herself by giving a perpetual. **50...♕g1+** 50...♕xe4 51.♕c8+, mating; 50...♕b8 51.♕xh7#; 50...♔g8 51.♗d5+ ♔h8 52.♕c8+ ♗f8 53.♕xf8#. **51.♔xg1 d1♕+ 52.♔h2 ♔g8 53.♗d5+ ♕xd5** 53...♔h8 54.♕c8+ ♗f8 55.♕xf8#. **54.♕xd5+ ♔f8** 54...♔h8 55.♕d8+ ♗f8 56.♕xf8#. **55.♕d6+/c5++–.**

999 36.♘xd5! Luring away the pawn or the knight. **36...exd5** 36...♘xd5 37.♕xh6+ ♔g8 38.♖xg7+ ♖xg7 39.♖xg7+ ♕xg7 40.♕xg7#; 36...♗xe5 37.♘xe7 ♗xf4+ 38.♔h1 ♖xe7 39.♖c2+–. **37.♕xh6+!** Again, luring away an important defender! 1-0 Kovchan-Korobov, Kiev ch-UKR 2018; 37...gxh6 (if 37...♔g8, 38.♖xg7+ ♖xg7 39.♗e6+! ♔f8 (39...♕xe6 40.♖xg7#) 40.♕h8+ ♘g8 41.♕xg8+ ♖xg8 42.♖xg8#; 37...♘h7 38.♖xg7 and Black will get mated soon) 38.♖g8+ (the pinned knight is a bad defender!) 38...♔h7 39.♗f5#. And here we see why the e6-pawn had to be lured away!

1000 38...♕xb4! The game Ju Wenjun-Stefanova, Teheran W 2016, continued 38...♖xb4 39.♗a3 ♘c6 40.♖c1! ♘e6 41.♖xc6 ♕xc6 42.♕xb4 and Black had to resign soon. **39.♕xb4 ♖xb4 40.♖xe7+** 40.♗a3 ♖b7 41.♗xa6 ♘c7!∓ (41...♖d7? 42.♗b5 ♖b7 43.a6 ♖c7 (43...♖xb5 44.♖xe7+ ♔f6 45.♖xa7+–) 44.♗d6± **40...♔xe7 41.♗a3 ♗c5!–+**

1001 29...f5! Clearing the f7-square for the knight. **30.e4** 30.♖ed1 ♘f7–+. **30...f4!** Shutting off the c1-h6 diagonal. 30...♘f7? 31.♕d2±. **31.♖xd5 ♖xd5 32.♗b3** 32.exd5 ♕h4! (threatening 33...♘g3+, winning the queen; 32...♘f7? 33.♖xe8+ ♕xe8 34.♗xg6! and here Black is happy to escape with a draw: 34...♘g3+ 35.♔h2 (35.♔g1? ♕e3+ 36.♔h2 ♘xh6–+) 35...♘f1+ 36.♔h1 ♘g3+) 33.♔g1 (33.♖xe5 ♖xe5 34.♗xe5 ♘g3+ 35.♔h2 ♕xh6–+; 33.♔h2 ♘xf3+ 34.gxf3 ♕f2+ 35.♔h1 ♘g3#) 33...♘xf3+ 34.gxf3 ♖xe1+ 35.♗xe1 ♕xe1+ 36.♔g2 ♕d2+–+. **32...♘f7 33.♗xd5 ♕xd5! 34.exd5 ♖xe1+ 35.♗xe1 ♘xh6–+** and Black won, I.Sokolov-Fluvia Poyatos, Barcelona 2012.

Glossary

Terms marked with * can also be found in an entry of their own in this glossary.

A
attracting
Luring the king (see also 'magnet').

B
battery
A formation consisting of a front piece and a back piece on the same line (rank, file or diagonal), with which a *discovered attack can be executed.

blocking
Forcing an opposing piece to move to a square that the opponent badly needs for other purposes.

C
capturing
Taking away one of the opponent's pieces.

chasing
Forcing the king or a piece to a bad square or line by attacking it. On that bad square or line, the piece or king will be a target for a tactic.

chasing away
Forcing a piece to move by attacking it.

check
A direct attack on the enemy king.

checkmate
When a king is under direct attack and it cannot parry this attack in any way.

clearance
Freeing a line (a file, rank or diagonal; = line clearance) or a square (= square clearance) by moving away one of the one's own pieces that is obstructing that line or square. The removal and/or *sacrifice of this piece is followed by a tactical blow.

combination
A forced series of tactical motifs, often involving a *sacrifice.

cross-pin
A situation in which one piece is pinned in multiple directions. Various forms of a cross-pin are the St Andrew's Cross, the Maltese Cross and the Oblique Cross.

D
decoying
Luring an enemy piece onto a poisoned square by means of a *sacrifice on that square.

deflection
Drawing the guard away from a square where it is protecting a piece.

desperado
A piece that is under attack or trapped, is *sacrificed by first capturing an enemy piece.

discovered attack
A *double attack for which the attacker uses two pieces forming a *battery. By moving the front piece, an attack by the back piece is 'discovered'.

discovered check

A form of *discovered attack. Moving away the front piece unmasks a *check given by the back piece.

double attack

When one piece attacks two targets at the same time, or one move creates two different threats at the same time.

double check

A form of *discovered attack where both the front piece and the back piece give *check at the same time. The opponent cannot parry the check by interposing a piece or by *capturing one of the pieces that give check.

E
elimination of the defence

Forcing a protecting piece to disappear, or preventing the escape of a piece by blocking its flight square/route. The goal is to win material or to deliver *checkmate. Elimination of the defence can take on different forms: *capturing, *chasing away, *luring away, *interference and *blocking.

escape square

An unoccupied square that is available for an attacked piece to escape to.

exchange

1) Trading one of one's own men for one of the enemy men with the same value;
2) The value of a rook as opposed to that of a minor piece (knight or bishop).

F
forcing move

A move which limits the opponent's options by giving *check, *capturing a piece or making a concrete threat.

fork

An attack on two pieces at the same time.

G, H
hanging piece An undefined piece that is under attack

I
interference Interrupting the connection between the enemy pieces by interposing an own piece. Novotny and Plachutta are various types of interference.

intermediate move (also: zwischenzug, in-between move) An unexpected move in the midst of a planned tactical sequence.

J, K, L
liquidation

A purposeful transition into an ending by *exchanging pieces.

loose piece

An undefended piece that is not under immediate attack.

luring

Forcing an opponent's *targeted piece or his king to move to a bad square or line (rank, file or diagonal), most of the time by means of an *exchange or a *sacrifice, after which the position of the *targeted piece or king can be exploited by a tactic.

luring away

Eliminating a defender by forcing it to move with a *sacrifice or an *exchange.

M
magnet

Attracting the enemy king by a *sacrifice in order to deliver *checkmate.

mating net
When a king is trapped in order to deliver *checkmate. Sometimes this can be achieved with quiet moves.

N, O
overloading
When a piece has more defensive tasks than it can cope with.

P
perpetual check
When a draw is forced by an unending series of *checks.

perpetual pursuit
When a draw is forced by a continuous attack on an enemy piece (see also *perpetual check).

pin
A situation in which a piece attacks an enemy piece and indirectly threatens a more valuable enemy piece or square behind it.

promotion
When a pawn reaches the last rank, it can (and must) be substituted by any other piece except the king.

Q
quiet move A move that does not give *check, does not *capture an enemy piece, and often does not pose an obvious threat to the opponent.

R, S
sacrifice
When a player gives up a piece for nothing, or *exchanges it for a less valuable enemy piece, to gain a subsequent tactical or strategic benefit.

skewer
A form of *double attack, also known as 'x-ray attack': a piece attacks an enemy square or piece 'through' another enemy piece along a line (file, rank or diagonal). With a skewer, either the more valuable enemy piece is the one standing in front, or the front and back pieces are of the same value.

stalemate
When a player's king is not in *check and he cannot make a legal move. The result is a draw.

T
targeting
Setting up a favourable tactic to enable the attacking piece to move to its purpose square with gain of tempo.

theoretical draw
A known endgame position where a draw is the inevitable result of best play.

trapping Attacking a piece which cannot escape.

U
underpromotion
When a pawn reaches the last rank and is substituted by a knight, bishop or rook.

V, W, X, Y, Z
zugzwang
A position in which any move made by the player whose turn it is, will have negative consequences.

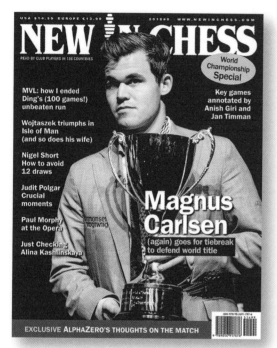
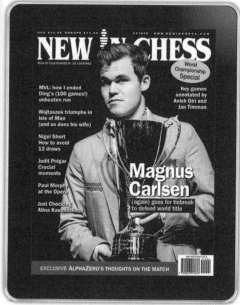

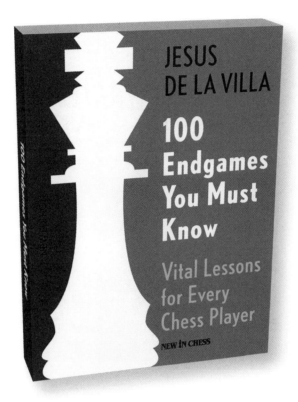

Not just another collection of interesting positions

paperback ◆ 464 pages ◆ €27.95 ◆ available at your local (chess)bookseller or at newinchess.com ◆ a NEW IN CHESS publication

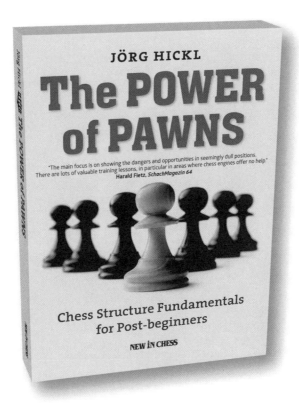